ENDING THE DEPRESSION CYCLE

A STEP-BY-STEP GUIDE FOR PREVENTING RELAPSE

Peter J. Bieling, Ph.D. • Martin M. Antony, Ph.D.
FOREWORD BY AARON T. BECK, MD

New Harbinger Publications, Inc.

Distributed in Canada by Raincoast Books

Copyright © 2003 by Peter J. Bieling and Martin M. Antony
     New Harbinger Publications, Inc.
     5674 Shattuck Avenue
     Oakland, CA 94609

Cover design by Amy Shoup
Edited by Wendy Millstine
Text design by Tracy Marie Carlson

ISBN 1-57224-333-3 Paperback

New Harbinger Publications' Web site address: www.newharbinger.com

05 04 03

10 9 8 7 6 5 4 3 2 1

First printing

For my parents
　　　—P. J. B.

For Cynthia
　　　—M. M. A.

Contents

Foreword

We have come a long way in understanding and treating depression over the last four decades. Careful research has documented the devastating impact of this illness on people's lives, in the way they think, act, and feel. The good news is that depression is treatable. For example, through the development of cognitive behavioral therapy we have demonstrated that a relatively short-term and focused therapy dealing with people's negative thinking can be very powerful in reducing symptoms and helping people to resume their lives. But, for so many people, depression is a recurring illness that threatens to return even after a person feels well again. This book tries to address this problem and provides many useful and documented techniques.

For the first time perhaps, this book offers readers ideas and strategies that can be used after they have recovered from depression to stay well and to protect themselves from the return of depression. Each chapter emphasizes a specific area, describing why it is related to relapse and what can be done, practically, so that a person can help him- or herself. Chapters on pleasant activities and thinking in a balanced way were inspired by research on cognitive behavioral therapies, known to offer protection from relapse, especially when continued into a period of wellness. The authors have adapted these strategies to be used when people are feeling well, which may prevent the return of symptoms. But the authors provide more than information. Bieling and Antony give the reader many different exercises and worksheets to take this information from the written page and into the reader's everyday life in a meaningful way.

Ultimately, the real strength of what the authors have done lies in the fact that they have carefully surveyed the existing research and theory on relapse and prevention and then boiled those ideas down to simple-to-use strategies in every chapter. Anyone who has suffered from depression in the past will find something useful in the chapters of this book that will enable them to begin to make changes in their life.

 —Aaron T. Beck, M.D.
 University of Pennsylvania

Acknowledgments

The authors wish to thank the following people who helped contribute to this work. Thanks to David Grant and Sandra Sagrati for helping with locating source material. Various people read specific chapters and offered important expert feedback for which we are grateful: Lawrence Martin, Zindel Segal, and Steven Wesley. Thanks also to Cynthia Crawford for proofing the text, and Andrea Ashbaugh, who combed each chapter for mistakes large and small. Finally, thanks to Karen Rowa for allowing use of her computer on many, many weekends.

Preface

The purpose of a preface, it seems to us, is to explain why a book was written. In explaining this, authors also foreshadow the content of the book and tell a story of how the book came to be. Critical to all these bits are the motivations of the authors: why was this subject compelling enough to write about? This is an especially important question when one considers the topic of depression, specifically self-help books for depression. Of all the categories of problems, depression has probably been written about the most. There are many great books that try to help people cope with depression and reduce the devastating symptoms of this disorder. The best of these books rely on scientific findings and help translate these into a "how-to" format. Certainly, our intent here is to take the best and most robust research and present it in such a way that a reader gets the information and can make practical use of it.

But that's not what is new about this book; instead, this book is really all about playing catch-up—catching up the reader with the science of depression., which has changed dramatically in the last ten years. For such a long time, the key areas in depression research involved recognition of depression, understanding the causes of the disorder, and developing and studying treatments that work. We have made great strides in each of these areas, and these topics have been written about extensively, from both academic and consumer perspectives. But the field has also undergone a tremendous shift, one that was borne of both good news and bad news. The good news is that depression can be accurately identified and systematically diagnosed; this is no small feat when you think of how complicated a disorder it is. Additionally, we have excellent and very effective treatments available that will fairly quickly offer relief for the majority of people who seek assistance. We also are lucky to have a variety of treatments to offer, depending on the person's needs, wishes, and level of response to other treatments. If one strategy doesn't work, others are available. This is seriously good news.

But as researchers were showing the dramatic and positive treatment effects that happened after weeks or months of medications and/or therapy, they also began to follow their treated subjects over time to see what would happen next. Without any strong expectations going in, researchers certainly hoped that successful treatment would result in gains that were maintained over time. But they were not. The treatments worked well in the short term, but, even after a few months, significant numbers of apparently well people began to have symptoms again. As collectively as possible in science, researchers of various stripes turned their attention to this unexpected fact: many people who get well after an episode of depression will have another. It turns out that the more episodes one has, the more serious the consequences for the person and the more likely that he or she will have even more episodes. In fact, it seems that having two episodes is more than twice as bad as having one episode. In the case of depression, one plus one does not equal two; it's more like one plus one equals three.

This little equation is why we wrote this book. Relapse is serious business, and not much has been written about it that is accessible to the reading public. This is understandable to some extent, since those within the field are still in the process of learning new things every day and, perhaps just as importantly, coming to grips with the scope of the problem. Another reason for the lack of consumer-oriented books on relapse is something we ourselves discovered; in many cases, the answers are still unknown and often very complex. However, there is also a large and growing mass of work on what predicts relapse in depression, and many of the things that have been shown to predict relapse, thankfully, are what the field might call "modifiable" or changeable factors. But even better than knowing what some of the risk factors are, research is beginning to emerge that suggests that certain kinds of treatments (for example, mindfulness-based cognitive therapy) can actually reduce the risk of relapse. Putting all this together, we felt that it was high time to share this information and disseminate what is known to the people who are most affected. That's the why of this book.

We have tried to stick to the science of relapse as much as possible, with the proviso that what we offer the reader is something practical and something that wrests the control away from mysterious processes and back into the hands of the affected person. In each chapter, there are some stories, some facts, and some suggestions. We encourage the reader to learn as much as possible, and we hope that the reading will be not only for a purpose but also enjoyable. However, this is not a book to be read and put down; simple reading of it may do very little. Each chapter has information about how you can take action. We do not have all of the answers on relapse yet, but this is a start, and we hope this book will help you.

—Peter J. Bieling, Ph.D.
—Martin M. Antony, Ph.D.

Chapter 1

What Is Depression and How Can It Be Overcome?

Everyone experiences the emotion of sadness from time to time. The experience of sadness is as normal as the experience of any other emotions, including fear, anger, and happiness. While it might sound strange to talk about the benefits of sadness, emotional pain may motivate us to reflect on our behavior and make changes in our lives to prevent future losses. For example, experiencing sadness after the breakup of an unhealthy marriage may make us think twice about getting into another unhealthy relationship. Low mood in response to a difficult situation may also prevent us from making impulsive decisions that we might regret later. Difficulty making decisions and a lack of motivation are features of sadness that may help prevent us from making decisions too quickly.

Clearly though, not all sadness is helpful or adaptive. If you are reading this book, chances are that you or someone you care about has suffered from a more extreme form of sadness known as depression. As we will discuss later in this chapter, severe depression can have a devastating effect on a person's life. When depression is too intense, prolonged, or frequent, it can become a significant problem, affecting almost all areas of an individual's functioning (such as work, school, relationships, housework, social life, and hobbies). The goal of this book is to teach you strategies for preventing the recurrence of significant depression, not for preventing the occurrence of sadness, which is a normal and healthy part of life.

Although the topic of this book is the prevention of relapse and recurrence of depression, it is difficult to discuss how to prevent depression from returning without also discussing the nature of depression and how it is treated in the first place. That's what we will be doing in this chapter, which provides an overview of the nature of depression, theories about what causes depression, and a description of treatments that have been proven to be effective for reducing symptoms of depression.

What Is Depression?

The American Psychiatric Association has defined a number of different problems for which a key feature is depression. The specific symptoms that are associated with each condition are listed in the *Diagnostic and Statistical Manual of Mental Disorders, 4th edition, Text Revision* (American Psychiatric Association 2000). Although there are a number of different disorders that are associated with depression, two of the most commonly diagnosed problems are *major depressive disorder* and *dysthymic disorder*. It is these two problems that this book addresses most, although people suffering from other forms of depression may also find the strategies described in this book to be helpful. This section includes descriptions of major depressive disorder and dysthymic disorder, as well as a few other problems that are associated with depressed mood—such as seasonal affective disorder, bipolar disorder, and adjustment disorder.

Major Depressive Disorder

Major depressive disorder (MDD), the most common form of clinical depression, is a condition associated with periods of severe depression lasting at least two weeks, almost every day, most of the day. Untreated, the average episode of depression lasts four months or longer, usually followed by a complete remission of symptoms. However, about a quarter of people with MDD continue to experience some symptoms for a longer period of time, and about 5 to 10 percent of individuals with MDD experience severe depression chronically, for at least two years, without a significant break.

To receive a diagnosis of MDD, an individual must experience at least five symptoms from a list of nine, and at least one of the symptoms must be either (1) low mood or (2) a loss of interest or pleasure in almost all of his or her usual activities. In addition to having at least one of these two core features, there must also be at least four additional features from the following list: (3) increases or decreases in appetite or weight, (4) changes in sleep (either insomnia or sleeping too much), (5) changes in the rate of physical activity (moving very slowly or becoming physically agitated and fidgety), (6) feeling tired, (7) feeling worthless or excessively guilty, (8) difficulty concentrating or making decisions, (9) recurrent thoughts of death or suicide.

Although these are the official symptoms of MDD, a number of other features are also quite common in people with MDD, as well as other forms of depression. Some of these include

- worrying about minor matters

- feelings of helplessness and hopelessness about the future

- decreased interest in sex

- irritability and short temper

- crying

- social withdrawal

- feeling numb or empty

- feeling easily overwhelmed

- a tendency to be focused on oneself

- experiencing other associated problems (for example, anxiety or alcohol or drug abuse)

To receive a diagnosis of MDD, a number of alternative causes for the symptoms have to be ruled out. For example, if a loved one has recently died, an individual would normally be expected to experience symptoms of depression for several months, and the reaction wouldn't be called MDD if it is within the expected level of severity. Similarly, it is important to rule out any physical illnesses, such as certain thyroid conditions or cancer of the pancreas, or the use of any drugs (prescribed or recreational) that can directly cause symptoms of depression.

Dysthymic Disorder

Dysthymic disorder is a milder form of depression, in that the severity and the number of symptoms required for the diagnosis are less than are required for a diagnosis of MDD. However, unlike MDD, dysthymic disorder is, by definition, chronic or long lasting. In addition, although the depressed mood experienced in dysthymic disorder is sometimes less severe than that experienced in MDD, the level of depression can also be similar in these two problems. To receive this diagnosis, the symptoms of low mood must be present most of the day, more days than not, *for at least two years.* Without treatment, only about 10 percent of individuals with dysthymic disorder can expect to have a remission of their symptoms in any given year, whereas MDD symptoms tend to go away on their own, even without treatment (American Psychiatric Association 2000). For some individuals, the course of their depression may include more intense, brief, major depressive episodes superimposed on a chronic depression that persists over time. This combination of major depressive episodes and chronically dysthymic mood is sometimes referred to as *double depression.*

To receive a diagnosis of dysthymic disorder, an individual must have low mood for two years or more, with at least two of the following six symptoms:

1. poor appetite or overeating

2. insomnia or sleeping too much

3. low energy or feeling tired

4. low self-esteem

5. poor concentration or difficulty making decisions

6. feelings of hopelessness

As with MDD, we need to rule out any medical or drug-related causes before making a diagnosis of dysthymic disorder.

Seasonal Affective Disorder

Seasonal affective disorder (SAD) is a form of depression that is tied to a particular time of year—usually the winter months. Often, SAD is actually considered to be a form of MDD. However, there are a number of differences between SAD and more typical forms of depression (Howland and Thase 1999). First, SAD is more likely to be associated with increased appetite and sleep, whereas typical depression is more likely to be associated with a loss of appetite and decreased sleep. In addition, people with SAD often report cravings for carbohydrates, such as sweets and starches.

SAD appears to be related to the decreased sunlight that occurs during winter months and, therefore, this problem tends to be more prevalent in northern climates. Interestingly, exposure to bright light (also known as *phototherapy*) can be an effective therapy for reducing certain symptoms in people who suffer from SAD (Lee and Chan 1999). Although the hormone *melatonin* has been previously thought to be involved in SAD (melatonin is secreted from the *pineal gland* in response to darkness), scientists have found little evidence for the role of melatonin in causing this problem. Instead, a chemical in the brain called *serotonin* is thought to be involved, in combination with various hormones in the body (Howland and Thase 1999).

Bipolar Disorder

Like MDD, *bipolar disorder* (also known as *manic depressive illness*) is associated with periods of intense depression characterized by the same types of symptoms. However, unlike MDD, bipolar disorder is also associated with periods of intensely high, elevated, or irritable mood known as *manic* or *hypomanic* episodes (manic episodes are more severe than hypomanic episodes, last longer, and are associated with greater impairment). The types of symptoms that are experienced during manic and hypomanic episodes include unusually high self-esteem or a belief that one has special powers, a decreased need for sleep, a pressure to talk much more than usual, a feeling that one's thoughts are racing, being easily distracted, a dramatic increase in activity, and excessive involvement in pleasurable, though risky, activities, such as spending sprees and other impulsive behaviors.

Manic and hypomanic episodes typically last from a few days to a few weeks, and they are often preceded by an episode of depression. People with bipolar disorder may experience periods of normal mood in addition to periods of depressed mood and periods of mania or hypomania. Although bipolar disorder shares features with MDD, there are also important differences between these illnesses. Most important, the role of biological factors is much better established in bipolar disorder than in MDD, and it is generally accepted that effective treatment of bipolar disorder almost always includes medication as a component. Bipolar disorder is less prevalent than MDD, and this book doesn't discuss treatments for bipolar disorder in much detail.

Adjustment Disorder

Adjustment disorder is a condition in which an individual has experienced a negative emotional response to some sort of stressful event in his or her life (for example, a difficult period at work, a marital separation, or losing one's job). The symptoms begin soon after experiencing the stressful event (within three months) and usually improve over a relatively brief period (no more than six months) after the situation has ended. In addition, the reaction to the stressful event must be more intense than what would normally be expected. Adjustment disorder is often (but not always) associated with depressed mood. However, the depression is not severe enough to meet the criteria for MDD or another mood disorder. Adjustment disorder is thought to be fairly common in the general population.

Who Gets Depressed?

Depression is a relatively common problem. In one large study, almost 30 percent of Americans reported a period of extreme sadness lasting two weeks or longer at some point in their lives (Weissman et al. 1991), although the rates of particular depressive illnesses, with all the required symptoms, appear to be somewhat lower. For example, between 5 and 15 percent of individuals report a history of MDD at some time in their lives and between 3 and 6 percent of individuals have experienced periods of low mood meeting the criteria for dysthymic disorder (Kessler et al. 1994; Weissman et al. 1988). Bipolar disorder affects less than 2 percent of the general population (Kessler et al. 1994).

Just about anyone can develop depression, and there is some evidence that the prevalence of depression is increasing across the world. Although depression occurs in a wide range of people, there are certain factors that put some people at greater risk than others (Kaelber, Moul, and Farmer 1995). For example, women are two to three times as likely as men to suffer from depression. People who have experienced certain life stresses, such as divorce, unemployment, poor health, or low income are also at a greater risk than people who have not experienced these stresses. If you've had depression before, the likelihood of becoming depressed again is increased. The same is true if you've suffered from substance use problems or other emotional difficulties.

There is little evidence that age or ethnic background affect the risk of developing depression. However, a family history of depression is a significant risk factor. In all likelihood, as discussed in the next section, the transmission of depression across the generations is due to both *genetic factors* (the transmission of genes from parent to child) and *environmental factors* (for example, learning ineffective ways of dealing with stress).

Causes of Depression

You may have heard somewhere that depression is caused by a chemical imbalance in your brain. Or perhaps you have read that negative thoughts can lead to depression. You may also have heard that it's caused by the foods you eat, or by your genetic makeup. In fact, there have been dozens of attempts to explain why we get depressed.

Despite what you may have read in magazines or seen on television, we do not know *the* cause of depression. In fact, depression probably has no single cause and there is currently no theory that explains all cases of depression. For example, even though we know that certain patterns of genetic makeup and family history can increase a person's risk of developing depression, there are individuals with a strong family history of depression who never develop depression, and others who are depressed and yet have no family history of depression at all. In fact, two people can be genetically identical (as is the case for identical twins) and have very different experiences when it comes to depression.

Because we define depression by its symptoms (including sad mood, loss of interest, and poor sleep and appetite), rather than its underlying causes, there is no reason to think that each person's depression always has the same cause. Rather, it is likely that the same symptoms can be caused by many different factors. Just as abdominal pains can be caused by cramps, gas, excess acid, anxiety, too much exercise, constipation, ulcers, food poisoning, cancer, and many other conditions, the same is probably true of depression. There is now strong evidence that many different factors interact to cause this disorder, including biological factors, life events, patterns of negative thinking, lifestyle habits, and other variables. For any one individual, any combination of these factors may play a role. Let's review some of the variables that are thought to contribute to the development and maintenance of depression.

The Impact of Negative Life Events

In the 1970s, psychologist Martin Seligman demonstrated that dogs who were exposed to inescapable electrical shocks later developed a tendency to passively accept future electrical shocks without even trying to escape (even though these later shocks could be avoided), whereas dogs who did not first receive inescapable shocks were quick to learn how to avoid the escapable shocks to which they were later exposed (Seligman 1974). In fact, the dogs who underwent the unavoidable shocks showed a number of signs that we often associate with depression, including weight loss, a tendency to behave passively in the face of stress, and a tendency not to take actions that would potentially help them to cope. Seligman called this reaction to the unavoidable shock *learned helplessness,* and these experiments formed the basis of his theory of depression.

Based on the results of his now classic research, Seligman proposed that learned helplessness may account for why some people become depressed. Specifically, he hypothesized that depression is the result of repeated, unpredictable, and uncontrollable negative experiences. Since Seligman's original research was published, there have been numerous studies showing that negative life events do contribute to depression, anxiety, and other negative emotions, with unpredictable and uncontrollable negative events being particularly problematic. In addition, Seligman and his colleagues (Abramson, Seligman, and Teasdale 1978) have proposed that these events lead to depression by influencing the ways in which people interpret negative experiences in their lives. The influence of thoughts on depressed mood is discussed in the next section.

In the case of depression, the negative life events that are seen to be most relevant are those that involve some sort of loss in a person's life, although other life stresses are often triggers as well. Although negative life events and stressful circumstances can put an individual at risk for developing depression, they do not cause depression on their own. If they were the sole cause of depression, any individual who experiences a negative life event would become depressed. Rather, it is currently believed that negative life events interact with other variables to trigger depression in people who are vulnerable. Factors that might make an individual vulnerable include styles of interpreting negative events and biological vulnerabilities such as genetics.

Negative Thinking and Depression

There is now considerable evidence that depression is associated with negative thought patterns. In 1967, Dr. Aaron T. Beck, a psychiatrist at the University of Pennsylvania, described one of the first *cognitive* theories of depression, suggesting that depression stems from a tendency to interpret situations negatively ("cognitive" refers to thinking). According to Dr. Beck, there are three different levels of negative thinking that interact to cause depression: negative triad, negative schemas, and cognitive biases.

Negative Triad

Dr. Beck's negative triad refers to the tendency to have pessimistic views about three different areas of one's life: the self, the world, and the future. Below are examples of each.

- Pessimistic views of the self, such as "I am inadequate."

- Pessimistic views of the world, such as "People cannot be trusted."

- Pessimistic views of the future, such as "I will never find a job."

Dr. Beck's theory of depression is not the only theory to propose that negative thinking contributes to depression; however, it has been among the most influential. Although some aspects of Beck's model remain to be tested by researchers, it is now well established that patterns of thinking do influence the experience of depression and other negative moods. More importantly, researchers have demonstrated again and again that learning to change patterns of thinking can lead to improvements in depression. This book (particularly chapter 6) will help you to begin the process.

The Effects of Biology

Just as psychological and environmental factors such as life events and patterns of negative thinking appear to contribute to depression, there is strong evidence that biological factors also play a role (Howland and Thase 1999; Thase and Howland 1995). This evidence includes studies on the genetic transmission of depression, the role of brain chemistry and hormones in depression, the relationship between sleep patterns and depression, and various other biological processes. A comprehensive review of the scientific evidence on the role of biology in depression is beyond the scope of this book, but we summarize some of the key findings below.

Family and Genetics Studies

The rate of depression in those with a family member who is depressed is higher than the rate of depression in the general population, and genetics appears to play a role, along with other factors (Rehm, Wagner, and Ivens-Tyndal 2001; Rhee et al. 2001). The role of genetics is strongest in bipolar disorder (or manic depression), and more modest in people whose depression is not associated with occasional periods of mania or hypomania.

Brain Chemistry and Hormones

Brain chemistry appears to play a role in depression. There is evidence that certain *neurotransmitters* (chemicals that transfer information from one nerve cell to another) may be altered in depression. In particular, levels of the neurotransmitter serotonin tend to be lower on average in people who are depressed than in people are who are not depressed. In the case of bipolar disorder, the neurotransmitter *norepinephrine* also seems to play a role. Interestingly, drugs that increase the levels of these chemicals in the brain lead to decreases in depression (see chapter 4) for most individuals.

It should be noted that these findings do not mean that depression is *caused* by a chemical imbalance in the brain. Nor are there any tests to measure whether your levels of serotonin and norepinephrine are too low. Although scientists have been able to show differences between depressed and nondepressed groups with respect to these brain chemicals, there are also many exceptions within each group. In other words, although someone with low levels of serotonin is statistically more likely to be depressed than someone with higher levels, that doesn't mean that the person will necessarily be depressed. Depression and serotonin levels are related just as height and weight are related. Someone who is very heavy is *more likely* to be tall than someone who weighs very little. Still, there are many heavy people who are not particularly tall and many tall people who are not particularly heavy.

Hormones in the body also appear to play a role. In particular, levels of *cortisol* (a hormone that is released when a person is under stress) tend to be higher in people who are depressed than in nondepressed individuals. Changes in certain thyroid hormones may also be involved. In other words, one way in which stress can lead to depression may be through its effect on hormones, which ultimately leads to changes in brain functioning.

Sleep and Depression

Insomnia and oversleeping are common in people who are depressed. In addition, depression is associated with a tendency for people to enter what is known as *rapid eye movement* (REM) sleep more quickly than people who are not depressed (REM sleep is the stage of sleep during which dreaming occurs). Depression is also associated with a tendency to spend less time in the deepest stages of sleep. Finally, depriving individuals of sleep, particularly during the second half of the night, has been shown to cause temporary improvements in depressed mood.

Effective Treatments for Depression

Fortunately, as reviewed earlier, depression does not typically last forever. Even without treatment, the average episode of major depression lasts no more than a few months, although some symptoms of depression may continue even after the problem has improved. If depression is likely to improve without treatment, why bother treating it at all? There are several reasons for obtaining treatment for depression:

- Treatment can result in improvements that would not occur otherwise (remember, not everyone's depression improves without treatment).

- Treatment is likely to result in a quicker recovery.

- Treatment can result in a more complete recovery, with fewer leftover symptoms.

- Treatment can help to prevent relapse.

Although there are claims supporting the effectiveness of many different treatment approaches for depression, there are relatively few treatments that have been tested and supported through well-controlled research studies. Proven treatments for depression include *cognitive behavioral therapy, interpersonal psychotherapy,* antidepressant medications, and *electroconvulsive therapy.* In addition, there is evidence supporting certain alternative treatments such as herbal products, as well as changing lifestyle habits (for example, exercising regularly) for depression. Finally, recent evidence suggests that mindfulness-based meditation may be helpful, particularly for preventing depression from returning in people who have recently overcome a bout of major depression.

Cognitive Behavioral Therapy

Cognitive behavioral therapy (CBT) is a brief treatment for depression that involves two main types of strategies—*cognitive* and *behavioral*. Cognitive therapy is designed to teach individuals to (1) identify depressive patterns of thinking, and (2) replace negative thinking with more realistic interpretations, predictions, and assumptions. Through cognitive therapy, people are taught to not automatically assume their beliefs are true, but rather to challenge their thoughts by examining the evidence supporting and contradicting their negative beliefs. By broadening one's perspective and shifting one's thinking, cognitive therapy can be an effective tool for combating depression.

The other group of strategies that are used in CBT are more behavioral in nature. These involve changing depression by changing one's behavior. One behavioral technique, known as *behavioral activation,* involves forcing yourself to do things even though you lack the interest, energy, or motivation. For example, you might go to a party even though you are feeling too tired and you are convinced you will not enjoy yourself. Or, despite feeling overwhelmed with the idea of applying for a new job, you might still prepare a new résumé and send it out. More often than not, forcing yourself to confront a situation instead of avoiding it leads to more enjoyment than you might expect, as well as other benefits.

CBT is a relatively brief form of treatment, lasting from ten to twenty sessions. In addition to being taught CBT strategies by a therapist, there are several excellent self-help books on the market that have primarily a CBT emphasis. For example, *Mind over Mood: Change How You Feel by Changing the Way You Think* (Greenberger and Padesky 1995) and *The Feeling Good Handbook* (Burns 1999) are two popular books on using cognitive strategies to combat negative thinking. In addition, the book *Messages: The Communications Skills Book* (McKay, Davis, and Fanning 1995) is an excellent book on improving communication skills.

Interpersonal Psychotherapy

Interpersonal psychotherapy (IPT) is a relatively new treatment for depression developed by Drs. Myrna Weissman and Gerald Klerman and their colleagues (Weissman, Markowitz, and Klerman 2000). Problems in relationships can often trigger feelings of depression. The underlying theme of IPT is to help individuals to improve their current relationships and develop new relationships, and thereby improve their mood. Research on IPT is very promising, showing gains that are comparable or better than those seen following CBT or medication for depression.

Like CBT, IPT is a relatively brief form of psychotherapy, lasting fifteen to twenty sessions. If you were to get involved in IPT, you would end up working on one or more of the following four relationship areas:

1. Dealing with interpersonal role disputes (for example, marital problems and conflicts at work).

2. Adjusting to the loss of a relationship (death of a loved one or a divorce).

3. Acquiring new relationships (meeting new friends or getting married).

4. Improving social skills (for example, learning to be more assertive).

Unlike CBT, there are very few books designed to teach individuals to use the IPT techniques in a self-help format. One exception is a patient manual written by Myrna Weissman (2000). This manual, although written for the person who suffers from depression, is meant to be used in conjunction with IPT sessions with a trained therapist. Seeing a therapist is really the best way to benefit from IPT, and there is information about how to choose a therapist at the back of this book (see Additional Resources).

Medication

The first antidepressant drugs were discovered in the late 1950s. Although some of these earliest medications, such as imipramine (Tofranil) are still in use, there are now also many newer medications that are effective for reducing depression, often with fewer side effects than the older drugs. In fact, dozens of different medications, with somewhat different mechanisms of action, may be useful for reducing symptoms of depression. Medications can be useful for treating depression and preventing relapse, both on their own and in combination with psychological treatments. In addition to traditional medications, there is also evidence supporting the use of certain natural products for depression, including St. John's wort. Chapter 4 contains a detailed discussion of medications, as well as certain herbal products.

Electroconvulsive Therapy

Electroconvulsive therapy (ECT) is perhaps the most controversial treatment for depression. It was introduced in the early 1900s as a method of inducing seizures by researchers interested in studying epilepsy. ECT involves inducing a seizure and brief unconsciousness by passing a current through the brain of the patient, either on one side or on both sides. Although ECT was used to treat schizophrenia many years ago, today it is used primarily as a treatment for severe depression. The patient is unconscious during the procedure and, because muscle relaxants are used, the convulsions undergone by the body are barely noticeable.

ECT is controversial because it has been portrayed very negatively in the media. Perhaps this is because the idea of hooking electrodes to a person's head and shocking them looks highly invasive, punishing, and downright scary. But then again, many medical procedures, including diagnostic tests and surgeries that are very common and very effective, look scary. The data on ECT are fairly strong. It seems to be effective, particularly for people in whom neither therapy nor medications have worked. Some individuals may claim that ECT can cause all kinds of emotional and physical problems, but those claims are not substantiated by the research. That is, the vast majority of people who undergo ECT will not experience important negative effects on their health, although temporary memory loss is common. All medical procedures have complications and side effects; for example, some people become very ill from common vaccinations. But the chances of ECT working for someone who is deeply depressed are high, and the chances of having severe complications from ECT are very low when patients are screened carefully and when the treatment is administered by an expert.

Compared to medications and psychotherapy, which can take weeks to work, the beneficial effects of ECT are experienced much more quickly. In addition, many people who do not respond to medications or psychotherapy will experience a positive response to ECT. However, the relapse rate after stopping ECT treatment is quite high, especially if the individual does not continue to take medications. The most common side effect of ECT is temporary memory loss. Although it is clear that ECT is an effective treatment for depression, we still do not understand how it works.

Staying Free of Depression

Episodes of depression tend to improve even without treatment. However, almost half of patients who recover from an initial episode of depression will experience at least one more depressive episode in the future, and the likelihood is even higher if some symptoms remain after the initial recovery (Paykel et al. 1995). Furthermore, with each additional episode of depression, the chances of having more episodes increases. For example, individuals with a history of two or more past episodes of depression have a 70 to 80 percent likelihood of having another episode of depression in their lifetimes (Judd 1997). Helping you to protect yourself from relapse is the goal of this book. In the next chapter, we describe this problem of returning depression in more detail. By the time you're done working through *Ending the Depression Cycle,* you'll have some excellent strategies to help defend yourself from relapse.

Why Does Depression Come Back?

As mentioned previously, people who are depressed tend to engage in negative, pessimistic thinking. Furthermore, as their depression improves, their thinking tends to become less negative. However, people who have experienced depression in the past appear to be at risk for having their negative thinking patterns reactivated under certain circumstances. One trigger for reactivating negative thinking patterns is a period of sad mood. Although everyone experiences sadness from time to time, people with a history of depression are more likely than people without a history of depression to react strongly to such an experience. They are more likely to enter into a spiral of negative thinking and to worry that they may be sinking into a deep depression.

A number of factors have been identified that predict whether depression will return for a given individual who has recovered from an episode (Coryell, Endicott, and Keller 1991; Daley, Hammen, and Rao 2000; Giles et al. 1989; Hart, Craighead, and Craighead 2001; Lin et al. 1998; Wilhelm et al. 1999). The other chapters in this book describe in great detail most of these factors and what can be done about them. A partial list includes

- a history of previous depressions (particularly at younger ages)

- certain personality styles

- the presence of other psychological problems

- frequent stress in one's life

- low levels of social support (from family and friends, for example)

- the presence of continuing, mild depression symptoms

Preventing the Recurrence of Depression

Understanding the reasons why depression often returns is key to preventing its recurrence. In recent years, a number of researchers have focused their efforts on trying to prevent the recurrence of depression.

One method of preventing the return of depression is continuing to use the strategies that have been shown to treat depression in the first place. These include continuing to take maintenance medications (see chapter 4), continuing "booster" sessions of maintenance psychotherapy (chapter 5), continuing to challenge negative thinking patterns (chapter 6), and maintaining positive interpersonal relationships (chapter 13). However, there are other things that you can do to prevent the return of your depression.

For example, based on the work of Jon Kabat-Zinn and colleagues (1990), psychologists Zindel Segal, Mark Williams, and John Teasdale (2002) have developed a new treatment for preventing the recurrence of depression using mindfulness-based meditation. The treatment focuses on helping individuals to recognize negative moods early on, before they become overwhelming, and to let go of negative thinking rather than getting caught up in the spiral of pessimism that characterizes depression. A study based on this treatment found that for patients who had experienced three or more depressive episodes in the past, mindfulness training reduced the rate of relapse by half in the year following recovery from the most recent episode (Teasdale et al. 2000). Mindfulness training is discussed in chapter 8 of this book.

Attention to lifestyle habits may also pay off when it comes to preventing depression. For example, there is evidence that regular exercise can improve mood, which may help to prevent depression (Lane and Lovejoy 2001). Recently, researchers have also investigated a combined treatment package involving exercise, exposure to light, and daily vitamins for benefiting mood in women suffering from mild to moderate depression (Brown et al. 2001a). Compared to a group that just took a *placebo* (a "dummy" pill containing no real medication or nutrients), the group that received the combined treatment experienced significant improvements in mood. It is not clear from this study which components of the treatment (the exercise, light, or vitamins) were responsible for the improvement.

As we've described, stress can also lead to the recurrence of depression. We've known about this factor for several decades and are learning more about the ways in which stress might trigger depression. In chapter 9, we will discuss some ways to examine your stress levels and to limit stress. There are also factors related to the risk for becoming depressed that have more to do with one's personality. Two main types of personality styles that appear to increase one's likelihood of suffering from depression are *dependency* and *perfectionism* (Beck 1983; Blatt and Zuroff 1992). Dependency seems to put people at risk because it makes them rely too much on other people, so they may not develop the skills to look out for themselves. Perfectionism puts people at risk because having expectations that are too high and too strict increases the likelihood of being disappointed. In chapters 11 and 12, we discuss these personality styles and what can be done about them. In the final chapter, we examine the issue of meaning in our lives, because finding meaning in one's existence has been shown to lead to and maintain good physical and mental health.

Summary

Depression is a serious condition that can interfere significantly with your functioning across a wide range of life domains. Also, depressed mood is often associated with other problems and symptoms, such as anxiety, fatigue, lack of interest, pessimistic thinking, suicidal thoughts, and disturbances in appetite, sleep, and concentration. Fortunately, there are a number of effective treatments for depression, including cognitive behavioral therapy, interpersonal psychotherapy, antidepressant medications, and electroconvulsive therapy. However, a high percentage of individuals who overcome depression experience a return of their symptoms at some point in the future. If you have a history of depression, the strategies taught in this book should help you to break the cycle and ultimately to prevent your depression from returning.

Chapter 2

The Nature of Relapse
in Depression

In the first chapter, we described and defined depression. For those who have been depressed or are depressed, many of the points we raised would not have been a surprise. Instead you may have found your own experiences reflected in that chapter, whether this had to do with different symptoms you have had, limitations on your ability to function, or your sense of self. You may also have benefited from some of the treatments we described. In any case, the important point is that we have now put into context the difficulties faced by people with depression, and some of the options for finding help. In fact, there are many kinds of materials that describe depression, ranging from self-help books to Web sites to advertisements for antidepressant medications. However, information about relapse is much less readily available to the average person suffering from or recovering from depression. Our aim for this book is to provide you with an understanding of what relapse is, the problems it can bring about, and, even more importantly, what can be done about relapse before it happens.

In this chapter, we'll define what relapse is and describe why it is so critical to understand and prevent. In some ways, this information reflects a kind of story about our scientific understanding of depression, especially what we have learned over the years from carefully conducted research. We'll describe how this new information contradicts some of the conventional wisdom that was, and still is, provided to many patients recovering from depression.

Depression As an "Episodic" Illness

It may be surprising to learn that up until about twenty-five years ago, depression wasn't taken all that seriously by many people, including many mental health researchers and academics. Going back to the early 1900s, the earliest thinkers in psychiatry were, perhaps understandably, more preoccupied with understanding and treating illnesses like schizophrenia. After all, people with schizophrenia and other psychotic illnesses often have bizarre thoughts, emotions, and behaviors that are very noticeable, and they are often unable to live independently. Also, people with schizophrenia do not seem to spontaneously recover, and they can spend a lot of time in the hospital. Looking back on the history of psychiatry in the first half of the twentieth century, almost all psychiatrists were working in big state and university-based psychiatric hospitals. It's not surprising then that schizophrenia and related illnesses were such a prominent focus for decades. For those early psychiatrists, depressed individuals were lumped into a category called "neurotic," which encompassed a broad range of problems, including anxiety disorders. The notion of being "neurotic" meant that, although a person might be in distress, he or she was in touch with reality and able to function reasonably well in everyday life. The forefathers of modern psychiatry thought that most depressed people would do quite well over time, especially if they received *psychoanalysis,* a form of psychotherapy developed by Sigmund Freud to uncover the unconscious roots of psychological problems.

The trouble was, these ideas were just plain wrong. Depression is very serious, both because the person suffers greatly and because the illness undermines his or her ability to function. For verification, we have to look no further than the World Health Organization, which sees depression as one of the leading causes of disability worldwide, even considering all other medical illnesses (Parikh and Lam 2001). Also, psychoanalysis, the so called "talking cure," doesn't work well for depression. In fact, starting in the 1950s, many of the ideas underlying the field of psychoanalysis began to come under attack, because the theories are very complicated and hard to prove or disprove, and because the treatment was not as helpful as Freud and others had claimed (Bergin and Lambert 1978; Eysenck 1952). In the last three decades we have come to understand the seriousness of depression and to realize how important it is to treat depression as aggressively as possible. In addition, we have come to recognize the importance of not making assumptions based simply on "expert" opinion or theory, but rather to study the disorder and its treatment very carefully.

There are other reasons why depression wasn't well understood until more recently. First, people with depression may not display any outward signs that they are unwell, so a casual observer may not detect that anything is wrong. Second, as described in chapter 1, many people sometimes feel "blue," and for decades mental health experts overlooked the many critical differences between sadness, which we can all experience, and clinical depression. Third, many depressed people can function during at least part of their illness and may never need to be hospitalized. As a result, psychiatrists in the past thought that people with depression would improve over time and would have a high likelihood of feeling fine in the future. We still see signs of this in some of the stigma around depression, such as the belief that depression is just feeling a little blue, and, if a person is patient and waits long enough, he or she will "get over it." If there is any grain of truth to this thinking, it is this—depression is an *episodic* illness (Clark, Beck, and Alford 1999). The term "episodic" refers to an illness that comes and goes. The symptoms may last for some time and then lessen, often to the point that the person feels like his or her usual self (Coryell et al. 1995). In fact, in the past, without the benefit of any decent studies on the course of depression, it seemed that most currently depressed people would feel better spontaneously after only a few months, and would continue to feel well in the future.

However, when more careful studies were conducted, our understanding of depression changed radically. We still believe that most depressions are episodic; however, we now know that for at least 50 percent of sufferers, depression comes back some time after an episode has ended, and about a quarter of people with depression will have more than six episodes (Angst 1986). Also, after each subsequent episode of depression, the risk for having a further episode goes up (Belsher and Costello 1988). During a recent five-year study of depression, the average patient in that study was well for only twenty months, and the odds of a person remaining well for the entire five years was only about one in five (Keller 1994). About 66 percent of people treated for depression report periods of depressive symptoms that come and go even between their full-blown episodes (Keller et al. 1995). Finally, in 10 percent of cases, depression becomes *chronic,* meaning that it lasts for years at a time, and the person may no longer have periods of feeling like his or her usual self.

Our improved knowledge regarding the course of depression was made possible by carefully following large groups of patients over many years. This is a great example of an area in which research brought a whole new understanding to mental illness and really drew our attention to a problem we didn't know was there. Unlike past generations of psychiatrists and psychologists who were somewhat in the dark, the mental health community can no longer be blasé about the risk of depression returning. Clearly, we need to do something active to try to understand the problem of relapse and to stop it before it happens.

There are probably several unanswered questions in your mind as you read this. One question might be, How long do episodes of depression typically last and what happens to this illness when people get treatment? As discussed in chapter 1, untreated episodes of depression typically last several weeks to several months (Coryell et al. 1995). We know this from studies in which individuals with depression are followed *naturalistically,* meaning that the researchers simply observe very carefully what happens over time, without any intervention or treatment. Based on this research, we know that depressions do seem to end spontaneously in many instances. However, this same research has shown that for many people depression comes back, often only weeks or months later. In a way, this is a classic "good news/bad news" scenario. If you're currently depressed and for whatever reason you receive no treatment, chances are you'll feel better at some point in the future. On the other hand, there is at least a 50 percent chance (and perhaps much higher, depending on your history), that you will become depressed again sometime after you recover from a given episode. Clearly, something active must be done to prevent the recurrence of depression, which naturally leads people to consider the issue of treatment.

Although episodes of depression often eventually improve without any intervention, treatment is critically important. As we discussed in chapter 1, there are a number of treatments that are effective enough that most people feel normal after the treatment ends. These gains are substantial, as those who have recovered will know. Also, the earlier one seeks treatment, the less time one has to suffer. For years, the generally positive outcomes in treatment research for depression have been a source of satisfaction to those who work in this area. After all, researchers could point to dozens of studies showing very large decreases in symptoms as a result of a variety of antidepressant medications, psychotherapies (such as interpersonal therapy and cognitive behavioral therapy), and combinations of these approaches. This meant that we not only had good treatments for depression, but we also had a variety of choices to suit the individual. Once these treatments were shown to be effective in the short-term, researchers started to look at what happened to people in the months and years following treatment. They were particularly interested in what happened to those who recovered as a result of the treatment. Would these people stay well in the long run?

Unfortunately, the data on the return of depression in the period following the end of treatment were quite shocking, even to experts in the field. One of the most thorough studies on the treatment of depression was conducted under the auspices of the National Institute of Mental Health in the 1980s. In this study, which involved hundreds of patients in different settings across the United States, three active treatments were compared, medication (imipramine), cognitive behavioral therapy, and interpersonal therapy. All of the treatments worked equally well, and all succeeded in making people better. However, the people in the study were closely monitored even after the treatment part of the study had ended, and about eighteen months after the treatment ended, only around 30 percent of the patients had remained well (Shea et al. 1992). The other 70 percent had significant difficulties over the follow-up period. In other words, a year and a half after receiving state-of-the-art treatment that seemed to work well initially, more than two-thirds of the participants had already relapsed. There are now many more studies that suggest a similar trend. It seems that getting effective treatment for a current episode of depression is not very good protection against the return of symptoms once that treatment has ended. We write this not to scare you, but rather to let you know the facts as best as we understand them. These figures are obviously worrisome for people who have been depressed, and are the motivation for much of the work and ideas described throughout this book.

A natural question, having read these disturbing statistics is, "What is *my* risk for relapse?" Unfortunately, we don't yet know how to predict whether any particular person is likely to have more than one episode of depression. Even after an individual has had more than one depression, there is no diagnostic test or indicator of the individual's risk for having further depressions in the future. However, researchers are now setting their sights on the question of who is vulnerable to relapse, and answers to these questions will likely emerge in time. For now, we would encourage anyone who has suffered from an episode of depression to consider what they might do to protect themselves from becoming depressed again. In large part, this book is based on the strongest theories and research on relapse prevention, and the factors that we know to be associated with return of symptoms. If you're wondering what you can do to help yourself, using the strategies in this book is a good start!

On this same topic of the return of depression, it is also important to note that as people have more episodes, the impact on their life is greater and greater. This is not too surprising. As people spend more time being depressed, their ability to live a productive life decreases, relationships can be damaged or eroded, and sometimes people no longer feel well at all, even when they are not actively depressed (Gotlib and Hammen 1992). Chronic depression is also associated with a number of physical problems, including the experience of certain kinds of pain conditions, poor general health, and the development of other psychiatric and medical disorders (Clark, Beck, and Alford 1999). Again, the idea here is not to scare you, but rather to set the stage for making changes that will protect you from recurrent or chronic depression.

One of the difficulties with recovering from depression is a lack of motivation that often sets in as the depression improves. We probably need to explain this statement, because it may seem counterintuitive. We have found that when people recover from an episode of depression, their motivation to help themselves often decreases. In some ways, this is understandable. The person may have been morose, unfocused, despondent, lethargic, and hopeless for weeks and months. The return of energy, pleasure, concentration, and hope may make a person want to put the experience of depression in the past as quickly as possible. Thinking about the depression is often the last thing a recovered person wants to do. At this stage, a typical thought may be, "It was bad enough to go through it once—why rehash the experience?" This line of thinking, while understandable, can also be problematic. Once recovery has taken place, it is important to spare some of your newfound energy, hope, and focus on protecting yourself from relapse precisely because of the sobering statistics presented earlier. This is a message we will return to throughout this book, as many of our suggestions take careful thought, planning, time, and effort. Our suggestions may not always be fun either; at times, it will take hard work to build a future without depression. On the other hand, we think this small investment will pay huge dividends in your life.

Defining Relapse and Related Terms

Now that we have provided an overview of why the notion of relapse is so important, perhaps we should step back and define exactly what we are talking about when we use this term. *Relapse* is generally defined as a return of symptoms of a disease after there has been improvement. This may seem straightforward enough, but actually it can be very difficult to define a relapse in depression, or in most other mental illnesses. In fact, researchers have only had a consistent definition of relapse in the area of depression for the last twelve years or so (Frank et al. 1991). Prior to this, researchers tended to define relapse in very different ways. Although the field did tend to agree that the return of depression symptoms was problematic, the exact terms used to define what was being studied were not very consistent. For example, whereas some studies might have defined a relapse as an increase in the severity of depressed mood, other studies might have defined a relapse in terms of the number of symptoms (such as loss of interest or sleep problems) that returned. This lack of consistency has made it hard for scientists to communicate what they were learning about relapse, because they were often comparing apples and oranges (Prien, Carpenter, and Kupfer 1991).

There are a few important problems that need to be considered to ensure that the term "relapse" is used in a meaningful and useful way. First, if one can only have a relapse after some initial improvement, how much improvement is needed before a return of symptoms is a relapse? What if a person was to feel entirely well for a day or two? This often occurs for some people with clinical depression. If the symptoms return in full force after two days of feeling well, has the person had a relapse? What about if a person reports moderate improvement over a long period—for example, the depression is 50 percent better for a period of many weeks? Has the person recovered? What if the symptoms return in full force after having been at a 50 percent level for several weeks? Is this now a relapse?

These points, and many other technical issues (such as how we define symptoms or how we rate a person's condition), have plagued the field for many years, and scientists and clinicians continue to debate these issues to some extent. However, recent guidelines for defining relapse are now gaining popularity and improving consistency across the litera-ture. In fact, there is now pretty fair consensus among experts around how terms such as relapse, recurrence, recovery, and remission should be used (Frank et al. 1991). What's confusing is that the terms relapse and recurrence seem similar, as do the terms recovery and remission. However, when it comes to studying depression, these terms now have very precise and technical meanings.

All of these terms are currently defined based on the symptoms that an individual is experiencing. Because we don't understand the ultimate cause of depression (compared to knowing that a virus causes the common cold), the best thing we can do is track the symptoms carefully and define the state of the illness by the presence and absence of, or changes in, symptoms. Of course, symptoms don't cause depression, and depression is about much more than just symptoms. In fact, even when symptoms go away completely, some people experience lingering effects of depression on their ability to function, their relationships, or their quality of life. However, symptoms are the most reliable and observ-able signs of depression we have, so for now we must rely on symptoms, such as low mood, poor concentration, and feelings of worthlessness, to monitor the state of a person's illness.

Before we can define the four terms (relapse, recurrence, recovery, and remission), we also need to describe the different levels of symptoms that people experience. These can range from very severe to none, but, for the purpose of this discussion, we will describe three different ranges. The term *fully symptomatic* refers to a situation in which the person has all of the symptoms necessary to meet the diagnosis of depression according to the *DSM-IV* (American Psychiatric Association 2000). The term *asymptomatic* refers to the situation in which a person has no symptoms of depression and is essentially normal. Finally, the term *partially symptomatic* is a term used to describe people who fall somewhere in between—they don't have enough symptoms to be considered fully symptomatic, but they do have some symptoms that are significant and bothersome. Together, these terms define the range of symptom severity.

There is also the variable of duration, which refers to how long a person has been in one of the three ranges (for example, whether they have been asymptomatic for a week, fully symptomatic for a month). Unfortunately, the terms we described earlier are not currently associated with very clear time periods. We don't yet know whether being asymptomatic for two weeks is much different (in terms of predicting the future course of depression) than being asymptomatic for three or four weeks. The *DSM-IV* uses two months (eight weeks) as a guide for determining whether someone has overcome their depression, whereas some researchers have recommended as few as two weeks for making this determination (Frank et al. 1991).

Defining Remission

Remission can be of two kinds, either *full remission* or *partial remission*. Full remission is when a person previously diagnosed with depression improves to the point where he or she is asymptomatic for a specified period. We recommend the use of two weeks or fourteen days in a row as the period needed for full remission. There is also the possibility of partial remission in which the person has moved from being fully symptomatic to being partially symptomatic; again, we recommend using two weeks as the period needed for partial remission. In other words, the person whose depression is in partial remission feels much improved for some time, but not completely back to normal.

Defining Recovery

Recovery can be thought of as a period of remission that lasts for much longer. For example, we recommend that a period of six months be used to define the cutoff for recovery. A depressed individual who improves completely and feels normal would initially be considered to be in full remission. If the depression remains in remission for long enough (at least six months), then the individual would be said to have recovered from the depression. So, for our purposes, recovery is different from remission only because more time has gone by and the individual has continued to feel well. The rationale for this distinction between remission and recovery is that if a person is not symptomatic for six months, it is very likely that the episode of depression is over (recall that the natural lifespan of most depressive episodes is a few weeks to a few months). On the other hand, if a person goes into remission for three weeks and the symptoms suddenly return, we might say that the current episode of depression has emerged or broken through again.

Defining Relapse

Relapse is said to have occurred when the full symptoms of depression reoccur after the person's depression has been in remission. In other words, the individual had all the necessary symptoms for a diagnosis of depression, was then much improved for at least two weeks, and then experienced a return of all his or her depression symptoms. Essentially, relapse is thought to be a reemerging of the same episode of depression.

Defining Recurrence

Recurrence of depression refers to the emergence of a new depressive episode long after an individual has recovered from a previous episode. In other words, before the depression recurs, the individual has not only reached a state of remission, but has also recovered from the previous depression. For example, a person whose symptoms go away completely for several years, who then suddenly begins to feel depressed again, would be said to have experienced a recurrence of depression. The notion of recurrence is related to relapse, with the main difference being the length of time separating the new depressive episode from the earlier one.

Even the most careful reader might be a little confused at this point; that's okay. In our experience, even mental health professionals easily mix up these terms and need to constantly remind themselves of the definitions. Also, whereas one professional may be using the timelines suggested by the *DSM-IV,* another professional might use the criteria that Dr. Frank and colleagues created in 1991 (and on which our recommendations are based). These various definitions may also make you wonder about your own level of symptoms or whether your depression is in full remission, partial remission, or some other state. In fact, the next chapter is designed to help you understand where your depression is at currently.

Our purpose in providing these definitions is to help you to understand some of the terminology used by professionals who work in the area of depression. In many cases, it may not matter whether a return of symptoms is in fact a relapse or a recurrence. The strategies described in this book are designed to prevent the return of depression, regardless of whether your symptoms are in remission or you have reached the point of recovery.

The Conventional Wisdom on Relapse

Having digested the previous section, you are now armed with some new terms and lots of information. As we've already suggested, some of these terms and ideas fly in the face of conventional wisdom and may contradict things you have heard as you've navigated the world of depression. In our experience, the data demonstrating a high rate of relapse are still not very well known, nor is information about prevention readily available. Therefore, a lack of accurate information and an excess of misinformation sometimes get in the way of providing people with the best advice. In the next section, we describe some of the ideas that still seem to be in circulation, and how the information we now have contradicts these views.

Myths about Depression and Relapse

Myth: Partial recovery is good enough.

One problematic idea that we still run across has to do with the treatment of depression, particularly the goals of treatment. This line of thinking says that the most important thing for a person getting treatment is to notice substantial improvement, and that as long as the improvement is significant, it is good enough. We have seen situations in which patients are told that, because their sleep has improved or their appetite is better, they should be satisfied with their progress even when other symptoms are still troubling them. In cases like this, the treating physician, counselor, or other professional may see the treatment as a success, even when the patient is ambivalent and uncertain about how much better he or she is feeling. Sometimes the treating professional may be thinking that the patient doesn't appreciate how far he or she has come, and may try to make the progress seem much greater than it really is. For some people, this means being left with at least some remaining symptoms, which has been identified as an important problem even when the person's improvement is substantial. We now recognize that even limited symptoms of depression bring about many difficulties. Not the least of these is that if one is partially symptomatic, the risk of having a full relapse to depression is much higher (Clark, Beck, and Alford 1999). Also, the limited symptoms themselves can still cause substantial impairment in interpersonal and vocational functioning, as well as in overall medical health (Clark, Beck, and Alford 1999; Wagner et al. 2000). It is more desirable that treatment leads to a full recovery, with minimal or no symptoms remaining. This may require longer periods of psychotherapy or more aggressive medication management. In any case, it is important to make sure that the treatment you are provided is sufficient, and to be persistent in working on the symptoms until they are almost all gone.

Having said that, we also need to say that some amount of negative emotion is part of daily living, and treatment cannot make anyone's life perfect. This is especially true when someone is undergoing a stressor, for example, a disagreement in a relationship or pressure in a work setting. Some amount of upset is normal and probably quite healthy: being sad or upset is supposed to help you identify that a problem in your life needs to be addressed. Everyone struggles at times, and in subsequent chapters we will describe the differences between normal negative emotions and depressed mood that may signal a relapse.

Myth: Treatment should stop just as soon as you're feeling better.

Another piece of conventional wisdom has to do with ending treatment. It is still not unusual for people to stop taking medication as soon as they feel well, or to terminate psychotherapy when their mood returns to normal. We are not suggesting that psychotherapy needs to go on forever, nor that if you've had depression you must take medication for the rest of your life. However, the data on relapse after successful treatment speak for themselves. Just because a person has recovered from the current episode does not mean that he or she is protected from future episodes. In fact, continuing treatment beyond the time when the depression symptoms improve appears to protect an individual from experiencing a return of depression. We suggest that whatever decisions are made about when to end treatment or stop medication occur between you and your treating professional. Also, it is never too early to plan for relapse prevention, or to at least put relapse prevention on the agenda to be discussed with the person treating you. Having a relapse prevention plan in place emphasizes the importance of staying well and will facilitate this new focus to the treatment once normal mood returns. It may also be useful to have a plan in place if you notice your mood worsening once treatment ends. For example, in psychotherapy it may be possible to have "booster sessions" when one is struggling. Here again, it is motivation that is critical. Sticking with a relapse prevention plan may seem onerous when things are going well. Clearly though, carrying out a relapse prevention plan is well worth the effort.

Myth: There is a single way to prevent depression from returning.

One of the major reasons for writing this book relates to another type of conventional wisdom having to do with identifying a single, "magical" way to stay well. For example, we have seen patients who have been told that the secret to staying well is one of the following: physical exercise, rigid dietary restrictions, a low dose of antidepressant X, Y, or Z, religious conversion, and, in one case, finding a boyfriend. Obviously, we see the process of prevention as a multifaceted one and we urge you to think about all the possible ways to stay well, rather than just one. In fact, we think it is likely that, for most people, the way to stay well will involve a combination of factors, some of which they might not previously have thought of. We certainly would encourage keeping an open mind as you come up with a prevention plan. At the same time, we are particularly keen on methods that have been shown by research to be related to reducing risk of relapse and reemergence of symptoms. As in so many areas of health, there are unscrupulous individuals who will try to sell a cure or prevention for profit motives. It is important to ask what the person's credentials are for what he or she is doing. On what information are his or her ideas based? Is there any research to support what he or she is saying? Perhaps most important, does the "cure" sound too good to be true? If so, it probably is. Just as in any area of life in which we receive goods or services, it's important to ask questions and practice the maxim "buyer beware."

Myth: Depression is a trivial problem for which people shouldn't bother getting treated.

Another myth we sometimes hear about is frequently spread at a societal level through the media, popular culture, and other sources. It is a bit more complicated, and perhaps also more dangerous than the other myths discussed so far, because it contributes to the stigma surrounding mental illness and keeps people from getting help. We will refer to this myth as the "Prozac culture" myth. The premise of this myth is that Western society is obsessed with seeking happiness, and that mental health care is really just a reaction to a craving we all have to eliminate sadness. We have been approached at least half a dozen times by journalists writing stories about people who have too much time on their hands and seek treatment because they think it will make them happy. The underlying assumption of these reporters has been that we, as a culture, have been overly influenced by advertising, television, and movies to expect our lives to be perfect—filled with fabulous friends, an ideal romance, a great job, and a well-toned abdomen! These reporters argue that when our lives aren't perfect (which is inevitable), we run off and become "pill-poppers" or psychotherapy devotees rather than simply adjusting our expectations. People who share this belief may also assume that there was once a time (for example, the "good old days") when life was simpler and people expected little and made the best of what they had.

This myth will likely seem absurd to anyone who has treated people who suffer from depression. First, it is clear that people who really suffer from depression are not simply dissatisfied or feeling less than perfect—they are miserable, unable to function, and may wish to end their lives. Second, in the "good old days" life may have been simpler, but serious mental illness was ignored or, worse, punished as a sign of wickedness, sin, or some character flaw. Third, and perhaps most important, we know that the majority of people with clinical depression do not get diagnosed and are not treated.

In our opinion, the Prozac culture myth can cause harm by discouraging people from seeking treatment. In fact, depressed people, who often doubt themselves, may be the most vulnerable of all to being persuaded that their problems are trivial. In addition, this same myth could keep someone from trying to stay well by continuing to help themselves, whether by pursuing more professional treatment or using self-help strategies. Staying well is not a trivial or minor pursuit. Rather, there is a lot at stake!

The point of describing these myths is to bring attention to how dangerous depression can be, and how important relapse prevention is. Even some mental health professionals may not be as aware as they should be of prevention information, and you may find that you have to be assertive to get what you need. Don't allow yourself to be dissuaded by these myths, and make sure you pursue a comprehensive wellness plan.

Summary

In this chapter, we have described some of the history concerning our understanding of depression and particularly the problem of relapse in depression. We have tried to describe carefully how our view of depression has changed over time, and how the field, as a whole, has been trying to tackle the issue of depression being a recurrent and episodic illness. Detailed definitions were provided for relevant terms, such as remission, recovery, relapse, and recurrence. We saw that most people suffering from depression experience episodes that last several weeks to several months but eventually end, hopefully because of successful diagnosis and treatment. However, even when one has recovered from depression completely, there is a good probability that depression will return, and we know that the more depressive episodes a person has, the more difficulties they will experience in the future. Obviously then, the goal is to be able to prevent the return of depression, and the rest of the book focuses on this very issue.

The remainder of the chapter described a number of myths regarding depression and relapse prevention held by individuals who suffer from depression, mental health professionals, and society at large. On the one hand, it is not surprising that these misconceptions exist. New research findings regarding particular health problems and their treatments take years to trickle down from academic publications to professionals who work on the front lines. People involved in everyday practice cannot possibly keep up with all the latest developments in their field. To do so, they would have to give up their jobs to do nothing else but read! What we have tried to do for readers of this book is to give them a head start—to be proactive about their own care and to be as informed as possible about relapse. If you feel it's warranted, you may want to share what you've learned here with the professional who works with you. We hope that as you read the rest of the book you will begin to make a plan to help protect yourself from the return of depression.

Chapter 3

Understanding Where You've Been and Where You Can Go Next

Now that you are knowledgeable about what relapse is and hopefully have learned a lot more about the nature of depression, we turn our attention to understanding your own illness. As we've said, this book is designed to work best for people who are recovering from depression and are interested in preventing a relapse or recurrence. Because of this, it's important to know the state of your own depression right now. Of course, we don't want to recommend that you try to diagnose yourself; if you have any concerns about what your diagnosis is, it's best to seek an assessment by a physician or a psychologist (both of whom can formally diagnose a psychiatric disorder). Our aim in this chapter is to provide some tools so that you can better understand where you are and make informed decisions about what might be the best options for you.

First, we want to describe again the criteria for clinical depression. From the *DSM-IV* (American Psychiatric Association 2000), they are

- sad or low mood for more than two weeks

or

- loss of interest or pleasure in almost all activities for more than two weeks

Plus at least four of the following over that same two-week period:

- appetite or weight changes (either increases or decreases)

- changes in sleep (either insomnia or sleeping too much)

- noticeable agitation (for example, fidgeting) or moving more slowly than usual

- fatigue

- feelings of worthlessness or excessive guilt

- difficulties concentrating or making decisions

- thoughts of death or suicide

These are the criteria that a mental health professional would use to make a diagnosis. In addition, as discussed in chapter 2, it is important to know the actual level, intensity, or severity of the symptoms you are experiencing right now, and this is just as important as knowing whether your symptoms would formally meet the criteria for depression.

The self-assessment printed below will help you get a handle on how you're feeling right now. You will see a list of items that describe the different symptoms of depression and a rating scale for describing the extent to which you have the symptom. To use this survey, simply think about how things have been in the last week and circle the number that fits most closely with your experience. Once you have rated all ten items add the ten circled numbers together. The range of scores on this informal survey should be anywhere from 0 to 40.

Self-Assessment

Considering all the days of the last week, circle the number that best fits you for each item:

1. I feel sad.

0	1	2	3	4
Not at all true	Slightly/rarely true	Moderately/ occasionally true	Very much/ frequently true	Extremely/ constantly true

2. I am not interested in things that usually interest me.

0	1	2	3	4
Not at all true	Slightly/rarely true	Moderately/ occasionally true	Very much/ frequently true	Extremely/ constantly true

3. My appetite is different—I want to eat more or less than usual, or my weight has changed.

0	1	2	3	4
Not at all true	Slightly/rarely true	Moderately/ occasionally true	Very much/ frequently true	Extremely/ constantly true

4. My sleep is different—I sleep more or less than what was usual for me.

0	1	2	3	4
Not at all true	Slightly/rarely true	Moderately/ occasionally true	Very much/ frequently true	Extremely/ constantly true

5. I am more agitated than usual, or I am moving or talking much more slowly than usual.

0	1	2	3	4
Not at all true	Slightly/rarely true	Moderately/ occasionally true	Very much/ frequently true	Extremely/ constantly true

6. I am more tired or fatigued than usual.

0	1	2	3	4
Not at all true	Slightly/rarely true	Moderately/ occasionally true	Very much/ frequently true	Extremely/ constantly true

7. I feel worthless or I feel more guilty about things I have done or not done.

0	1	2	3	4
Not at all true	Slightly/rarely true	Moderately/ occasionally true	Very much/ frequently true	Extremely/ constantly true

8. I have difficulty concentrating on things or making even small decisions.

0	1	2	3	4
Not at all true	Slightly/rarely true	Moderately/ occasionally true	Very much/ frequently true	Extremely/ constantly true

9. I have thoughts of death or dying.

0	1	2	3	4
Not at all true	Slightly/rarely true	Moderately/ occasionally true	Very much/ frequently true	Extremely/ constantly true

10. I am less interested in sex than usual.

0	1	2	3	4
Not at all true	Slightly/rarely true	Moderately/ occasionally true	Very much/ frequently true	Extremely/ constantly true

What the Scores Mean

This scale should not be used to diagnose clinical depression, and there is no single cutoff to indicate that an individual is definitely suffering from depression. Rather, this scale can be used to provide ranges of scores that might indicate the severity of your depression during a given week. You can also use the scale to assess the severity of depression symptoms over a different period (for example, a month). Remember, depression is not considered "clinical" unless the symptoms have been present for at least two weeks. Using this self-assessment scale to observe your pattern of symptoms over time will add a lot to your understanding of where you are. Here are some suggested ranges that can be used to interpret your scores.

Scores of 21 to 40: Fully Symptomatic

If your score is greater than 20 (meaning that on average you've rated the symptoms as at least moderate in severity in the last week), you are probably experiencing substantial symptoms of depression and may currently be in a depressive episode. Recalling the terminology discussed in chapter 2, a score above 20 would be indicative of being fully symptomatic. If your score is in this range, you are likely to be feeling either sad or disinterested (or both), with numerous other physical and emotional manifestations of depression. Problems with mood are likely interfering with many of your usual activities, and you may not be able to work or function well in your usual roles (for example, as a parent, friend, or spouse). People in this state are often in need of assessment and treatment. If treatment has been started and is ongoing, scores in this range may signal the need to continue treatment and to do so actively. Unless scores decrease over time, the type or dosage of medications may need to be altered, or psychotherapy may need to be stepped up.

Scores of 6 to 20: Partially Symptomatic

If your score is between 6 and 20, it is likely that you have some symptoms of depression. Although your symptoms are probably not at their worst, they may still be present and bothersome. People who are in this range (partially symptomatic) may recall a time when their depression was much worse, but they may still feel different than their usual self. People in this range may have received treatment that they found helpful, and the reduction in their symptoms may have allowed them to return to work or get back into those things that were important to them, like family, friends, and hobbies. At the same time, people who are partially symptomatic may have some days that aren't so great. There is the potential for their symptoms to hamper their functioning in various ways. For example, they may have so much trouble waking some mornings that they are late for work. Or they may feel fatigued enough to skip their physical exercise routine. Or they may find themselves overeating some days, especially on days when they experience sadness or a loss of interest in things. Or they may have some days at work when things seem harder than usual, noticeably impairing their productivity. Obviously, reducing these difficulties and working toward minimal symptoms is still going to be important for anyone who is partially symptomatic.

Scores of 0 to 5: Asymptomatic

If your score was 5 or less, you may have symptoms that are mild or absent, and may well be in the asymptomatic range. People in this range are not necessarily always happy; rather, we would say that their depression symptoms are for the more part absent. Remember that most people have moments, even days, when they feel sad or have one of the other depression symptoms. There are also other things that can cause certain depression-like symptoms for a short period, aside from the usual slings and arrows of living. For example, if you've had a cold in the last week, you may have had a bad night of sleep, a sense of fatigue, or trouble concentrating, and this may be worth a rating of "2" on some items from the self-assessment. However, overall these experiences would fall into the normal range and are not signs that anything is seriously wrong. It is while in the asymptomatic range that most patients will report that they are back to normal and may consider ending treatment because it has been successful. They may feel as productive as ever at work, and may have "rediscovered" their strong relationships with family and friends. In some cases, if these people have been very depressed in the past, that time will seem like a distant and hazy memory even if it was only weeks ago. They may in fact describe themselves as a different person from the one who was despondent, hopeless, and unable to function during the worst period of their depression.

Your Current Status and What to Do about It

After calculating your score and considering the descriptions provided for the three severity ranges (fully symptomatic, partially symptomatic, and asymptomatic), you probably have a pretty good sense of the range in which your own symptoms fall. Completing the self-assessment on a regular basis for a longer period (such as one month) may provide you with information about changes in your depression symptoms. For example, you may find that in the first two weeks you are partially symptomatic, and in subsequent weeks your scores decrease to the asymptomatic range. This may mean that a depressive period is ending and you may be heading toward remission. On the other hand, you may find that in the first week you are partially symptomatic, and the next two weeks you are fully symptomatic. In this case, although the first week may represent somewhat of an improvement, you may still be in a full episode of depression, overall. If you are not clear in which range your symptoms fall, we would encourage you to carry on with the ratings and read over the descriptions again. It is very important to get some understanding of where you currently are, because the actions you take, even the way you read this book, may be affected whether you are fully symptomatic, partially symptomatic, or asymptomatic. Next, we discuss the different stages of depression, what to do about them, and then how this book may be useful.

If You Are Symptomatic

If you scored more than 20 on the self-assessment and the description of that symptomatic range fits your level of depression, your first action should be to seek assessment and treatment. If you are already in an appropriate form of treatment, continuing on this course is the best thing you can do right now. If you are not in treatment, the best place to start is with your doctor. He or she may want to refer you on to a specialist, perhaps a psychologist or a psychiatrist, or another kind of expert in the area of depression. Hopefully, this person will provide you with treatment that works and will be someone whose advice and ideas you trust. However, it also pays to be an informed consumer. You may want to review chapter 1 and focus on those methods that have been shown to be effective in careful research. Don't be afraid to ask the professional you are seeing whether the methods (or medications) they are going to use have been shown in research studies to be effective for depression. Most practitioners are already oriented to the use of what is typically called *evidence-based practice,* and may well make most of their treatment decisions on the basis of what has been shown to work best with the fewest side effects or complications. If the professional you see is unable to answer questions about the evidence supporting his or her approach to treatment, you may want to reconsider whether he or she is the kind of professional you want to continue seeing. Using an evidence-based approach to make treatment decisions is critical, not just in mental health, but in health care more generally. If a health care professional is not willing or able to rely on properly controlled research to guide treatment decisions, he or she is, in effect, using techniques that are unproven and, in the end, is really conducting a kind of experiment—with you as a test case! This is not a position most people want to be in; nor should they be.

If you are currently in treatment, you may still wish to review those treatments that work best for depression. If there is some particular treatment that you are not currently getting and you believe that it might help, don't be afraid to ask whether this other approach might be added to the treatment that you are already receiving. For example, if you are in interpersonal therapy and think an antidepressant medication may also help, ask your therapist about this. Most practitioners are very open to combinations of treatments and may even suggest them straightaway. Remember, you are your own advocate, so it's important to arm yourself with information and ask for what you want.

You may also want to access other resources that will be helpful during the acute phase of depression. We have included a list of Additional Resources at the end of this book. Many books have been written that are specifically designed for people who are currently depressed and want to help themselves. Many of these are workbooks that describe some useful strategies and then provide worksheets to help guide the reader through using the ideas to facilitate change in emotions, thoughts, or behaviors. Some books also provide specific problem-solving strategies and suggestions for coping.

As far as this book is concerned, we suggest that if you are currently in a severe depression, you may want to hold off on further reading until you are feeling better. There are several reasons for this. First, the intent of this book is to develop a wellness plan, and it will be less useful for reducing or controlling symptoms of acute depression. Second, during an acute phase of depression, getting better comes first; staying well is the next step once things are better. Third, reading this book about staying well may feel overwhelming if you are currently depressed. For example, it may be hard to imagine making certain lifestyle changes when you are already feeling low. Making these changes will seem more manageable when you have more energy and feel more hopeful about the future.

If You Are Partially Symptomatic

If you scored between 6 and 20 on the self-assessment and found that the description of the partially symptomatic range fits your level of depression, you have a number of choices and options. First, there's the good news that things are probably quite a bit better than they have been or could be. As we've said, being partially symptomatic means that substantial improvement has taken place. At the same time, you may not be back to your normal self. Your symptoms may still be difficult at times, and it may seem important to control your symptoms so they do not increase in severity. It may be that your symptoms have changed because an episode of depression is coming to an end. Or, perhaps you have found a treatment that is working for you. In either case, it may be important to review the next section on treatment strategies and find out what has worked in the past and what you think might be useful in the future. You may want to consider stepping up treatment (such as increasing your dosage of a medication or increasing the intensity or frequency of psychotherapy) to bring your symptoms down to the lowest possible point. At the same time, it may not be too early to start to think about staying well and using a relapse prevention plan. In fact, reading this book may offer you some important ideas about things you can do to reduce your vulnerability and may help you get to the point where you feel well. Using the strategies in this book will also help you to stay well.

If You Are Asymptomatic

If you scored between one and five, this is the situation for which this book is probably going to be most useful—when you've had a depression that has gone away and you are interested in trying to avoid getting depressed again. You'll see in the chapters ahead that we have lots of suggestions for staying well and warding off relapse and recurrence. Some of these ideas are things you can do yourself, like lifestyle changes, whereas others require the assistance of a professional (for example, using medications to prevent relapse). Not everything we describe will be something you will need or want to do; instead, you may find that some chapters are more relevant than others. That's exactly how it should be because relapse is a multifaceted issue and not all people who are prone to depression are alike. We would encourage you to have an open mind as you read, and to experiment with some of the strategies we suggest as you develop your own unique plan.

If you are asymptomatic, the main difficulty you may encounter in your use of this book is likely to be lack of motivation. We referred to this issue in chapter 2, but mention it again now that you have completed the self-assessment. As horrible as your depression might have been, it may now be a vague memory that you'd just as soon forget. We understand the need or wish that people might have to move ahead and look forward, to get into living their life without constantly thinking about "the illness" or "the depression." That's fine and, in fact, we heartily encourage the idea of reengaging with life and not ruminating about what you went through. But at the same time, we believe that it is important and reasonable to take active steps to stay well, and sometimes this may mean thinking about your depression and taking some time to understand it. It may be helpful to think of your depression as a problem that needs to be understood, broken down into its parts, and worked on step-by-step. The more you can approach the issue with a rational and perhaps even scientific mindset, the less onerous the task will be. We encourage you to be a student of your problem but not to let the problem become your life.

Just as important, thinking about a past depression can be frightening, and we know that fear usually leads to avoidance. Although avoidance often leads to a reduction in fear in the short term, it will not reduce your fear in the long term. In fact, in the long term, avoidance can actually make the fear much worse. So what is the cure for fear? The most powerful way to reduce fear and avoidance is to gradually confront the feared object or situation (Antony and Swinson 2000). Fortunately, the fact that you are reading this book is an excellent confirmation of your motivation. Putting into practice the ideas and suggestions in this book should take you a long way toward preventing your depression from returning.

Differentiating between a Sad Mood and a Relapse

One other important issue that needs to be discussed before we look at strategies to prevent relapse is the issue of normal or expected mood changes. First, everyone experiences sad periods over the course of his or her emotional life. These sad periods can happen as a result of many things, including stress, physical illness (such as a cold or flu), tiredness, lack of certain nutrients, conflicts, disappointments, or even a sad movie or book. In some people who have had depression or are currently depressed, we've noted a tendency to wish that life was never disappointing or that they could insulate themselves from sadness. Other people who have been depressed often see sad mood as a signal that depression has returned. They may even develop a fear of feeling sad. Indeed, some depressed people believe that others are *never* sad and that the ideal state is to always maintain a positive outlook. This is unlikely to be realistic for anyone, and negative emotions are a necessary part of life. The bigger question of course is what emotions are really supposed to do for us. That is, why do we feel emotions at all?

The most common answer to this question has to do with motivation. Emotions are powerful motivators that, as discussed in chapter 1, probably developed to help us function more efficiently. In fact, all emotions can be described as having a function. For example, the emotion of fear is thought to have developed to protect us from threat or danger, functioning much like an alarm system that gets us ready to flee from a dangerous situation or to fight back against a threat. Our prehistoric ancestors, who may have been faced daily with threats from animals or the natural environment, would have benefited greatly from this kind of alarm system, and would been more likely to survive as a result of being able to experience fear. Similarly, positive emotions may have developed because they reinforce things that are good for our survival or reproduction. For example, we often feel positive when eating or having sex, both functions that obviously help our species to survive.

It is easy to see how positive emotions might have a function in our survival, and even how certain negative emotions, such as fear, might help us to survive. The relationship between survival and other negative emotions may not be as clear. One possible explanation is that negative emotional states alert us to problems that must be solved. For example, jealousy in intimate relationships is thought to exist because it helps us protect the investment we have in our mate. Similarly, sadness may point out that there is a problem that needs to be solved for us to be in an optimal position. Another negative emotion, loneliness or a sense of isolation, may motivate us to seek the company of others and may also tell us that being alone is somehow risky or problematic. Anthropologists and evolutionary psychologists would point out that being part of a clan or group in prehistoric times was critical for survival, and hence loneliness is a kind of alarm signal for us.

In a nutshell, negative emotions probably exist to help motivate us to solve problems or to point out areas that are important for us. This doesn't in any way make them more fun to bear, but does suggest that they are not useless; nor should we try to never feel bad or sad. There are a number of critical factors or questions to ask yourself to differentiate between normal sadness and the first signs of a return of depression. First, you may ask yourself, "Do I understand what event or factor is responsible for the way I am feeling?" If it is difficult to pinpoint the trigger for your bad mood, this may mean that the sad mood is not connected to an event, but instead could be a sign of depression. Also, if you are able to identify the source of the negative emotion, you should ask yourself, "How would an average person respond in the same situation?" Would almost anyone feel the same way you do right now? If so, chances are you have, for lack of a better term, a normal bad mood. Second, and perhaps more important, is how long the sad mood lasts. For example, let's imagine you've applied for a job and discover you didn't get it, even though you were qualified and you wanted very much to get the job. Anyone is likely to feel sad, or perhaps even be tearful. They might want to talk to someone else about how upset they are. The question is, as several days go by, does the sad mood start to diminish? Four days later do you think about what happened as much as you did the day of the event? If, after several days, the emotion feels just as raw as it did initially, you think about it constantly, or the sad mood spreads and you start to feel bad about other areas of your life that have nothing to do with the job you applied for, this could be the first sign of an oncoming relapse.

If you determine that a sad mood is not normal, it is time to take out the wellness plan that we describe below. You may also want to complete the self-assessment and see whether other symptoms are present. Review the wellness plan carefully and choose the strategies that you think would be helpful right now, then take action without delay on the plan you've made.

Creating a Comprehensive Wellness Plan

In the subsequent chapters of this book, you will learn about specific strategies for preventing the return of depression. These strategies will form an important part of the wellness plan that you begin to develop in this chapter. Although you will not be in a position to develop a comprehensive wellness plan until you have finished reading this book, this is a good time to *begin* the process of developing the plan. The idea at this stage is to review what you've discovered in the first two chapters and to keep this information in mind as you read on. For now, you'll want to complete sections A, B, C, and D of the preliminary wellness plan worksheet below. Completing section A will help you see what to do next, based on your self-assessment. In section B, you record the age at which you had your first episode of depression, and also how many episodes you have had. This can be difficult, especially if you are going back several years or decades. But as you will see throughout this book, the number of episodes you have had, how long those episodes were, and what triggered them are all important pieces of information for looking at a wellness plan. In section C, we ask you to record treatment strategies that have worked in the past because you may want to consider using a similar approach if you begin to feel depressed again in the future. In section D, we ask you to think about ways to make sure that whatever resources have been helpful in the past will be available should you need them. Finally, in section E, you will record any obstacles that may arise in trying to access the help you need (for example, a previous therapist moved away).

Wellness Plan Worksheet

A. Taking into account your Self-Assessment completed earlier in this chapter, your current status is (circle only one)

1. Currently symptomatic (score 21 to 40)

2. Partially symptomatic (score 6 to 21)

3. Asymptomatic (score 0 to 5)

If you circled

1. Your priority should be obtaining an assessment and comprehensive treatment. You may want to hold off reading this book until this is completed.

2. You may want to consider getting additional treatment, modifying your treatment, and beginning to develop a comprehensive wellness plan based on the strategies described throughout the rest of this book.

3. Develop a comprehensive wellness plan based on the strategies described throughout the rest of this book.

B. Review of episodes

The first episode of depression (more than two weeks of symptoms) you recall when you were _____ years old.

Up until now, you can identify that you have had _____ episodes of depression. Below write some details about each episode, such as when it started, how long it lasted, and how it turned out:

_____

_____

_____

C. Review of treatments that have worked for you

Based on treatments that you have tried in the past, what has helped improve your depression?

Medication or biological treatments (such as antidepressants, herbal supplements, or electroconvulsive therapy):

_____

_____

Provider of these treatments is/was:

_____

Therapy or counseling (such as CBT or IPT):

_____

_____

_____

Provider of these treatments is/was:

_____

Lifestyle changes that have been useful (such as exercise or nutrition):

_____

_____

Provider of these treatments is/was:

_____

D. Are the providers of the helpful interventions listed in section C available and ready to assist you in the future? (circle YES or NO)

YES   NO

If NO, describe ways to contact new providers or reestablish contact:

_____

_____

_____

E. Are there any other obstacles you can think of that would interfere with your accessing treatments or therapists that have helped you in the past? (circle YES or NO)

YES   NO

If YES, describe potential ways to overcome these obstacles:

_____

_____

_____

Developing a Wellness Plan with This Book

Up to this point in the plan, you have had to review your history of depression and past treatments. These will be critical pieces of information in your wellness plan. Now we turn to what is in this book and what you can take from your reading to create a plan that is unique and works for you. Each of the subsequent chapters covers different topics, all of which are related to the theme of staying well. To complete the wellness plan we have provided, you will have an opportunity to summarize what we call the "bottom line" for each chapter, and what that bottom line means for you. We call this the Summary Exercise and it is a critical part of the wellness plan. After reading each chapter, the idea of the Summary Exercise is for you to come up with your own bottom line, just a couple of sentences about what you take away from that chapter as a central message. If some of the chapters are more applicable to you than others, go ahead and note that in your bottom line. It's possible that for some chapters you may write little, or you may simply state that this is not an area that seems important for you. That's okay too, as long as that doesn't become a pattern for all the chapters. The reason we ask you to write out this bottom line is that the act of doing so will trigger an important learning process; you may find that you have to reread portions of the chapter before you can formulate your own thoughts. Plus, your own words will have more significance to you later than ours.

The second section in the Summary Exercise for each chapter asks you to write down what examples, exercises, practices, or worksheets you found useful, and whether these need to be added to your life in some way. Again, you may not have something for each chapter, but over the remaining chapters there should be a number of things you can take action on. Preventing relapse is a multifaceted process. There is likely to be no single magic solution, but rather a combination of wellness strategies. When you finish the book, you may want to look over each of your bottom lines and the actions you will take. That information will also be there when you return to look at this book in the future. In essence, this book, tailored by you, will become your wellness plan.

Summary

In this chapter, we helped you to review the current status of your depression and how the stage of depression you are in relates to how you should use this book. Perhaps more importantly, you've begun to consider whether you should be focused on acute treatment for reducing symptoms, or whether you are ready to develop a wellness plan and put your energy into relapse prevention and staying well. You have also begun to take action by beginning to complete a wellness plan. In the next chapter, we describe the first strategies for preventing relapse and recurrence of depression.

Chapter 4

Using Medications to Stay Well

Medications are one of several treatments that have been shown to be effective for the majority of people who suffer from depression. In addition, medications are useful for preventing the return of depression. Yet, despite the benefits of antidepressant treatments, people are often reluctant to take medications for a number of reasons, many of which are unfounded. Before deciding whether to take medications, it can be useful to consider the advantages and disadvantages of these treatments.

Advantages and Disadvantages of Taking Medications for Depression

Medications have several advantages over other approaches to treatment, such as psychological treatments. They are easy to obtain (any physician can prescribe antidepressants), they may be covered by prescription drug plans, they are easy to use (one just needs to remember to take a pill or capsule), they may work more quickly than other forms of treatment, and they are often less expensive—at least in the short term. However, there are a number of disadvantages of medications as well, compared to other forms of treatment. In the long term, medications may be more expensive than other approaches to treatment; they are sometimes associated with side effects and interactions with other medications and drugs (including alcohol); and some antidepressants may be unsafe for people who have particular medical conditions or who want to get pregnant.

Although medications and psychological treatments (such as cognitive behavioral therapy and interpersonal psychotherapy) are about equally effective, especially for mild and moderate levels of depression, some people do better with one approach or the other. It is often difficult to predict beforehand who is likely to respond best to antidepressants, psychological treatment, or a combination. To some extent, the only way to find out is to try one of these approaches and see what happens. A person's own expectation regarding what will work is one factor that seems to predict outcome following treatment, so the decision of what type of treatment to try should be based in part on your own preferences, as well as recommendations from your doctor. The more severe your depression, the more likely it is that you will need medication or a combination of psychotherapy and medication.

Stages of Medication Treatment

There are five stages involved in medication treatments for depression: assessment, medication initiation, dose escalation, maintenance, and discontinuation.

Assessment

Before starting a new medication, it is important for your doctor to conduct a thorough assessment. The purpose of the assessment is to determine whether you are a good candidate for treatment with antidepressants and to select an antidepressant that is most likely to be useful. To determine whether you are a candidate for antidepressants, your doctor will likely want to first confirm that you are in fact suffering from depression. He or she will also want to obtain details of any current or past medical conditions that you have, as well as information about any other medications you are taking (including herbal preparations and dietary supplements). In addition, your doctor will likely ask you a number of questions to help determine the best choice of medications for your particular case. Issues that should be considered when choosing among medications are discussed later in this chapter.

Medication Initiation

When starting an antidepressant, it is important to start low and go slow. For many antidepressants, side effects are often at their worst in the first few days or weeks of treatment. If side effects occur, they can be minimized by first lowering the dosage, and then increasing the dosage slowly. During this initial phase of treatment, it is important for you to stay in close contact with your doctor, especially if you notice any side effects. During this phase, you will not likely notice much improvement in your depression symptoms.

Dose Escalation

Most newer antidepressants are effective at their introductory dose. However, if you do not notice any improvement after three to four weeks, your doctor will instruct you to increase the dosage of medication in small steps until your mood has improved. These adjustments may be made over several weeks. With each increase in dosage, you may also notice a return of, or an increase in, side effects. However, in most cases side effects improve as your body gets used to the new dosage. Some side effects may not improve over time, in which case your doctor may decrease the prescribed dosage or provide other suggestions for managing these symptoms. The goal of dose escalation is to find an ideal dosage that maximizes the antidepressant effect while minimizing the side effects. If the first antidepressant is not fully effective, it may be necessary to try other medications, or to combine several medications to obtain the maximum benefit.

Maintenance

Once an effective medication regimen has been established, the next stage of treatment is the maintenance phase. During this phase, an individual continues to take the medication. Visits to your doctor may be less frequent during the maintenance stage, particularly if everything is going well. Generally, it is recommended that treatment with antidepressants continue for a year or more. Stopping too early will increase the chances of your depression coming back. You should expect to continue at the dose of medication that you got you better; lowering the dose during this phase puts you at risk of falling back into depression. During this phase, you should also notice further gradual improvement in your mood.

Discontinuation

The final stage of medication treatment is discontinuation. After having taken an antidepressant for a while, many people are able to come off their medication without experiencing a significant return of symptoms. However, if you are considering stopping your antidepressants, it is important to do this under close supervision of your doctor. With several of the antidepressants, it is important for the discontinuation to be gradual, decreasing the dosage in small steps over a period of several weeks. Stopping medications abruptly, particularly at high doses, may lead to uncomfortable or dangerous withdrawal symptoms.

For some people, it is best to continue to take medications for a long time, and some people may never reach a point at which they can come off their medications without experiencing a return of their depression. Experts suggest (Greden 2000) that continuing to take medications is most important for people who

- have experienced three or more episodes of depression

- have had at least one or two severe episodes (for example, episodes with suicidal behavior, hallucinations or delusions, or a poor treatment response)

- have chronic depression

- have a history of relapsing upon discontinuing their medication

- have late-onset depression (first episode after age fifty)

- would find relapse to be unacceptable, perhaps because of their work or their life circumstances.

So some people can successfully come off their medications, whereas others are better off if they continue to take their medications over a long period. The decision to come off your medications should be made in consultation with your doctor.

An Overview of Medications That Work for Depression

Before we discuss what is known about antidepressant medications, we will start with a review of some misconceptions and myths about medications that people often believe, as well as responses to these misconceptions. Next, we provide a discussion of how antidepressants work, followed by an overview of available antidepressants and their key features. Information presented in these sections may change as new research findings become available. Some of the information presented (for example, whether particular medications are available, the brand names of medications, and available tablet strengths) varies from country to country and may not apply where you live.

Myths and Misconceptions about Medications

Below are five commonly held myths about taking medications for depression, as well as the truth concerning these misconceptions.

Myth: The side effects of medications, such as weight gain and sexual dysfunction, will be unbearable.

Response: Of course, it is not a myth that medications cause side effects. However, this should not automatically be a reason not to try antidepressants, at least initially. Although side effects may be unpleasant for some individuals, many people are able to take antidepressants without experiencing significant side effects. When side effects are a problem, they can be minimized by increasing the dosage very slowly at first, reducing the dosage, switching to a different antidepressant, taking another medication that counteracts the side effect, or stopping the medication altogether. In other words, you are not necessarily stuck with unpleasant side effects.

Myth: Medication is a sign of weakness and I should be able to get over this without medication.

Response: Having to take medication for depression is no more a sign of weakness than having to take medication for other illnesses. Although there are alternative treatments for depression, such as cognitive behavioral therapy, for some individuals medication is the only treatment that seems to work.

Myth: I shouldn't take medication because of the stigma attached to these treatments. Others will be critical or reject me if they find out I am taking medication for depression.

Response: Although this may be true in some cases, this belief may also be an example of the exaggerated negative thinking that often characterizes depression (see chapter 6). Antidepressants are among the most commonly prescribed medications, and we all have friends, family members, and coworkers in our lives who take antidepressants (even if we don't know it). You have the right to obtain effective treatment for your depression and it is important not to let the possible stigma associated with the treatment stop you from getting better. The benefits of treatment usually outweigh the costs.

Myth: Medication will not lead to an improvement in my mood.

Response: Most people who take medications for depression do notice an improvement in their mood and have a lowered risk of having their depression return as long as they continue to take the medications. If a particular medication doesn't work for you, there are many other treatment options, including trying a different medication, improving upon the effects of the medication by adding a second drug, or trying a nonmedication approach to treatment.

Myth: There are long-term risks in taking medication for depression.

Response: To the best of our knowledge, antidepressants are safe when taken over a period of many years. Medications such as fluoxetine (Prozac) have been available since the early 1980s, and other antidepressants, such as imipramine (Tofranil), have been available since the 1950s. When taken as prescribed, long-term use of these drugs appears to be quite safe.

How Antidepressants Work

The exact mechanism by which antidepressants work is not completely understood, although scientists continue to make progress in understanding how medications affect mood. All of the antidepressants appear to work by changing levels of neurotransmitters, the chemical messengers that pass information from one nerve cell (or *neuron*) to another, across a gap between neurons called the *synapse*. In depression, the neurotransmitters that seem to be most involved are serotonin and norepinephrine, although others, such as *dopamine*, may play a role as well. Neurotransmitters are released from one neuron and are then picked up by *receptors* on the second neuron, which allows the message to be passed from one cell to another.

Neurotransmitters that do not attach to the receiving cell are reabsorbed or recycled by the neuron that released them, a process known as *reuptake*. They are then broken down by *monoamine oxidase,* and made into new neurotransmitters. Some antidepressants (such as the momoamine oxidase inhibitors) probably work by preventing monoamine oxidase from breaking down neurotransmitters, thereby increasing the amount of neurotransmitters available. However, most antidepressants act by preventing the reuptake of one or more neurotransmitters. The net result is that more neurotransmitters are available for longer periods of time in the synapse between neurons. These changes in neurotransmitter levels lead to changes in the sensitivity and number of neurotransmitter receptors in the brain, which may be involved in the mood changes that occur several weeks after someone has started taking an antidepressant medication.

Common Features for All Antidepressants

There are a number of features that are common to all antidepressants. Rather than repeat these in our description of each medication class, we will describe these features first, in this section:

- All of the antidepressants take time to work. Usually, patients taking antidepressants will notice some improvement in the first three weeks, but significant improvement should continue during the first six to eight weeks. Improvement after this period is more gradual.

- All antidepressants may potentially cause side effects. In our descriptions of each drug, we focus on the most common side effects, which are generally not dangerous. However, in rare cases antidepressants can be associated with more serious side effects.

- It is important that individuals taking antidepressants be monitored closely by their physicians, particularly early in treatment.

- All antidepressants have potential interactions with medical illnesses. Therefore, it is important that your physician be aware of your medical history. For example, some medications may make seizures more likely in people suffering from epilepsy, or may increase the risk of liver failure in people who have problems with their liver.

- Antidepressants can also interact with various substances, including over-the-counter medications, other prescription medications, nutritional supplements, alcohol, caffeine, illegal or recreational drugs, and even certain foods. It's important to check with your doctor about any possible interactions between the antidepressants you are taking and these other substances.

- The safety and effectiveness of antidepressants may vary in different groups of people. For example, although some antidepressants have been shown to be safe and effective across age groups (children, younger adults, and older adults), others may not have been tested as extensively in children or older adults. The dosages indicated in this chapter are primarily for adults between the ages of eighteen and sixty-five. They may vary for children and older adults, either because of lower weight (children) or differences in the rate at which medications are processed or metabolized by the body (in older adults). Larger adults may also require higher dosages than smaller adults. Medications also vary with respect to their safety in women who are pregnant or breast-feeding. Finally, antidepressants may trigger a manic episode in people with bipolar (manic depressive) disorder. Check with your doctor if any of these issues are relevant for you.

Table 4.1 contains the generic name and trade name for each antidepressant medication and information on the available strengths and typical daily dose for each. In addition to the brand name formulations of these drugs, many of these medications are available in generic versions for a fraction of the cost.

If you are interested in a very comprehensive guide to medications for depression, anxiety, and related problems, one of the best books available is the *Clinical Handbook of Psychotropic Drugs* (Bezchlibnyk-Butler and Jeffries 2002). This book is written for a professional audience and is somewhat technical, but it is also among the most thorough books on the market. David Burns has a comprehensive but easy-to-read overview of medications in his book *The Feeling Good Handbook* (1999). There are also a number of excellent Web sites that provide comprehensive information on medications (see Additional Resources).

Selective Serotonin Reuptake Inhibitor

The Selective Serotonin Reuptake Inhibitors (SSRIs) are the most popular of the antidepressants. In addition to being effective for treating depression, SSRIs also have the official stamp of approval from the Food and Drug Administration (FDA) for preventing the recurrence of depression. SSRIs are also effective for treating problems with anxiety, obsessive-compulsive disorder, bulimia, and various other problems.

Common side effects of SSRIs include nausea and other abdominal symptoms, sexual dysfunction, dizziness, tremor, rash, insomnia, nervousness, fatigue, dry mouth, sweating, and palpitations. In very rare cases, more serious side effects may occur. Many of the most common symptoms tend to improve after the first few weeks of treatment, although sexual side effects often persist over time. Recent research suggests that sildenafil citrate (Viagra) can reduce sexual dysfunction in men who are taking SSRIs (Nurnberg et al. 2001).

Most of the SSRIs are easy to discontinue. Fluoxetine (Prozac) is particularly easy to stop because it naturally breaks down very slowly and therefore the body has a chance to get used to the gradual reduction in medication levels after the drug is no longer being taken. In contrast, paroxetine (Paxil) is processed very quickly by the body, and therefore discontinuation is associated with a number of withdrawal symptoms, particularly when the drug is stopped abruptly. Discontinuation from paroxetine and other SSRIs may entail such symptoms as insomnia, agitation, tremor, anxiety, nausea, diarrhea, dry mouth, weakness, sweating, or abnormal ejaculation. If this should happen, resumption of the medication usually reverses these symptoms within hours.

Norepinephrine Dopamine Reuptake Inhibitor

At this point in time, the only available Norepinephrine Dopamine Reuptake Inhibitor (NDRI) antidepressant is bupropion (Wellbutrin). This medication is approved for the treatment of depression, as well as the prevention of relapse and recurrence in depression. Bupropion is also marketed to help people quit smoking under the brand name Zyban. Side effects for bupropion may include tremor, dizziness, poor coordination, and increased libido. Compared to the SSRIs and other antidepressants, bupropion use is not usually associated with sexual dysfunction or weight gain. However, there is a higher risk of seizures with this medication, particularly early in treatment, at higher doses, and in people who have a prior history of eating disorders or seizures. Unlike the SSRIs and certain other antidepressants, bupropion does not appear to be especially helpful for problems with anxiety and related disorders. Withdrawal symptoms are generally not a problem when discontinuing bupropion.

Selective Serotonin Norepinephrine Reuptake Inhibitors

At this point in time, the only available Selective Serotonin Norepinephrine Reuptake Inhibitors (SNRIs), antidepressant is venlafaxine (Effexor). The extended release formula (Effexor XR) has the advantage of not having to be taken as frequently, and may be taken once a day. In addition to treating depression, venlafaxine is also useful for treating generalized anxiety disorder and other anxiety-based problems. Side effects are generally worse at higher dosages. Common side effects include nausea, sexual dysfunction, insomnia, dizziness, tremor, weakness, and dry mouth. Abrupt discontinuation can be associated with temporary withdrawal symptoms including insomnia, dizziness, nervousness, dry mouth, headache, weakness, sweating, or sexual dysfunction. These symptoms usually begin within the first eight to sixteen hours after stopping the medication and may continue for a week or more.

Serotonin-2 Antagonists/Reuptake Inhibitors

Serotonin-2 Antagonists/Reuptake Inhibitor (SARIs) include nefazodone (Serzone) and trazodone (Desyrel). These drugs are approved for the treatment of depression and the prevention of future depressive episodes. In addition, there is preliminary evidence that nefazodone is useful for treating certain types of anxiety and other psychological problems, although it doesn't have official FDA approval for treating these conditions.

Commonly reported side effects include headache, drowsiness, dizziness, weakness, and abnormal vision. These medications can be problematic for individuals with liver disease or for people who have recently experienced a heart attack.

Noradrenergic/Specific Serotonergic Antidepressants

Noradrenergic/Specific Serotonergic Antidepressant (NaSSAs) are the newest class of antidepressants to be introduced in North America and the only one currently available is mirtazapine (Remeron). Unlike many other antidepressants, there is not yet much research on the effectiveness of mirtazapine for other problems such as anxiety. Common side effects for mirtazapine include drowsiness, dry mouth, increased appetite, weight gain, and dizziness. Sexual side effects are generally not a problem with mirtazapine. Withdrawal effects upon discontinuation are usually mild, and may include drowsiness, nausea, dizziness, anxiety, and insomnia.

Tricyclic and Other Non-Selective Cyclic Antidepressants

Tricyclic antidepressants were the first medications to be introduced specifically for the treatment of depression. These medications have been around since the mid-1950s, and for many years they were one of the few available treatments for depression. Today, these medications are not prescribed as frequently as some of the newer antidepressants, but they are still an effective option for treating depression or for preventing depression from returning. They are also useful for treating certain anxiety disorders, such as panic disorder (imipramine, clomipramine) and obsessive-compulsive disorder (clomipramine), and a number of other psychological problems. Because these medications are older and are all available generically, they tend to be less expensive than many newer anti-depressants.

Side effects differ considerably across these medications, but some that seem to occur frequently across most of the tricyclic antidepressants include dry mouth, constipation, blurred vision, sedation, sexual dysfunction, sweating, and dizziness. Information on side effects for particular non-selective cyclic antidepressants is available in the *Clinical Handbook of Psychotropic Drugs* (Bezchlibnyk-Butler and Jeffries 2002).

Monoamine Oxidase Inhibitors

Monoamine Oxidase Inhibitor (MAOIs) have been around for almost as long as the tricyclic antidepressants. Despite the fact that they are effective treatments for depression (as well as certain anxiety disorders, such as social phobia), they are not often prescribed and should be considered only after other treatment options have been tried. The main reasons for the drop in the number of people being treated with MAOIs are that these drugs can be dangerous when taken with other prescription medications (for example, SSRIs), they may interact with certain over-the-counter medications (including cold medications), and they may produce severe increases in blood pressure when mixed with foods containing a substance called *tyramine*. Because of these potential interactions with tyramine, a prescription for an MAOIs comes with dietary restrictions. The list of forbidden foods includes aged cheeses (such as Cheddar and blue cheese), certain beans (such as fava), certain aged meats (such as sausage, pepperoni, and salami), certain soy products (such as tofu and soy sauce), and draft beer. In addition, one needs to maintain dietary and drug restrictions for at least ten days after stopping these drugs. Stopping MAOIs is sometimes associated with withdrawal symptoms.

Reversible Inhibitors of MAO-A

In Canada, the only Reversible Inhibitor of MAO-A (RIMAs) that is currently available is a drug called moclobemide (Manerix). In the United States, RIMAs such as moclobemide are not available. Moclobemide works in much the same way as the traditional MAOIs, but there are some important differences that make this medication a much better option than other MAOIs for many patients. The side effects of the RIMAs are much fewer than those of the traditional MAOIs, and interactions with foods and other medications are of little concern. Withdrawal symptoms are rarely a problem when stopping moclobemide.

When a Particular Medication Doesn't Work

Although antidepressant medications are usually effective for combating depression and for preventing relapse, there are times when a particular medication is not helpful for an individual. This can occur for a number of reasons, including

- an inaccurate diagnosis

- intolerable side effects

- inadequate time to see an effect (less than four weeks at a therapeutic dosage)

- too low a dosage

- inconsistent use of the medication (for example, forgetting to take some pills)

- interactions with other medications or drugs that a person is using

- the presence of certain other psychological problems

- the presence of certain environmental factors such as life stress

If you and your doctor are able to identify the factors interfering with your response to medication, it may be easy to correct the problem. However, it is often impossible to know why treatment with medication is not fully effective for a particular person.

When treatment with a specific medication is ineffective or just partially effective, there are several options, including

- switching to another medication (about two-thirds of people who do not respond to a particular antidepressant will respond to a different antidepressant)

- combining the ineffective antidepressant with another medication that boosts its effect (such as lithium)

- combining the antidepressant with another antidepressant

- combining the antidepressant with an effective psychological treatment (such as cognitive behavioral therapy or interpersonal psychotherapy)

- adding electroconvulsive therapy

If you decide to switch from one antidepressant to another, this should be done under close supervision by your doctor. Depending on the type of medication you have been taking and the type of medication you are switching to, it may be necessary to have a period of days or even weeks when you are taking neither drug, to give the first medication a chance to leave your system before starting the new drug. Most often, however, medications can be directly switched or even given simultaneously as the first is being stopped and the second started.

Natural and Herbal Treatments for Depression

Many cultures use natural or herbal products to treat various medical and psychiatric conditions. However, very few of these products have been subjected to rigorous scientific study and, in many cases, whether they are effective remains unknown. In addition, little is known about their safety, side effects, withdrawal effects, and interactions with medications, although this information is slowly becoming available (Davidson and Connor 2000; Kuhn and Winston 2000; Miller 1998; Russo 2001; Wong, Smith, and Boon 1998). In fact, because these products are not well regulated in North America (where they are considered nutritional supplements rather than medications), it is even difficult to know whether the concentration of the product indicated on the label matches the concentration in the bottle.

Despite these cautions, there are a number of herbal products that have at least preliminary evidence for treating depression. The best understood of these is St. John's wort, which is discussed below, followed by a review of several other natural products that have preliminary support for the treatment of depression. Note that although these products may be useful for treating depression, little is known about their long-term effectiveness. In other words, whether herbal products can be used as a long-term strategy for preventing relapse and recurrence in depression remains to be studied.

St. John's Wort

St. John's wort *(Hypericum perforatum)* is the most studied herb for depression. It contains several different chemical components that are likely responsible for its effects. Some of these chemicals appear to inhibit the activity of monoamine oxidase in the brain, which is also how MAOI antidepressants work. However, when St. John's wort is taken orally, this effect is relatively small. The antidepressant effect of St. John's wort probably has more to do with components of the herb that block the reuptake of serotonin, norepinephrine, and dopamine, which is similar to the mechanism of several antidepressant medications including the SSRIs, which block reuptake of serotonin in particular.

St. John's wort is relatively safe and appears to have few side effects. However, studies examining its effectiveness have yielded mixed results. Although a number of studies have suggested it is an effective treatment for depression (Kalb, Trautmann-Sponsel, and Kieser 2001; Lecrubier et al. 2002; Linde et al. 1996; Philipp, Kohner, and Hiller 1999), several recent, large controlled studies have found St. John's wort to be no more effective than placebo (Hypericum Depression Trial Study Group 2002; Shelton et al. 2001). The largest of these studies (Hypericum Depression Trial Study Group 2002) was conducted at twelve research clinics across the United States. This study compared treatment with St. John's wort to treatment with either sertraline (Zoloft) or placebo. On the main outcome measures, neither sertraline nor St. John's wort were more effective than placebo. This finding was surprising in light of many previous studies showing both sertraline and St. John's wort to be useful treatments for depression. More research is needed to clarify the role of St. John's wort in the treatment of depression.

Other Natural Products

In addition to St. John's wort, there are a few other natural substances that when taken may help to improve mood. *S-adenosyl-methionine* (SAMe) is a naturally occurring substance in the brain that affects the processing of serotonin, norepinephrine, and dopamine. SAMe has been shown to be useful for reducing depression in a number of studies (Bressa 1994; Fava et al. 1995) and the side effects appear to be mild. More studies are needed to establish the safety of this product before it is recommended widely. Also, the cost of this compound is too high for many people.

Another product, *inositol* (a variant of the sugar *glucose* that occurs naturally in the body) was found in one study to be more effective than placebo for treating depression (Levine et al. 1995). In another study, adding inositol to an SSRI did not lead to better outcomes than adding a placebo to treatment with an SSRI (Levine et al. 1999), suggesting that this product is not particularly useful in combination with an SSRI, above the effects of the SSRI alone. Despite the initial study showing a positive effect of inositol, additional controlled studies are needed to determine whether inositol is a safe and effective treatment for depression.

Finally, there is now evidence that combining omega-3 fatty acids (found in fish oils and other natural sources) with standard antidepressant treatment improves outcomes in individuals who suffer from recurrent depression (Nemets, Stahl, and Belmaker 2002).

Choosing between Antidepressant Medications

For most types of depression, any antidepressant is equally likely to be effective, based on studies that have compared one medication to another. Therefore, choosing among medications is usually based on factors other than the proven effectiveness of the medication. Here are some issues that your doctor will likely consider when making the decision of which medication to prescribe:

Type of depression: Certain types of depression may respond better to one medication than another. For example, *atypical depression* (where a person's mood remains responsive to the individual's surroundings and is associated with increased appetite and sleep, extreme fatigue, and prior sensitivity to rejection throughout one's life) appears to respond better to SSRIs, venlafaxine, and MAOIs, and more poorly to tricyclic antidepressants (Greden 2000).

Presence of other psychological problems: If another psychological problem is present in addition to depression, it is preferable to choose an antidepressant that will treat both conditions. For example, in the case of obsessive-compulsive disorder, an SSRI such as fluoxetine will likely lead to improvement in both the depression and the obsessive-compulsive disorder, whereas a tricyclic antidepressant such as imipramine will likely help only the depression.

Side effect profile: Some medications are more likely than others to cause side effects for a particular individual. Often, it is difficult to know in advance which medications are more or less likely to be problematic, so the decision is based on a process of trial and error. However, in some cases known side effects of a medication can be used to influence the decision for a particular patient. Some antidepressants are more likely to cause weight gain, for example, and may be avoided in those for whom weight gain is a problem. A recent review of antidepressants concluded that bupropion is the best-tolerated antidepressant, based on information from the 1998 *Physicians' Desk Reference* (Dewan and Anand 1999).

Other safety concerns: If the individual is a child or an older adult, it is preferable to select a medication that is better established in these groups (some antidepressants have not been studied in children or older adults). Similarly, if the individual is pregnant or breast-feeding, one would be more likely to select a medication that has been shown to be safe for the developing fetus or the nursing infant.

Previous treatment response: If a specific antidepressant has worked for a particular individual in the past, with few side effects, a physician may be more likely to prescribe the same antidepressant again. Although there is no guarantee that it will work the second time, chances of it working may be higher than if a different medication were selected.

Past treatment response of a family member: In the absence of other information, physicians will often first recommend trying a medication that has worked previously for the same problem in one or more of the patient's family members. Given that people share many physical characteristics with their family members, including a genetic predisposition that helps to determine whether they will develop depression, it makes sense that family members might also have similar responses to treatment.

Cost: Older medications are considerably less expensive than newer medications. The cost of medications may be a factor in the decision of which medication to prescribe, particularly for people who do not have insurance to cover the cost of prescription drugs.

Interactions with medical conditions: If a patient has a particular medical condition, a prescribing physician is likely to choose an antidepressant that will not interact with the medical illness. For example, if a person has epilepsy, one would not select a medication that increases the risk of seizures. Similarly, for a patient with Parkinson's disease, one would not select a medication that can increase Parkinson's symptoms.

Interactions with other medications, drugs, and herbal remedies: If a patient is taking other medications or herbal preparations, it is important to choose antidepressants that will not interact with these other products, or to have the patient stop using the other product if possible.

Similarly, if the patient wants to continue to be able to have a glass of wine with dinner, it may be important to select a medication that can be consumed safely with modest amounts of alcohol.

Ease of discontinuation: When choosing between medications, physicians will often take into account how easy it will be in the future to discontinue the medication, particularly for an individual who has a history of experiencing withdrawal symptoms when coming off antidepressants.

Dosing issues: Physicians will often take into account the frequency with which the medication must be taken. Most antidepressants can be taken once per day, although a few are recommended to be taken more frequently.

Combining Medications with Other Treatments

Treatment with an antidepressant often occurs along with other treatments, including additional medications, psychological treatments, or electroconvulsive therapy. In the next section, we discuss these combination treatments for depression. We also include a brief description of transcranial magnetic stimulation, a new treatment that shows promise for depression.

Combining One Medication with Another Medication: Augmentation and Combination Treatments

Most of the research on the effectiveness of antidepressants is based on studies comparing a single medication to either a placebo or another medication. There is relatively less scientific research on combining more than one medication for depression. However, the research that does exist suggests that this may be a useful option for individuals who do not benefit from treatment with a single antidepressant or for those who obtain only partial benefits. In clinical practice, physicians often prescribe more than one medication in these cases.

Often, treatment with more than one medication involves combining more than one antidepressant (for example, an SSRI combined with a tricyclic antidepressant, or bupropion combined with venlafaxine or an SSRI, or mirtazapine combined with an SSRI). However, augmenting an antidepressant with other types of medication including lithium (a mood stabilizer normally used to treat bipolar disorder), thyroid hormone, buspirone (an antianxiety medication), or a novel antipsychotic medication such as olanzapine or risperidone (medications used to treat schizophrenia) may be useful when a person's depression does not respond to just one medication (Bezchlibnyk-Butler and Jeffries 2002). Also, as reviewed earlier, addition of omega-3 fatty acids has been shown to help boost the effect of antidepressants (Nemets, Stahl, and Belmaker 2002).

Combining Medication with a Psychological Treatment

For many people, the combination of an antidepressant and a psychological treatment seems to work best. For example, in one study (Evans et al. 1992) relapse rates were examined in the two years after being treated with imipramine, cognitive therapy, or the combination of these treatments. Relapse rates were highest (50 percent) for individuals who were treated with imipramine alone and then stopped the medication. Relapse rates were lowest (15 percent) for people who received imipramine and cognitive therapy and continued their medication during the two year follow-up phase. The rate of relapse for individuals who received cognitive therapy alone was 21 percent in the two years following treatment. A number of other studies have confirmed the long-term benefits of combining medications and psychological treatments (Boland and Keller 2001).

Combining Medication with Electroconvulsive Therapy (ECT)

Electroconvulsive Therapy (ECT) involves inducing a very mild seizure by delivering a shock to the brain lasting less than a second. Treatments usually occur two to three times per week, for a total of between six and twenty treatments. Antidepressants are typically continued after the ECT treatments have been completed. The main side effect of ECT is impaired short-term memory that improves over the first to second month after treatment stops. Despite this side effect, more than half of individuals who do not respond to medications alone may find ECT to be effective for depression.

This type of treatment is still somewhat controversial, mostly because of how it was administered in the past, and how it has been portrayed in the media (for example, ECT was depicted very graphically in a particularly disturbing scene from the film *One Flew Over the Cuckoo's Nest*). Today, ECT is administered under general anesthetic so the patient is unaware of the procedure when it is occurring. In addition, medications are used to minimize muscle convulsions and other unpleasant effects during the procedure. This treatment is usually viewed as a last resort, reserved for individuals with the most severe forms of depression who have not responded to other forms of treatment, such as medication and psychotherapy. Although ECT is an effective treatment for depression, its mechanisms of action remain unknown.

Transcranial Magnetic Stimulation (TMS)

Transcranial Magnetic Stimulation (TMS) is a new treatment for depression that has only been studied since the early to mid-1990s for this condition (George et al. 2001). Essentially, the procedure involves placing a powerful magnet over a person's scalp, which changes the electrical signals in the brain. Although a few studies have failed to show any benefit of this procedure, enough studies have shown a positive effect in depression to suggest that TMS may be useful. As the procedures become more refined, additional research will answer the question of whether TMS is an effective treatment for depression, as well as the question of how it works. There is still a lack of research on combining TMS with medications, so it unclear whether the procedure works better on its own or in combination with medications. In addition, more research is needed on the benefits of using TMS to prevent relapse in depression.

Using Medications to Stay Well

Up to three-quarters of people who experience two or more episodes of depression will experience another episode in the future. In addition, for some people with recurrent depression, the intensity and duration of the episodes tends to increase over time. Therefore, when selecting medications it is important to choose a drug (or combination of drugs) that will be effective not only for reducing depression, but also for preventing depression from returning in the future.

Until recently, researchers have ignored the need to develop strategies for preventing relapse and recurrence in depression. However, in recent years there have been a number of studies examining the continued use of antidepressants after individuals begin to feel better. In most cases, these studies have followed patients for up to two years, with relatively few studies following people for periods longer than that. Therefore, there is still a lack of research addressing the question of whether medications will continue to be helpful over very long periods (for example, five years or longer).

As summarized in a recent review by Greden (2000), there are now studies showing that a number of medications can be useful for preventing depression for periods of one to two years, including tricyclic antidepressants, NaSSAs, MAOIs, and SSRIs. For example, in a study of sertraline versus placebo (Doogan and Caillard 1992), 46 percent of those taking placebo experienced a relapse during the follow-up period, whereas only 13 percent of those taking medication experienced a relapse. Although a number of different medications have been shown to prevent relapse, there are relatively few studies comparing medications to see which ones are most effective for keeping depression away. Therefore, at this point in time it is difficult to recommend one medication over another for the purpose of relapse prevention. Instead, the issues raised in the earlier section on choosing among medications for initial treatment of depression need to be considered for the purpose of choosing maintenance medications as well.

Your Medication History

As you will have noticed, choosing and understanding medications for depression is pretty complex. There are lots of different medications, dosages, side effects, and other factors to consider. One of the things that will be important is to have a good record of your own history of taking medications. This will not only be important for you, but could also be very useful for the doctor treating you, who will undoubtedly want or need to know what you've tried in the past and what the effects were. Putting this information on paper when you are feeling well is important too. Depression can and will affect your memory and concentration. So if you have a return of depression, getting this information down may be a struggle, or you may forget something you tried. Take the time to note your history here so that it will always be ready when you need it.

Summary

This chapter reviewed issues related to the use of medications to treat depression and to prevent depression from returning. First, the issue of whether to take medication at all was raised, and the disadvantages and benefits of taking medication were reviewed. The stages of medication treatment were described, with a special emphasis on maintenance medications and discontinuation, since the topic of this book is the prevention of relapse and recurrence of depression. The chapter also reviewed myths about taking medications, and the key features of the various antidepressant types and herbal remedies that may be useful for depression. Suggestions for choosing between antidepressant medications were provided, followed by information on combining medications with other treatments in order to improve outcome, in both the short term and the long term. The chapter ended with a reminder that the goal of treatment is not just to overcome depression, but rather to prevent it from returning. Medications can be one of several tools for helping an individual remain well.

Summary Exercise

Record what you believe is the bottom line from this chapter, then record what practices, exercises, or worksheets you would adopt as part of your wellness plan.

Chapter 4, Using Medications to Stay Well, reviews medications that work and may offer protection from relapse. My bottom line in this chapter is:

_____

_____

The practices, exercises, or actions I will take from this chapter are:

_____

_____

Worksheet 4.1: Personal Medication History

STEP 1. What medications, if any, are you currently taking for depression?

Medication 1: _____ Dose: _____

Medication 2: _____ Dose: _____

Medication 3: _____ Dose: _____

Medication 4: _____ Dose: _____

STEP 2. What medications have you taken for depression in the past?

Medication 1: _____ Dose: _____ What Year(s): _____

Medication 2: _____ Dose: _____ What Year(s): _____

Medication 3: _____ Dose: _____ What Year(s): _____

Medication 4: _____ Dose: _____ What Year(s): _____

Medication 5: _____ Dose: _____ What Year(s): _____

Medication 6: _____ Dose: _____ What Year(s): _____

Medication 7: _____ Dose: _____ What Year(s): _____

Medication 8: _____ Dose: _____ What Year(s): _____

STEP 3. Which of these medications worked best?

_____

STEP 4. Which medications had little or no impact?

_____

STEP 5. Which medications caused the most problematic side effects?

Side Effect: _____ Medication: _____

Side Effect: _____ Medication: _____

Side Effect: _____ Medication: _____

Side Effect: _____ Medication: _____

Table 4.1: Summary of Antidepressants Available in the United States and their Typical Dosages

Selective Serotonin Reuptake Inhibitors (SSRIs)

Generic Name	Trade Name	Available Tablets/Capsules	Typical Daily Dosage
Citalopram	Celexa	20 or 40 mg	10–60 mg
Escitalopram	Lexapro	10 or 20 mg	10–50 mg
Fluoxetine	Prozac	10 or 20 mg	10–80 mg
Fluvoxamine	Luvox	50 or 100 mg	50–300 mg
Paroxetine	Paxil	10, 20, 30, or 40 mg	10–50 mg
	Paxil CR	12.5, 25, or 37.5 mg	25–62.5 mg
Sertraline	Zoloft	25, 50, or 100 mg	50–200 mg

Citalopram, fluoxetine, and paroxetine are also available in a liquid form.
There is also a new formulation of fluoxetine that can be taken once per week.
CR = controlled release

Norepinephrine Dopamine Reuptake Inhibitors (NDRIs)

Generic Name	Trade Name	Available Tablets	Typical Daily Dosage
Bupropion	Wellbutrin	75 or 100 mg	225–450 mg
	Wellbutrin SR	100 or 150 mg	150–300 mg

SR = sustained release

Table 4.1: Summary of Antidepressants Available in the United States and their Typical Dosages

Selective Serotonin Norepinephrine Reuptake Inhibitors (SNRIs)

Generic Name	Trade Name	Available Tablets	Typical Daily Dosage
Venlafaxine	Effexor	25, 37.5, 50, 75, or 100 mg	7–225 mg
	Effexor XR	37.5, 75, or 150 mg	

XR = extended release

Serotonin-2 Antagonists/Reuptake Inhibitors (SARIs)

Generic Name	Trade Name	Available Tablets	Typical Daily Dosage
Nefazodone	Serzone	50, 100, 150, 200, or 250 mg	100–600 mg
Trazodone	Desyrel	50, 100, or 300 mg	150–600 mg

Noradrenergic/Specific Serotonergic Antidepressants (NaSSAs)

Generic Name	Trade Name	Available Tablets	Typical Daily Dosage
Mirtazapine	Remeron	15, 30, or 45 mg	15–60 mg

Table 4.1: Summary of Antidepressants Available in the United States and their Typical Dosages

Tricyclic Antidepressants

Generic Name	Trade Name	Available Tablets/Capsules	Typical Daily Dosage
Amitriptyline	Elavil, Endep	10, 25, 50, 75, 100, or 150 mg	75–300 mg
Clomipramine	Anafranil	10, 25, 50, 75 mg	75–300 mg
Desipramine	Norpramin	10, 25, 50, 75, 100, or 150 mg	75–300 mg
Doxepin	Sinequan, Adapin	10, 25, 50, 75, 100, or 150 mg	75–300 mg
Imipramine	Tofranil	10, 25, 50, 75, 100, 125, or 150 mg	75–300 mg
Nortriptyline	Aventyl, Pamelor	10, 25, 50, or 75 mg	40–200 mg
Protriptyline	Triptil, Vivactil	5, or 10 mg	20–60 mg
Trimipramine	Surmontil	12.5, 25, 50, 75, or 100 mg	75–300 mg

Amitriptyline and nortriptyline are also available in a liquid form.
Amitriptyline and imipramine are also available in a injection form.

Table 4.1: Summary of Antidepressants Available in the United States and their Typical Dosages

Other Non-Selective Cyclic Antidepressants

Generic Name	Trade Name	Available Tablets	Typical Daily Dosage
Amoxapine	Asendin	25, 50, 100, or 150 mg	100–600 mg
Maprotiline	Ludiomil	10, 25, 50, or 75 mg	100–225 mg

Monoamine Oxidase Inhibitors (MAOIs)

Generic Name	Trade Name	Available Tablets	Typical Daily Dosage
Phenelzine	Nardil	15 mg	45–90 mg
Tranylcypromine	Parnate	10 mg	20–60 mg

Reversible Inhibitors of MAO-A (RIMAs)

Generic Name	Trade Name	Available Tablets	Typical Daily Dosage
Moclobemide	Manerix	150 or 300 mg	300–600 mg

Chapter 5

Maintenance Psychotherapy to Stay Well

Perhaps one of the first questions for someone trying to stay well and prevent relapse is, "Should I seek the help of a therapist?" This is a very practical question that has important implications. If the answer is "yes," you will need to consider other questions like what kind of therapist, how often you will see that person, what you will want to work on, and maybe how the expense will be covered. In this chapter, we first look at the question of whether therapy when you are well (we call it *maintenance psychotherapy*) is actually helpful for preventing relapse. We then look at some of the factors involved in selecting a therapist, as well as how maintenance psychotherapy could be structured and what kinds of things would be useful to work on to stay well.

Does Maintenance Psychotherapy Help Prevent Relapse?

The quick answer to the question of whether maintenance psychotherapy helps prevent relapse seems to be "yes." Unfortunately, the number of studies in this area is still small when compared to the number of studies looking at treating acute (current) depression. However, exactly because relapse rates for depression tend to be quite high, researchers have recently begun to look at whether ongoing psychotherapy can help people stay depression-free over the long term. For example, a seven-year-long study followed older adults who had previously suffered from depression and provided them with monthly maintenance sessions of interpersonal therapy (IPT) with medication, or medication alone, or IPT alone, or placebo. The results of the study suggested that the best method for keeping people well was the combination of medication and monthly IPT sessions (Reynolds et al. 1999). In fact, 80 percent of the people who received medication and IPT stayed well, which is a very high percentage considering the fact that these people were followed for seven years. The researchers conducting the study also found that the combination of medication and monthly IPT led to better interpersonal relationships and satisfaction in those relationships (Lenze et al. 2002).

A somewhat similar study has also shown benefits of ongoing cognitive behavioral therapy (CBT) for maintaining wellness. In this study, patients who had been depressed and then improved were either randomly assigned to receive what was called *continuation cognitive therapy* for eight months or they were simply evaluated for eight months without any treatment. The continuation cognitive therapy sessions occurred monthly on average, and the patients were followed by the researchers even after the eight continuation sessions were finished. The researchers found that over the total study duration (two years), individuals who had received continuation cognitive therapy had a 10 percent chance of relapse whereas the people who did not get the continuation treatment had a 31 percent chance of relapse (Jarrett et al. 2001). Thus having monthly sessions of CBT over eight months meant that one's chances of having a relapse were only a third of what they would have been without maintenance psychotherapy. From these studies we can say with some level of confidence that if you have recently suffered from a period of depression, it may make sense to seek out maintenance IPT (see chapter 13) or maintenance CBT (see chapter 6) to stay well. However, note that despite the evidence supporting the use of IPT and CBT for preventing relapse and recurrence of depression, not all psychotherapies are the same. There is no research we are aware of that has investigated the benefits of most other forms of psychotherapy for the purpose of relapse prevention.

Besides these very compelling studies showing the benefits of continuing psychotherapy even after one's depression has improved, there is also research supporting the value of beginning a new prevention-focused treatment after depression has ended. An example is a study, described in detail in chapter 8, in which previously depressed individuals were found to have a better chance of staying well when they learned to do a specific form of mindfulness meditation (Teasdale et al. 2000). It is likely that in the next decade or two we will see many more such studies in which researchers provide people who are well with a treatment that is designed to help them stay that way. Clearly, those in the field of psychotherapy believe that treatment, even when you are well, can offer important long-term benefits for reducing the risk of relapse.

If you are thinking about seeking maintenance psychotherapy, there are a number of issues to consider. In the section below, we discuss several of these issues.

Do I Need Maintenance Psychotherapy?

After reading the previous section, you may be wondering whether you, as an individual, should seek out maintenance psychotherapy. This is a difficult question to answer for any one person. The studies we described tell us about the probabilities of relapse across groups of people, but they cannot tell us whether psychotherapy is right for any given individual. In chapter 2, on predictors of relapse, we described how it is no simple task for researchers to estimate the odds of any one person having a return of depression. The same is true in the case of relapse rates for many medical problems, for which it is difficult to accurately estimate one's odds of getting sick again, although it may be possible to determine whether one is high risk or low risk. From the available research, it is fair to say that maintenance psychotherapy is likely to improve your chances of staying well, although there are no guarantees. In the next section we will describe some of the individual factors that may help you to make a more informed decision about whether you should pursue maintenance psychotherapy. Many of these same factors are also relevant when considering whether to take maintenance medications (see chapter 4).

Risk Level Based on Past Depression

One important factor to consider with respect to the risk of relapse and the need for maintenance psychotherapy is what your depressions have been like in the past. There is a general consensus in the field that if you have had multiple episodes or a very severe episode of depression, you are at higher risk of having another episode. Therefore, if you have had many episodes or a very severe episode (for example, one that resulted in a hospitalization), maintenance psychotherapy should be more of a priority. Not only could it help you stay better for longer, but also, if you are seeing someone regularly in therapy, they can be part of a helpful early warning system. Some people have very sudden onset of depression, and many do not even realize when they are slipping into a depression until it is too late. Having a therapist who knows you well and can track your moods with symptom inventories can be invaluable in these situations.

Past Positive Experience with Psychotherapy

A second factor to consider in deciding whether to pursue maintenance psychotherapy is whether psychotherapy has helped in the past. For example, if IPT or CBT has helped you to recover from a depression, continuing the treatment after you have become well may be useful. If your therapy has ended, you may want to find out whether your former therapist could help you with maintenance treatment and is willing to work with you on staying well. Most therapists will understand that goal and many therapists see relapse prevention as an important objective to build into the therapy, often right from the start.

Compatibility with Psychotherapy

Another factor to consider is to what extent approaches like IPT and CBT appeal to you. Not all therapies seem equally appealing to all people; certain therapies have more value to some people than others. The more an intervention makes sense to you, relates to your life, or is something you can believe in, the more likely it is that this intervention is going to be something you want to work with and will stick with. At the same time, some healthy amount of skepticism is just as important; not all interventions work for all people, and you should judge therapy by how well it works for you.

If you have not been in therapy before, or are unfamiliar with the IPT and CBT approaches, you may want to have a careful look at the chapters in this book that feature these approaches; these are the forms of psychotherapy with the most research support for treating depression. CBT (chapter 6) starts with the assumption that depression is associated with thoughts and perceptions that are biased in a negative direction, as if the depressed person is wearing a pair of dark sunglasses that filter information in a harsh and unnecessarily pessimistic way. A CBT therapist helps the person to become more skilled at detecting and correcting these kinds of negative thoughts and helps the person to develop behavior patterns that will help diminish feelings of depression. IPT (chapter 13) focuses on interpersonal relationships and how these contribute to mood problems and wellness. Traditionally, IPT therapists focus on one of four areas, working on the issues that are most important for the person. The four different areas are

1. issues surrounding grief or interpersonal loss (such as the death of a loved one or divorce)

2. interpersonal role disputes, in which there is some disagreement and conflict about what you want in a relationship and what other people expect from you

3. role transitions—difficulties with adjusting to life changes, particularly when these changes involve taking on new demands or a different kind of identity (such as getting married or losing a job)

4. improving interpersonal skills (such as patterns of communication) to help improve the quality of relationships in general.

We recommend reading chapters 6 and 13 to help you to decide whether either IPT or CBT appeals to you.

Triggers for Depression

A final issue to consider when deciding whether to seek maintenance psychotherapy has to do with what triggers your depressions. This can be difficult to establish with certainty, but sometimes it is possible to look back at the start of your episodes and notice specific factors that may have contributed to their onset. You may want to look at your wellness plan from chapter 3 and focus on each episode recorded there. If you can identify particular life events that preceded episodes of depression, this may indicate that maintenance psychotherapy is for you. Therapy could help you to cope more effectively with future stressful life events or to develop new problem-solving skills in an effort to ward off future depressions before they start. A therapist may help you to get a handle on problems before they grow larger, limiting the amount of instability you experience in your mood.

Finding a Therapist

Once you have decided that you would like to pursue the option of having maintenance therapy, the next challenge is to find a therapist. This is not always easy, but finding the right therapist is worth the investment of time and energy. If you have previously had a successful therapy experience, one of the simplest things you can do is to return to that therapist and work on staying well. Presumably, you already trust that therapist and have a good relationship with him or her, and the therapist's knowledge of you will provide an important head start. You may want to look at your wellness plan where we asked you to record therapists you've seen in the past and whether they helped. Perhaps a helpful therapist is still available to you, or perhaps a similar type of therapy is available. You may also want to look at what didn't work in therapy and make sure to steer clear of what you know does not work for you.

If you are in a position where you have to find a new therapist, there are several factors to consider. Below is a simple checklist, and we go into detail about each of these areas in the next section.

A maintenance therapist should be

- experienced and have good credentials in providing CBT or IPT

- someone who is willing and able to work on wellness with you

- someone with whom you can establish a good working relationship

CBT or IPT Experience and Credentials

Therapists come in many different forms, and there are more schools of therapy than one could ever imagine. In fact, some people have counted as many as four hundred different therapy approaches. Also, surveys of practicing psychotherapists show that most of them say they are "eclectic" therapists, meaning that they use a variety of theories and techniques suited to a particular situation or patient. The trouble with the different schools of therapy and eclectic approaches is that you will not necessarily know what you are getting, and it is sometimes hard to know whether one therapist's approach to the problem will work for you. In mental health, and in medicine in general, there is an increasing emphasis on evidence-based practice. In this approach, when your doctor makes a diagnosis, he or she consults the current research literature to identify the best treatment—the one that studies have shown to work most effectively for that condition with the fewest side effects and other downsides. Like medicine, psychotherapy is also moving more and more toward an evidence-based approach, using the techniques shown to work for particular problems, based on carefully done studies. Remember that the research on maintenance treatments support CBT and IPT, so your best bet, based on this evidence, is to find a therapist who practices either of these techniques.

This may seem straightforward enough, but there are ways in which therapists differ other than just in their approach to therapy. For example, therapists differ with respect to their professional backgrounds. A therapist could be a psychiatrist, psychologist, social worker, counselor, nurse, or other professional. In fact, most states and countries do not specify what kind of background is needed to call oneself a therapist or psychotherapist. When looking through listings of therapists in your area, keep in mind that you will want to ask about the training and experience that potential therapists have. Relevant facts to consider are: What kind of university program did they graduate from? How much experience, training, and supervision did they have? Do they have a particular specialty or area of expertise? Above all, the best question to ask is, "Do you use an evidence-based approach to treating depression, such as IPT or CBT?" If the therapist hesitates in response to that question, we suggest moving along to the next therapist.

One other thing to consider is that there are great differences in the level of training therapists have received. If someone tells you that they do IPT or CBT, you may also want to ask them how they learned these approaches and how much experience they have using these approaches. Some therapists will tell you that they do IPT or CBT, but they may have only attended a weekend workshop to learn the techniques. Other people who do CBT and IPT may have much more extensive training and supervision in providing these treatments. However, there are really no laws that limit what people can say they do, so it is a case of "buyer beware."

More recently, some schools of therapy have started voluntary programs whereby practitioners can present their qualifications and backgrounds and then get a "stamp of approval" from their peers. For example, in CBT there is now an Academy of Cognitive Therapy (ACT), which lists its members by location in part to help the public clearly identify practitioners who are expert in CBT (www.academyofct.org). The Association for Advancement of Behavior Therapy (AABT) can also provide excellent referrals to therapists who identify themselves as CBT practitioners, although unlike ACT, AABT does not verify thoroughly the credentials of its members (www.aabt.org).

Therapists Willing to Work on Wellness

There are two kinds of obstacles to finding a maintenance psychotherapist. The first has to do with therapists' comfort level with the notion of relapse prevention and techniques related to that goal. The second obstacle has to do with the way therapy services in mental health are structured; unfortunately, "wellness" is not necessarily something that is a common mission in some clinics. When you and a potential therapist have an initial meeting or telephone conversation, you may want to start off by telling the therapist that you are interested in focusing on wellness and relapse prevention. Most therapists will be familiar with these terms; however, they may also be more familiar and comfortable working with people who are actively depressed.

The second factor that may be important has to do with the practicalities of health care coverage and what treatment clinics see as their mission. For example, someone who has completely recovered from depression may not actually receive a psychiatric diagnosis and therefore may not be eligible for treatment funded through an HMO or other health care plan. From the perspectives of insurance providers, this kind of treatment may still be considered a luxury that is not absolutely necessary. Of course, one might argue logically that if treatment can prevent an episode of depression and all the associated costs (such as more intensive treatment, possible hospitalization, or lost productivity), prevention treatment would pay for itself many times over. But this argument may fall on deaf ears with both public and private health care plans. If no coverage is provided, or if you are not able to convince your health care insurance company that the treatment ought to be covered, there is the option of paying out of pocket. This may be affordable if the maintenance sessions occur once a month.

Another consideration is what a therapy clinic or a therapist sees as their mission. Here too, out of necessity, some therapists may focus on treating people who are currently very depressed and ill. Certainly in publicly funded clinics, the emphasis is usually on those people who are desperately ill, and these clinics may not have enough resources to provide help for people who are not presently experiencing symptoms. In some ways, the research on relapse and the importance of prevention has not yet caught up with the realities of how mental health services are provided. However, by asking the right questions and being persistent, you will eventually find someone willing and able to help you with a wellness plan.

Finding a Therapist and Establishing a Good Working Relationship

A fairly substantial body of research tells us that one of the best predictors of how well people do in therapy is the strength and quality of the relationship between themselves and their therapist. It is important that you have a sense of trust in the therapist, that you see the therapist as empathic, and that you believe that you and the therapist are working on the same goals. If these factors are not present, the therapist's level of expertise and experience are less important. You may find that you prefer a male or female therapist, or someone a little older or a little younger. This is perfectly okay. The relationship you form with a therapist is very important, and there is usually some level of choice in who you see. Remember that you are a consumer buying a service, and therefore you should exercise your right of choice. However, we recommend that you give a therapist with good credentials a solid try, say three or four sessions, before you make a final decision about whether the relationship with that therapist can be productive. We also recommend that, if you feel the relationship is not what you want, then you should switch before you have had too many sessions. Starting over with a new therapist can be costly and time-consuming.

Structuring Maintenance Psychotherapy

In this section we consider how to structure maintenance psychotherapy, that is, how often you should have sessions, what issues could be addressed, and how long treatment should last. Of course, the information you get from this chapter needs to be considered with your therapist as well. Whatever you work out will probably need to be flexible and will change as you go along.

How Often Should I Have Sessions?

One of the important practical points to consider is how often to meet. The research we reviewed in this chapter suggests that monthly sessions are sufficient for prevention, but that is not to say that biweekly sessions or a session every two months might not be the same or better. Also, consider as a point of departure that when a person is acutely depressed, sessions tend to occur once a week. If a depression is very serious, twice a week may be necessary. But when someone is well, once a week may be too often. An important consideration is motivation. When someone is very depressed, coming to a weekly session is very important to him or her, and that person will likely make the time no matter what else is going on. When someone is well, a weekly session may seem a little burdensome to get to; there may be other things the person would rather be doing, which is probably a sign that he or she is doing well. Also, when a person is well, it is only logical that he or she will not have as many distressing experiences as when depressed. Therefore there will be less to talk about during the therapy sessions.

If you and your maintenance therapist choose to meet monthly, the increased time between sessions can and should be used to do some work on your own. For example, each month you can select an area to work on (such as becoming less sensitive to criticism from others) and over the course of the month you can jot down points to discuss during your next session. The important thing is that the timing of sessions should be such that there is enough new material to talk about at each meeting, but not so much material that it cannot all be fit into the session. You can adjust session intervals too, but we suggest, based on the evidence, starting with monthly sessions.

What Do We Talk About?

This is another basic question, and one that will be answered by you and your therapist as you go along. To get the process started, we suggest that you use this book and your wellness plan and present these materials to your therapist. Undoubtedly your therapist will want to know what brought you to therapy and what you want to get out of the experience. Presumably you will already have put some time and effort into reading this book and following up on some of the ideas; this can be an important starting point for you and your therapist. As you will see at the end of the book, the wellness plan you develop can really be a kind of road map that you work on with the therapist so you could cover the points in order of their importance to you.

In addition to this preplanned discussion, it will be important to adapt the sessions to reflect your experiences. This is particularly true if during the maintenance therapy you notice any kind of downturn in your mood, or if a stressful situation starts to develop in your life. Remember, in addition to helping with long-term planning, maintenance therapy can function as a kind of early warning system that your mood is becoming less stable. In the end, maintenance sessions will probably be about a balance of working out long-term wellness strategies and taking care of problems that crop up in life, particularly problems that put you at risk of relapse.

How Long Should the Treatment Last?

This question can be partly answered using the maintenance therapy research, which suggests that even eight to ten monthly sessions can lead to a fairly healthy reduction in relapse rates. However, maintenance psychotherapy that lasts for a year or two is likely to have almost no downside, except practical factors like finding the time or money to attend the sessions. Of course, some people may not want to think of themselves as needing a lifetime of psychotherapy. In these cases, sessions that go on indeterminately may actually make the person think of him- or herself as someone who is "sick" or "dependent." In the same way that some people are uncomfortable with the idea of taking antidepressants for life, a person may be uncomfortable with maintenance therapy that goes on for too long. But there are other factors to consider. Therapy that occurs once a month and focuses ultimately on the person helping him- or herself to stay well will likely not foster dependency. The idea that getting therapy means one is "sick" or unable to cope on one's own is really rooted in stigma, and nothing more. Consider that many people see their family doctor for regular checkups, even when they feel completely well, and we all are encouraged to make regular visits to the dentist. Yet most people would not say that regular visits to a family doctor or dentist for maintaining health are a sign of dependence. Why should mental health be any different from physical health?

In fact, wellness or maintenance psychotherapy is very similar to the model of care a dentist might use. We visit the dentist regularly for checkups, even when our teeth look and feel just fine. This checkup involves some maintenance, cleaning, exaggerating to the hygienist about how often we floss, and a quick examination by the dentist to make sure nothing is cropping up that needs attention. Psychotherapy for people who are vulnerable to depression could follow this dentistry model even after monthly maintenance sessions are ended. A periodic checkup to delve into recent events, revisit your wellness plan, and anticipate future hurdles may be a good idea. Also, just as you would go see the dentist if you suddenly had a toothache between checkups, you could schedule a session with your therapist if a stressor crops up or if you note a lasting downturn in your mood.

Next, we will look at a now familiar topic, motivation. Once you've decided you would like maintenance psychotherapy, have found a therapist, and are working on a plan, motivation will be an important consideration.

Maintenance Motivation

We first raised the issue of motivation around the development of a wellness plan in chapter 2. Motivation is especially relevant when thinking about maintenance psychotherapy. We propose that there are two kinds of motivational processes that may get in the way of maintenance psychotherapy—*emotional avoidance* and *no-gain avoidance*. Both of these can undermine maintenance psychotherapy in different ways, and we discuss them in this section. Although we cannot offer a total cure for lack of motivation in a single book, knowledge is power. Being aware of what might happen can often help you to prevent it from happening. Ultimately, of course, motivation for wellness is rooted in the threat that if you do not actively do something to stay well, you may become depressed again. In an ideal world, this is not the best kind of motivation one could have. Doing something because it will help you get a powerful reward is probably more compelling than doing something that will help you avoid a negative consequence. Take physical exercise as an example: Many people struggle to add exercise to their life, perhaps because the rewards are not always obvious. Jogging three times a week will not give you a perfect body. However, jogging three times a week can have all kinds of hidden benefits, such as an improved cardiovascular system, which could mean you'll live longer. Just as exercise wards off negative outcomes in physical health, maintenance psychotherapy will help with staying mentally healthy. Sometimes you may have to consider the consequences of what another depression might do to your life in order to kick start the wellness process. This may sound like scare tactics, and although this might be partly true, the scare is not based on consequences we have dreamed up, nor are the consequences exaggerations of what could happen. An episode of depression is a risky, scary proposition. If that gets you motivated to pursue wellness, that is a good thing.

Emotional Avoidance

This first type of motivational problem around maintenance therapy has to do with what often happens to people immediately after they get over a depression. The person suddenly feels like his or her "old self." The physical and psychological limitations are suddenly gone and the person feels as if sprung from a trap. More than likely, many things that the individual has not been able to do, or has not wanted to do, are beckoning now that the depression has lifted—things such as work that needs to be finished, friends to catch up with, or obligations that need to be met. The last thing a person in that state may want to hear is the word "depression" and the last thing that person wants to consider is revisiting what they have gone through.

This seems like a very natural human response to a negative experience that you would like to get past. But the avoidance of thinking about the depression may also be related to some level of fear that if the depression is discussed it could reenergize those negative emotions and thoughts. As we describe elsewhere in the book, some people who recover from depression seek to never feel sad, and may view negative emotions as a sure sign of relapse. However, remember that in maintenance psychotherapy the central concern has nothing to do with dwelling on the episode that has passed, and the aim is not to poke or prod negative emotions, or even to revisit what went wrong. The bigger issue is how to prevent that state from coming back. This may indeed involve some discussion of what things were like when you were depressed, especially around the triggers of depression and your thoughts and feelings at that time. Maintenance psychotherapy has a distinctly positive side in that the emphasis is on prevention.

Another situation in which avoidance motivation can be a problem is when someone has recovered from depression but the problem that triggered or fueled the episode still has not really been talked about or resolved. In this case, the person may be motivated to avoid talking about the depression, yet recognizes in the back of his or her mind that the underlying problem has not been solved. Of course in cases like this, the underlying problem is unlikely to just go away, and the person's recovery may not be as stable as it would be if the problem were to be resolved or addressed. Emotional avoidance always needs to be looked at carefully. There may be some people who simply do not benefit from maintenance psychotherapy, and we cannot rule out the possibility of some people having a negative reaction to therapy or feeling uncomfortable about going to therapy. However, the only way to find out what the benefits of maintenance therapy might be for you is to give it a try.

No-Gain Avoidance

The second motivation issue that can arise in maintenance therapy tends to occur further along in the process. Here, a person may have already gone to the majority of the therapy sessions and has benefited from the treatment. As the person's mood improves, he or she may start to question what is being gained from continuing the therapy. In that state, it is only natural that the person will start to think about whether it is truly necessary to continue coming to sessions. After all, if months go by with no significant relapse, mood trouble, or stressors, it is easy to think that the worst has passed, that you've learned all that can be learned, and that maybe it's time you try things on your own. Hopefully all of the preceding statements are true, but, statistically speaking, several months may not be long enough to get an accurate picture.

In contrast, therapists know that there is something about a person being truly miserable that brings people to sessions week after week and keeps them working so hard. The suffering people go through is a powerful motivator for them to go to sessions, to work on the problems, and to really benefit from the therapist's feedback. When things are going well, people attend sessions less regularly. There is potential for sessions to be less focused, and to be more informal and conversational than an interaction that has specific goals. Therapists can fall into this pattern as well. It sometimes takes effort on the part of both therapist and patient to return their attention to the real goal, warding off relapse. We are not saying that maintenance sessions need to focus exclusively on all the things that might go wrong and spark a relapse. The real message is to make sure that, once you've decided that maintenance psychotherapy is for you, you trust the wellness plan you created and stick with it.

Summary

In this chapter we introduced the idea of maintenance psychotherapy, particularly IPT and CBT, that can be used to stay well and to help ward off relapses. So far, the evidence shows that a relatively small investment of time, perhaps an hour of therapy and a few hours of homework each month, will pay big dividends. In the future, we are likely to find out even more about the benefits of maintenance therapy including what is the optimal number of sessions to have and what is the best way to deliver that treatment. For now, seeking out an IPT or CBT therapist with whom you can meet monthly for a year or more to work on a wellness plan is the best option. Finding such a therapist is not always easy. Chances are you will have more success in doing so in a medium-sized or larger city, but remember that there are many different professionals who are skilled at delivering IPT or CBT. Shop around to find the combination of expertise and personal characteristics in a therapist that suits your needs. Also, keep in mind that this book and the wellness plan you create from it can be brought directly to your maintenance therapy sessions. The investment of time you make in reading this book and working on the exercises may help you work more efficiently with a therapist. Remember, too, that motivation is critical in maintenance therapy. After all, maintenance therapy is, in the end, a hopeful exercise that is aimed at making your life as good and as depression-free as it can possibly be. That is a worthwhile goal in which to invest your energy.

Summary Exercise

Record what you believe is the bottom line from this chapter, then record what practices or exercises you would adopt as part of your wellness plan.

Chapter 5, Maintenance Psychotherapy to Stay Well, reviews psychotherapy treatments that may offer protection from relapse. My bottom line in this chapter is:

_____

_____

The practices, exercises, or actions I will take from this chapter are:

_____

_____

Chapter 6

Realistic Thinking Each and Every Day

This chapter will focus on the way in which your thoughts relate to your emotions and behaviors, particularly the feelings and behaviors that are associated with negative moods. These thoughts are critical for understanding depression and relapse. Depression and patterns of thinking are closely linked, which is why modifying negative thinking patterns is a very effective way to beat depression. This link between thoughts and depression can be traced back to the work of Dr. Aaron T. Beck, who pioneered these ideas in the 1960s and went on to develop one of the best-known and most effective treatments for depression. In fact, Dr. Beck and his colleagues around the world have continued to study the causes and treatments of depression to the present day (Clark, Beck, and Alford 1999).

The work of Dr. Beck in the area of thinking and depression began when he was a practicing psychiatrist and was treating depressed people with psychoanalysis, a type of psychotherapy developed by Sigmund Freud that was the standard treatment at the time (Weishaar 1993). Beck had been taught, like other psychoanalysts, that the root of depression was anger turned inward, something Freud had described at the turn of the twentieth century. And yet Beck did not see such anger in his patients and he began to doubt the validity of Freud's explanation for why people get depressed. Instead, Beck stepped outside of the usual role of the psychoanalyst and began asking his patients more direct questions about some of their emotions and behaviors. What he discovered was completely new and quite controversial, at least in the 1960s. Rather than anger turned inward, his patients spoke to him about a stream of consciousness that they had just below the surface of everyday conversation. This stream of consciousness, which Beck later termed "automatic thoughts," seemed to be very negative in its tone. Depressed people were having an internal dialogue that was often pessimistic, hopeless, and much more negative than was realistic. It was as if the depressed person was wearing a set of glasses that were filtering out positive information from the environment and allowing only negative information to get through (Beck 1967; Clark, Beck, and Alford 1999).

Today we know that all of us have an internal dialogue going on more or less constantly. To find out how true this is, think back to the last time you were talking with someone at a social gathering and found that you were not completely focused on the conversation because it wasn't all that interesting or because you didn't have much in common with the other person. You might have found yourself thinking, "I wonder what time it is?" or "Perhaps there's someone more interesting here," or "I need to pick up some groceries before I go home." Of course, at the same time as you had these thoughts, you may have still been talking and listening to the person, but this internal conversation was running its course nonetheless. This internal dialogue may have influenced your behavior as well. For example, if you had the thought, "I need to pick up some groceries," and then realized that the grocery store closes in half an hour, you might have decided to wrap up the conversation and say your good-byes. So your internal dialogue often determines your next action. The internal dialogue can also happen while you are working on something, and it is rarely turned off completely. You may notice it even as you read this book. For example, you could find yourself reading these words but wondering, "I'm not sure I get what they are writing about," or "Where is this going?" or "How does this relate to me?" That's the internal dialogue that we want you to bring to the surface and begin to look at more closely.

The Thinking Approach to Depression

The notion that thoughts and behaviors influence negative feelings is often referred to as the *cognitive* or *cognitive behavioral* approach to understanding depression. The word "cognitive" just means thinking, or mental processing. When we feel well, our internal thoughts or cognitions tend to be positive or neutral. However, as we reviewed earlier, Beck's critical observation was that individuals who are depressed interpret many of their circumstances as negative, even though this negative view is often quite unrealistic and may not reflect how things really are. It may be difficult to control the spiral of negative thinking. In fact, you may not even notice that it has happened until it has been pointed out. For example, let's say that you are an employee working for a company and it is time for your annual performance review. A nondepressed person might have a variety of thoughts about this, including some that lead to positive feelings: "I might be due for a raise" or "This is going to be a good chance to tell the boss some of my ideas." Similarly, this person might have thoughts that lead to neutral feelings: "I wonder how long the review will take" or "I need to get my materials ready for the review." Or this person might have thoughts that lead to depressed or anxious feelings: "There might be some critical feed-back" or "The company could be affected by a downturn in the economy, and I may not get a bonus this time around." Overall, a person with such a broad range of thoughts may feel that the annual review is, on balance, a neutral event.

A depressed person facing the same annual review is likely to have very different thoughts and very few positive thoughts at all. Instead, he or she will often have negative thoughts such as, "I'm sure to get critical feedback and lose my bonus for the year" or "With the economy slowing, I'll be the first to go." The negative thoughts may spiral even further to include thoughts like, "How will I support my family without a job?" or "I'm going to give the boss a piece of my mind when he fires me." Obviously, the depressed person will face the annual review with a lot of tension, fear, and pessimism. Of course, nothing about the annual review is different between these two examples. The emotions of the depressed person are based on biased perceptions regarding the upcoming event. The trouble is, the depressed person is not likely to recognize that his or her thoughts are biased in this way. Like most people, individuals who feel depressed tend to see their thoughts as accurate forecasts that are likely to come true. They act and feel accordingly, and hence continue to have emotions of sadness and upset. In the example above, the depressed person may get so upset and fearful that he or she decides to quit rather than face the humiliation of being fired when, in reality, his or her performance is just fine.

It's important to say here that you need not just take our word for it that depressed people think this way and act accordingly. This kind of a scenario is all-too-familiar to professionals who work with individuals suffering from depression. Also, since the 1970s there have been literally hundreds of studies that confirm the idea that depressed people see the same event in a more negative way than nondepressed people, and that depressed people act in ways that are consistent with their negative views (Clark, Beck, and Alford 1999).

We still don't completely understand all of the factors that lead depressed people to think this way. We believe, based on careful studies, that it has something to do with early life experiences, and that these types of thinking and emotions are turned on when depression is active (Clark, Beck, and Alford 1999). But the good news is that this negative internal dialogue can be modified. That is, depressed people can learn to detect patterns of negative thinking and actually modify their thoughts to be more accurate. This is most often done with the help of a cognitive therapist, and this kind of treatment has been shown to be as useful for combating depression as antidepressant medications, even in severe cases (DeRubeis et al. 1999; Elkin et al. 1989).

Recently, there have also been some studies conducted that looked at cognitive therapy for staying well and relapse prevention. One study, described in chapter 5 on maintenance therapy, found that monthly sessions of cognitive therapy for people who had recovered from depression did substantially increase the probability of staying well (Jarrett et al. 2001). Another study, which looked more at relapse in people with some mild symptoms of depression, found that cognitive therapy cut relapse risk in half compared to normal clinical management (Paykel et al. 1999). The techniques of cognitive therapy can also be used in a self-help format. For example, Dennis Greenberger and Christine

Padesky (1995) have written an excellent book titled *Mind over Mood* that takes the reader step-by-step through the strategies that can help change depressed thinking. Another good resource is a book by David Burns (1999), *The Feeling Good Handbook,* that describes exercises that are related to thinking and depression. But our description and use of cognitive therapy techniques is somewhat different than the description in these books because we are specifically interested in relapse prevention. Below, we describe how these techniques can help you stay well.

Cognitive Therapy and Relapse Prevention

A person who has recovered from depression will, in most ways, have thoughts that are no different from those of a person who has never been depressed (Clark, Beck, and Alford 1999). How then are cognitive techniques helpful for those who want to stay well? Careful studies have shown that, in specific circumstances, people who have recovered from depression do think differently from people who have never been depressed (Ingram, Miranda, and Segal 1998; Segal, Gemar, and Williams 1999). The circumstances under which formerly depressed people may think differently than those who have never been depressed is when they are in a sad mood. The sad mood may not be long lasting. In fact, in experiments that look at these kinds of questions, the sad mood lasts for a matter of minutes. You may ask, "How do people who have recovered from depression think when they are sad?" The answer is that some of their negative beliefs about themselves, others, and the world get "activated" (Segal, Gemar, and Williams 1999). *Activation* means that these thoughts may become more present or more frequent, and may in turn start to affect emotion and behavior. Let's make this more concrete with an example. In studies of formerly depressed people, researchers sometimes have participants induce temporary feelings of sadness. This is typically done by having them listen to sad music or think about a sad time in their lives. Once they are in a sad mood, studies find that formerly depressed people believe more strongly that they have to be perfect, that it is critical to always please other people, and that their worth as a person depends only on their achievements. Researchers and clinicians are concerned that this negative thinking, once begun, might continue for longer and longer periods, thereby making a person's mood even worse. Eventually, changes in these thoughts and beliefs could lead to changes in behavior, and ultimately these thoughts become difficult to turn off. Moreover, if a person is put in a sad mood because of an ongoing stressor (for example, marital problems or job stress), the combination of stress and negative thinking may start a vicious cycle and trigger a whole new episode of depression. The lesson here is to become aware of negative thoughts and feelings early on, so that you can stop or slow down the process before it gets started.

As we said, it's important to become aware of changes in mood (especially changes in a negative direction) and to prevent the negative mood from spiraling. In cognitive therapy, we call these small changes in mood *mood shifts*, which are moments when you notice that your mood has shifted from feeling normal or positive to feeling bad. In the sections below, we describe this process in more detail and talk more about how you can identify a mood shift and work with it. You may also recall that in chapter 3 we talked about the importance of being able to tell the difference between a normal sad mood (for example, in response to watching a very sad movie or hearing that someone you know is ill or has passed away) and a sad mood that might be the first sign of a return of depression. The cognitive techniques described in this chapter should help you to identify whether a sad mood is normal or at least understandable, or if a sad mood might be the first sign that your depression is coming back.

How to Work with Your Thoughts

To work on your thoughts, even to get what you are thinking down on paper, you need to first practice paying attention to shifts in your mood. This might not seem difficult at first, but over the years of doing therapy, we've noted that some people find this easier than others. Some people are completely aware of what they are feeling and have a pretty good idea why a particular change in emotions has occurred. Other people experience a downturn in mood as if it has come out of the blue unless they take the time to carefully analyze what happened. Being able to step back and take note of your shifts in mood is a learned skill. However, it's not a skill that we learn in school or from other typical life experiences. Rather, it is a skill that one must take some time to learn.

Let's start with a simple example of watching a movie in which something happens in the plot that evokes a feeling of sadness. Most of us have found ourselves in tears while watching a movie about love and loss, illness and the fragility of life, the folly of war, or social or personal injustice. Why is it that, as we sit in the theater or in our living rooms, we are so emotional when, in actuality, absolutely nothing is even happening to us? It's because we identify with the film, and especially with the characters in the film, although we may not be consciously aware of this process. In a film, if someone is sick, dies, or experiences a loss, we briefly but powerfully feel like this is our own loss. We put ourselves in that situation, and again, without full awareness, think as if we were the person in the film. It is actually a sign of a good film when we feel this way, because the film has managed to make us believe that something real is happening. In contrast, if something sad happens in a film and you don't feel sad, it may be because you are not thinking like the character or your thoughts are elsewhere. In this case, no mood change would occur.

You may also have had the experience of having left a sad movie and then noticing that your mood has quickly changed away from the sadness you were feeling. For example, a minute or two after leaving a film, you may find that you have a parking ticket on your car. Your sad mood might then be replaced by anger. The change in mood has occurred because you are no longer thinking as if you were a character in the movie; you are thinking as someone with a parking fine who is now angry. You may also have found that after some films the sadness lingers, perhaps for hours. In that case, it's likely that the sad mood continues because, in some ways, you are still thinking about the characters in the movie. If a film is compelling emotionally, it's often because the characters stay with you. It's as if the characters have a life of their own that continues outside of the theater and in the back of your mind. The same thing can happen when we obtain negative information on the news. In fact, it is not uncommon for depressed people to avoid watching the news or reading the paper because stories about crime, injustice, or war lead them to feel very sad. Reading about the misfortune of others may lead the individual to think negative thoughts that may be difficult to turn off.

The Thought Worksheet

When we have just seen something sad or received sad news, it's usually pretty easy to relate the event to the mood. In cognitive therapy, we use a special diary called a *thought worksheet* to facilitate the process of understanding the relationship between events and low mood.

Let's examine a sample thought worksheet in order to better understand how this process can help you articulate your feelings. For now, we'll continue to use the example of a sad movie to help get you started on recording your thoughts. In sample worksheet 6.1, you'll notice the form has three steps that ask you to record (1) The Situation, (2) Emotions, and (3) Thoughts. There is space to record information in each step, and we encourage you to make photocopies of blank worksheet 6.2 for regular practice. Let's start with a simple example. Think about the last time you were sad or tearful while watching a movie. If that's not easy, think about the saddest movie you've ever seen. Now write the title of that movie and a very brief description of the saddest scene in that movie under step 1, The Situation. In sample worksheet 6.1, we've written "Watching the movie *Saving Private Ryan*—first scene with the D-day landing and the battle that ensues." Now think about what emotions you felt during that scene in the movie. In our example, under step 2, Emotions, we've listed sadness, despair, and frustration. Notice that each entry in this step consists of one word, and that's important. Emotions can almost always be described using a single word only.

Now comes the part that's a little bit harder for most people—recording one's thoughts when the mood shift was experienced (for example, while watching the sad movie scene). This part is not a simple process, and the first time you try this it will take a while. In our example, under step 3, Thoughts, we've written our thoughts and reactions to that particular scene in the movie. These thoughts, which involve projecting oneself into the story, explain why one might feel so moved at that moment. Try this with the movie and emotions you recorded on your thought worksheet. At the beginning, it may take you anywhere from a few minutes to a half hour to complete the form. You will become faster at it as you go along.

Also, before moving on, try the following: Read the thoughts that you recorded back to yourself, perhaps even imagine you are in the movie theater and experiencing those thoughts. If you feel the emotions you recorded stirring up a little bit, you have recorded the correct thoughts. Those emotions coming back, even a little bit, tell us that the thoughts you've recorded were relevant. So, using this example of a movie, you've illustrated a central point in cognitive therapy—that our emotions in a given situation are related to our thoughts about the situation. The next step will be to go beyond our movie example and to record a recent event in which something happened and then your mood shifted.

Worksheet 6.1
Sample Thought Worksheet

Step 1. The Situation

Record what was happening as your mood shifted. What was going on? Was anyone else involved? Where were you?

Watching the movie Saving Private Ryan—*first scene with the D-day landing and*

the battle that ensues.

Step 2. Emotions

What were you feeling? What emotion words would you use to describe what you felt?

sadness, despair, frustration

Step 3. Thoughts

What was going through your mind just then? What were you saying to yourself?

War is futile; so many lives were wasted. Those guys never had a chance. I can't

imagine having to get out of those landing crafts, these people were heroes.

So many never came home.

Worksheet 6.2
Thought Worksheet

Step 1. The Situation

Record what was happening as your mood shifted. What was going on? Was anyone else involved? Where were you?

Step 2. Emotions

What were you feeling? What emotion words would you use to describe what you felt?

_____

_____

Step 3. Thoughts

What was going through your mind just then? What were you saying to yourself?

_____

_____

_____

_____

Using the Thought Worksheet to Monitor a Mood Shift

Try to recall the last time you experienced a strong change in feelings—a shift into sadness, fear, or anxiety. On a blank copy of the thought worksheet, consider the following questions to help you to complete step 1, The Situation: When did the shift occur? What time of day was it, what was going on, and who was around? Often, recording the situation is relatively easy; you may have had a disagreement with someone, gotten a phone call or letter with some bad news, or made a mistake while doing something that was important to you. However, at times the situation is more subtle and it may be difficult to identify what triggered your negative mood. In fact, sometimes there really isn't even much of a triggering situation at all. Instead, something really minor happens that triggers a negative thought, and it's actually the thought that triggers the emotions, and perhaps more sad thoughts.

Now it's time to move on to step 2, Emotions. For the situation you recorded, what were the most troubling emotions? Remember that most emotions can be described with one word, and it is perfectly fine if you wish to record multiple emotions. For example, it is not uncommon for people to feel angry and sad at the same time, or to feel one emotion right after another. It may also make sense to write down more physical feelings, especially if these feelings relate to fear or dread. Emotions affect us physically, and sometimes the way we feel physically affects our emotions. Keep in mind that there are no right or wrong responses when you practice with the worksheet. You'll find that the process of describing your emotions becomes easier and quicker with practice.

Finally, in the third step, write down your thoughts in the situation. If you prefer, this can take the form of a *stream of consciousness,* in which you just record whatever thoughts pop into your mind. Remember, these internal dialogues or automatic thoughts are not necessarily fully formed sentences. Instead, these thoughts occur quickly, may seem beyond your conscious control, and are often biased or extreme in some way. You may want to ask yourself some questions to facilitate the process, such as, "What was going through my head as this was happening?" or "As I was feeling like this, what was I saying to myself?" For most of us, there is something very personal, perhaps even embarrassing, about writing down our innermost private thoughts. You may write down a thought and then find yourself thinking "that's not right" or "that sounds silly," but it's really important that you don't censor yourself. The fact that some of the thoughts you write down don't seem to jibe with reality or the way you see things now is actually part of the process. Later in this chapter, we will discuss strategies for analyzing your negative automatic thoughts to determine whether they are realistic.

Most experts agree that it is very important to write down your thoughts on a thought worksheet, rather than just doing this exercise in your head. Writing things down may well be important because writing involves brain processes that are very different than those that are involved when one does these exercises mentally. As a final check to make sure that what you have recorded is related to the emotions you wrote down, read the thoughts you recorded aloud. Now, imagine that you or someone you know was thinking these thoughts. Would they have the same kinds of emotions you wrote down? If so, you've probably captured the thoughts that were most relevant to the situation and the emotions you experienced. For a while (a few days at least), you should practice using the three-step thought worksheet. In the next section, we discuss an expanded thought worksheet that can be used once you have mastered the three-step version.

Expanding the Thought Worksheet to Change Your Negative Thinking

For many people with depression, the most troubling aspect of their lives is their difficulties with negative emotions and low mood. But as you have seen, one's negative moods are driven by one's negative thoughts. So when it comes to changing your negative emotions, the best way to do this is to actually begin to work with your thoughts. In preventing relapse and recurrence of depression, the key is to watch out for situations and thoughts that cause a lasting change in your mood. Working with these kinds of thoughts will help to keep negative moods at bay, in both the short and long term.

The kinds of thoughts that cause strong emotions, also known as *hot thoughts,* are often unrealistic, especially when an individual is already in a sad mood. So rather than accepting the hot thoughts as true, it is important to slow down and carefully check to make sure that one's thinking is accurate.

Using the Evidence to Discover the Truth

Evidence gathering is a powerful method for discovering whether your thinking is realistic. The idea behind this strategy is simple, but the results are often profound. Evidence gathering asks you to become a more objective observer by having you carefully examine the *facts* of a situation. In addition, evidence gathering asks you to consider both the facts that may support your original interpretation (the hot thought) and those that support one or more alternative interpretations (alternative thoughts). In worksheet 6.4, you'll see a blank version of an expanded thought worksheet that includes new steps for facilitating evidence gathering and for recording alternative thoughts.

Before continuing on, an example might be useful. Let's say that Annette had made plans to speak to a friend over the weekend and Annette hasn't heard from that person. In sample worksheet 6.3 we show you a thought worksheet with the situation, "Jane was supposed to call this weekend, but now it's Monday and she hasn't called." Under emotions, Annette recorded "upset," "hurt," and "angry." Under step 3, Annette recorded thoughts such as "She's so inconsiderate" and "She probably doesn't like me and doesn't want to talk to me"; she then circled the second thought as the most hurtful one.

If we were going to engage in the process of evidence gathering here, we would step back and ask Annette, "What are the facts?" One fact is that the friend, Jane, didn't call over the period of time that she had agreed to call. Interestingly, that's about the only fact we have. Next, we would encourage Annette to ask herself, "Does that fact support my thought that Jane doesn't want to talk to me?" The answer is maybe, but not necessarily. The interpretation that Jane doesn't want to talk to Annette goes beyond the fact that she didn't call. What we really need is more information. Does Annette have other reasons to suspect that Jane didn't call because she didn't want to talk to Annette? We could find out about the history of the friendship. It may be that Jane often doesn't call when she says she will. That might speak to Jane's personal style, and not to whether Jane likes Annette. Similarly, Jane may be the kind of person who always calls when she says she will, but didn't in this case. Now should we conclude that Jane no longer likes Annette? Not really—the fact that Jane didn't call this one time may just as easily suggest extraordinary circumstances that have nothing to do with Annette. Jane might have had an emergency at home, a problem with her phone line, or a fight with her husband, or perhaps she simply forgot. All in all, the thought that "Jane doesn't want to talk to me" goes beyond what we know for sure, and therefore the emotions of hurt, sadness, and anger, though understandable, are really premature.

In this example, the next logical step might be for Annette to phone Jane to better understand why Jane didn't call. This would probably answer all of the questions we've posed here. One final question is important: What if it's true that Jane really doesn't like Annette anymore? In other words, isn't it possible that some negative thoughts are actually realistic? The answer to this is yes, some negative thoughts are realistic. Later in this chapter, we will return to the issue of how to handle such a scenario. However, the key to using cognitive strategies to cope with negative moods is to take note of any thought that causes a lot of sadness and to evaluate whether the thought is in fact true.

The example of Annette and Jane illustrated in worksheet 6.3 might seem simple, but it's pretty typical of the kinds of thoughts often reported by people who feel depressed. One way to think about the evidence-gathering process is that it helps you to step outside of yourself and to be a neutral observer of your hot thoughts. When using this strategy, some people find it useful to imagine that they are putting their thought on trial and that they are both the defendant and prosecutor in the trial. The prosecutor role involves identifying the facts that support the negative conclusion. The defense role involves examining the facts that do not support the hot thought, or that raise doubts about whether the hot thought is true. Sometimes it is helpful to take the attitude of wanting to "poke holes" in the story of the prosecutor. That is, some facts that seem to support the hot thought may not hold water. As the judge, you can then weigh both sides of the story and come up with a fair verdict (usually the alternative thought).

Another way to think about this exercise is to imagine that your best friend has come to you with this completed thought worksheet. This may give you some of the necessary distance and objectivity to help with evidence gathering. And it will also show you that we often have a different standard for other people than we do for ourselves. It is often easier to see the biases in someone else's negative thinking than it is to recognize one's own biases.

In step 4 of blank thought worksheet 6.4, we have included a number of questions and suggestions to help you gather the evidence you may need. However, the best questions often have to do with the situation itself. Some more general suggestions and questions that might be helpful include:

- Getting more information about the context: What is the background of the situation? What are some of the elements of the situation that are not known or that are beyond your control or responsibility?

- Taking a more objective view: Would your best friend or a trusted family member see this the same way?

- Taking a more long-range view of the situation: How will you see this situation in a month, in a year, or in five years from now? Does the situation need to develop over time before you have a complete picture? Are you looking at just a single moment in time and not taking into account the longer term?

For each thought you analyze, once a more complete picture of the situation emerges, you can write down a more balanced, alternative thought that takes into account all of the information and evidence you gathered. Chances are high that this thought will be much less emotionally upsetting than your hot thought. The evidence-gathering technique, like so many other skills, depends on practice. Once you have completed about fifty of these worksheets, the process will become almost automatic.

Checking One's Thoughts for Distortions

Related to the evidence-gathering process is the idea of making sure that thoughts are not distorted or biased. The idea that depressed people might think in biased ways goes back to Dr. Beck's original work in which he tried to specify the nature of depressive thinking. What Beck noted was that when thoughts produced sadness, there were systematic errors in thinking that the individual was typically not aware of. Cognitive therapy involves helping people become attuned to these errors. This not only leads to more balanced thoughts (especially when coupled with evidence gathering), but also provides a nice way for people to become aware of what their thinking patterns are and the kinds of thoughts they need to watch out for.

These errors in thinking, called *cognitive distortions,* occur when a person does not take into account all of the information in a given situation. Some of the typical distortions include

Arbitrary inference: Arbitrary inference means drawing a specific conclusion without supporting evidence, or even in the face of contradictory evidence. Example: A harried worker cannot accomplish all of his or her tasks and thinks, "I'm a horrible employee."

Selective abstraction: Selective abstraction is seeing a situation in terms of a single detail taken out of context and ignoring other information in the situation. Example: An employee focuses on a single piece of negative feedback from a performance evaluation that is otherwise filled with positive feedback, and then becomes sad and hopeless.

Overgeneralization: To overgeneralize is to take a rule that applies to one situation or perhaps a few isolated incidents, and then apply it more generally to situations in which the rule is not appropriate. Example: After having difficulty with a single unruly child in a class, a teacher concludes, "All of these children are ill-mannered."

Magnification and minimization: Magnification involves seeing certain things (usually one's own faults or flaws) as far more significant than they actually are. Example: A woman on a date mentions unintentionally that her former boyfriend had left her, and then thinks to herself, "Now I've done it. Now he knows there's something wrong with me." Minimization involves seeing certain things (usually someone else's flaws or faults) as far less significant than they actually are. Example: A husband downplays or ignores the fact that his wife has had an affair, and perhaps even blames himself for what happened.

Personalization: Personalization involves attributing external events to oneself without evidence supporting such a causal connection. Example: At a party, a woman overhears a man saying that there aren't enough interesting people at the gathering, and she has the thought, "I know he's talking about me."

Dichotomous thinking or black-and-white thinking: This type of thinking involves categorizing experiences in one of two extremes (such as right or wrong, good or bad, complete success or total failure). Example: A woman cooking a family dinner feels that one of her dishes has not turned out perfectly and thinks, "The entire dinner is ruined."

Mind Reading: Mind reading is believing that one knows what another person is thinking despite a lack of any direct evidence. Example: While having a conversation at a party, one assumes that the other person finds the conversation boring, despite the fact that there is no evidence to support such an assumption.

Keeping this list of distortions in mind, let's return briefly to the sample thought worksheet with Annette and Jane. Recall that Annette thought that Jane didn't like her anymore because Jane did not call when she said she would. This thought could involve several distortions, depending on the bigger situation. Arbitrary inference seems to apply because Annette's conclusion that Jane didn't like her was based on information that was not really very conclusive at all. Perhaps the cognitive distortion that most clearly applies here is mind reading. At some level, Annette believed that she knew what Jane was thinking, and if what Annette suspected had really been true, then Jane's behavior (not calling Annette) makes perfect sense. However, this conclusion is based on a faulty premise: there is simply no way for Annette to know what Jane, or anyone else for that matter, is thinking if they haven't verbally shared their thoughts. In the absence of strong evidence one way or the other, Annette might benefit from checking out the situation before deciding whether her negative interpretations and the resulting emotions were justified.

Keeping these distortions in mind as you complete the thought worksheets will facilitate the process of changing your thoughts. When you complete a thought worksheet, identifying the distortion you've made (step 5) may speed up the process of evidence gathering. Moreover, gathering evidence may help you with the process of identifying your distortions. With practice, the processes of evidence gathering and identifying distortions will become more efficient, particularly after you have begun to identify patterns in your thinking.

Identifying the Alternative Thought

After you've carefully reviewed the evidence and have examined possible distortions in your hot thoughts, the next step is to develop a new thought that incorporates all of your hard work. This new thought, called the *alternative thought* (step 6), is based on more facts and information than the original hot thought you started with. Often, the alternative thought leads to quite different, and more positive, emotions than the hot thought. Some people struggle with trying to identify alternative or more balanced thoughts. This is especially true when people are very depressed and have a lot of trouble saying or thinking almost anything that is positive about themselves or about their lives. But if you're using these thought worksheets for the purpose of preventing a relapse or recurrence of your depression, you may have a somewhat easier time coming up with a balanced alternative viewpoint. The simplest way to write this kind of thought is to summarize all of the facts under the evidence section, and then consider what distortion occurred. This will often suggest a new perspective on the experience. Going back to the example of Annette in sample worksheet 6.3, Annette's alternative, balanced thought was, "There are many reasons Jane might not have called. I should be careful not to mind read, and I need to check into this before I reach a conclusion." This led Annette to feel much less emotional about the situation, and led to the curiosity that resulted in her calling Jane.

In practice, completing a thought worksheet will have three different outcomes:

1. You may uncover evidence that completely undermines your hot thought. This may have been a fact you missed when the situation arose, or something you discovered as you completed the worksheet. If your hot thought is definitely not true, it's often easy to come up with an alternative thought that does reflect the reality of the situation.

2. The second possible outcome is that the evidence may go both ways. That is, there's a possibility that your hot thought is partially true, and yet there is also evidence that your hot thought is not true. In that case, what's probably needed is more information. In cognitive therapy, we call the process of seeking additional information to test the validity of one's beliefs an *experiment;* an experiment can be as simple as asking someone a question. In the Annette and Jane example, Annette calling Jane herself was an experiment in which Annette was seeking more information. The point of the experiment is to try to get information that tells you what is actually going on. An experiment typically involves identifying two distinct predictions, one involving the negative thought and one involving a more balanced or positive thought. You will find that experiments are especially helpful when you are making negative predictions about the future. Often the experiment can be as simple as letting time go by to see how things turn out.

3. The third possible outcome of a thought worksheet is discovering that the automatic thought is true. As we've said throughout this book, bad things can happen to people, sometimes randomly. For example, let's say that Annette speaks to Jane about the unreturned phone call and Jane tells Annette that, in fact, she's not sure about maintaining the friendship. In that case, there would have been some truth to Annette's original thought. When a hot thought is found to be true, it should be a signal to you that there is a problem that needs to be solved. Following a real loss or some other negative event (for example, you have lost your job, a relationship has soured, or something bad happened to someone you love), it is natural to have some negative thoughts and feelings. In that case, the next step is to consider the question, "What can I do about it?" That is, are there active steps you can take to repair the situation? If this is a problem that you have control over, you may also ask yourself some questions: "What do those problem-solving steps look like? When do I want to begin? What supports do I need to solve the problem?" If the situation is beyond your control (for example, someone you love is diagnosed with a physical illness), you may have to practice acceptance and try to find something positive in the situation. You may also want to consult chapter 9 on coping with stressors and problem-solving techniques.

Reexamining Your Mood

To complete a thought worksheet, the final step is to examine whether your mood has changed. Think about how you felt at the time the situation occurred, focusing on the specific emotions you experienced. Now that you have an alternative thought or have considered a more realistic appraisal of the situation, do you still feel the same way you did when you started? Most often, the answer will be no. More likely, your emotions will have changed after going through the process of completing the thought worksheet. Step 7 on the worksheet allows you to record changes in emotions.

If you find no change in your emotions following the exercise, there are some other possibilities you should consider. First, it may be that some part of the worksheet isn't quite right. For example, the thought you were working with may not be the hot thought. Or perhaps you were not been able to identify important pieces of evidence or to develop an alternative perspective. Some of these problems can be solved with simple practice on the worksheet. You may also want to consult other, more detailed references on cognitive therapy, such as *The Feeling Good Handbook* (Burns 1999) or *Mind over Mood* (Greenberger and Padesky 1995), that may help to clarify some of these matters. Both of these books have many more details, worksheets, and exercises for cognitive therapy that are easy to use and effective. Finally, you may want to locate a cognitive therapist in your area who can help you with completing the thought worksheets and developing other strategies for changing depressive thoughts.

Worksheet 6.3
Example of a Completed Thought Worksheet

Step 1. The Situation

Record what was happening as your mood shifted. What was going on? Was anyone else involved? Where were you?

Jane was supposed to call this weekend. Now it's Monday and she hasn't called.

Step 2. Emotions

What were you feeling? What emotion words would you use to describe what you felt?

upset, hurt, angry

Step 3. Thoughts

What was going through your mind just then? What were you saying to yourself? Circle the *hot thought* (the thought that is most responsible for the emotions).

She's so inconsiderate. She probably doesn't like me and doesn't want to talk to me.

Step 4. Evidence

What are the known facts? Are there some facts that support the hot thought? Are there some facts that don't support the hot thought? Are the facts supporting the hot thought beyond any doubt or could they also support another thought? What's the big picture? What advice would I give to a loved one, or what questions would I encourage another person to ask themselves?

Jane didn't call when she was supposed to have called. I have no other

information about why she didn't call. The fact that she didn't call may mean many

things I suppose. If this happened to someone else, I'd encourage them to check

out what really happened.

Step 5. Distortions

Is my thought a distortion? If so, what is the distortion?

I seem to have made an arbitrary conclusion or inference about what it means that

Jane didn't call. I'm trying to mind read what Jane was thinking.

Step 6. Alternative or Balanced Thought

Write a new thought that takes into account the evidence you found and the distortions you made. The thought should summarize everything you've discovered with the evidence gathering.

There are many reasons why Jane might not have called. I should be careful not

to mind read, and I need to check into this before I reach a conclusion.

Step 7. New Emotions

What emotions do you now have about the situation? Do you notice that you feel different? Write out how your emotions have changed.

I'm now curious about what really happened, so I feel less hurt and less angry.

Worksheet 6.4
Thought Worksheet

Step 1. The Situation

Record what was happening as your mood shifted. What was going on? Was anyone else involved? Where were you?

_____

_____

Step 2. Emotions

What were you feeling? What emotion words would you use to describe what you felt?

_____

Step 3. Thoughts

What was going through your mind just then? What were you saying to yourself? Circle the *hot thought* (the thought that is most responsible for the emotions).

_____

Step 4. Evidence

What are the known facts? Are there some facts that support the hot thought? Are there some facts that don't support the hot thought? Are the facts supporting the hot thought beyond any doubt or could they also support another thought? What's the big picture? What advice would I give to a loved one, or what questions would I encourage another person to ask themselves?

_____

_____

_____

_____

Step 5. Distortions

Is my thought a distortion? If so, what is the distortion?

_____

_____

Step 6. Alternative or Balanced Thought

Write a new thought that takes into account the evidence you found and the distortions you made. The thought should summarize everything you've discovered with the evidence gathering.

_____

_____

Step 7. New Emotions

What emotions do you now have about the situation? Do you notice that you feel different? Write out how your emotions have changed.

_____

_____

Some Thoughtful Conclusions

This section of the chapter provided a step-by-step approach to noticing negative thoughts and moods and then intervening to try to change sad mood states by making sure that underlying thoughts are not needlessly biased or negative. Being able to use a thought worksheet "on the fly" in any situation that arises is probably one of the most useful skills you will gain to help maintain your positive mood and to avoid spiraling negative moods. In fact, research on cognitive therapy for depression suggests that cognitive therapy is somewhat better at preventing relapse and recurrence compared to antidepressant medication (Evans et al. 1992; Shea et al. 1992). Why would that be? We believe that this is because cognitive therapy teaches specific skills like completing the thought worksheets, conducting experiments, and acquiring problem-solving strategies that a person can use for months and years after the therapy has ended. In contrast, when a person stops taking medication, the benefits of the drug often decrease as the drug is used up by the body.

People who have been through cognitive therapy are likely to use the cognitive therapy skills they learned when they notice mood shifts occurring, even after treatment is over. Most cognitive therapists working with depressed patients spend some time in the treatment discussing relapse prevention in an effort to help their clients come up with a plan in case their mood takes a turn for the worse. What we've done here is to describe briefly some of the most critical skills in cognitive therapy and to present these skills in a user-friendly manner. Utilizing these skills will make it easier for you to stay well and to not let sad moods get the best of you.

In wrapping up this section, we have one final piece of advice: Practice using the thought worksheet! Reading this book may be interesting but it is doubtful that reading alone will be terribly helpful. To take advantage of the strategies discussed in this book, it is essential to put them into practice. Just as reading a book on physical fitness will not make you fit, reading a book on preventing relapse in depression will not prevent relapse, in and of itself. There is no substitute for completing the thought worksheets on a regular basis. The more you do this, the more benefit you get from completing them, and the more likely they will be to help you when you need help the most.

Going beyond Thoughts: Understanding Beliefs

For most of us, negative thoughts and moods are not one-time events. Rather, the kinds of moods we experience and the triggers for those moods have a pattern, repeating themselves across situations and over time. If you find that your thought worksheets sometimes look similar, or that you write about the same situation again and again, you are not alone. The same would be true for most people. The negative thoughts we experience are neither accidental nor random. Instead, there is a distinct pattern to our thoughts that has more to do with the kind of person we are and our deeply held rules and beliefs about ourselves, others, and the world (Beck et al. 1979). If you think of automatic thoughts and hot thoughts as being at one level of your mind or consciousness, we also need to consider that there is a level of thinking that is deeper and sometimes harder to get to. Cognitive therapists call this the *belief* level, and sometimes these more deeply held assumptions are referred to as *core beliefs* or *schemas*. These beliefs are usually quite stable over time and are with us in a variety of situations. It is the stability of these beliefs that may explain why so many of our negative emotions and thoughts are repeated over time. However, unlike negative automatic thoughts, beliefs are a little bit trickier to access or analyze. Sometimes we have these beliefs for most of our lives and have never even said them aloud. Nonetheless, once you uncover your beliefs, you'll quickly recognize that they drive a lot of your behavior and emotions.

The best way to illustrate what we mean by a belief is with a couple of examples. First, let's introduce Carol, a college student who became depressed in her sophomore year of college and now, as a senior, is trying to use cognitive techniques to stay well. In completing the thought worksheet described in this chapter, Carol notices that her sad moods and thoughts often occur around schoolwork. In fact, almost anytime Carol gets feedback on her performance, like a grade on a test or feedback about her participation in seminars, she gets an uneasy feeling. Her sadness is especially prominent when she does not do as well as she would have wanted, and in those circumstances she's prone to have thoughts like "I'm not smart enough," "I'm stupid," or "I'm lazy." When Carol examines the evidence for these thoughts, she is able to notice that she tends to overgeneralize, to see things in a black-and-white way, and to ignore disconfirming evidence, such as the fact that her grade point average is quite good, that there are lots of times when her marks are near perfect, and that, in reality, she's done very well at a college with a good reputation. What accounts for the fact that Carol keeps having these negative thoughts? Looking at

Carol's beliefs, we might wonder what she has set as her standard or expectation and what her rules are for performance. What is Carol's rule for evaluating herself? It seems that what might be going on for Carol could be summed up like this, "If my performance is not perfect, it has no worth at all." If Carol were helped to verbalize this belief, she might acknowledge that it's a very strict rule and one that could do much more harm than good.

Beliefs often take the form of an "if . . . then" statement, rather like a rule or a law. However, laws of emotion are different than legal laws because we are responsible for our emotions, and our emotions have consequences only for us. This means that, unlike legal laws, we can change our own laws or beliefs if they do not serve us well, or if they lead us to feel sad.

Just like with automatic thoughts, in order to change one's beliefs using cognitive therapy, the belief must first be brought out and examined. To challenge those rules that sometimes lead you to sad moods you have to ask yourself some questions. Does this kind of belief make sense for me? Is it a fair rule? Would I suggest to people I love (for example, a family member or best friend) that they should adopt this rule in order to improve their lives? If the answer to any of these questions is no, then this may be a rule you want to change.

Let's examine another example to help you get the hang of it. Ellen, a homemaker with teenage children, was using the thought worksheets to try to figure out what makes her sad most often. Most of the situations she recorded were related to things that her family, her husband, and her kids had said to her. But one incident was especially clear for her and helped her to figure out what her beliefs were. Ellen's family had an annual reunion during which everyone got together for a traditional chili cookout and softball game. For years Ellen had prepared the traditional family chili recipe, making very large quantities to feed the family. Excited about the party, Ellen packed up all of the food and for most of the day had an enjoyable time. However, her mood shifted dramatically when, after the meal, Ellen's aunt approached her, complained of some stomach pain, told her that the chili had been a little too spicy, and asked whether Ellen had done something different this year. Ellen was crestfallen, and she later completed a belief worksheet with thoughts like, "The chili was horrible, and the party was a disaster" (see sample worksheet 6.5). On reflection, Ellen believed that she had personalized her aunt's comments and she found that she had very little evidence that anyone else had a problem with the chili. She couldn't even be sure that her aunt's upset stomach was actually due to the chili, and not some other food or drink at the party. However, completing this thought worksheet did lead Ellen to reflect on her rule that "I must make everyone satisfied at the party or I'm a bad hostess." In fact, Ellen then realized that a similar rule was governing her reaction to her husband and children. Ellen assumed that she was responsible for making sure that her family was always 100 percent satisfied with almost every aspect of their home life. If there was a problem that she couldn't fix, Ellen typically blamed herself for the situation. After becoming more aware of her beliefs, Ellen began to recognize that there was no way to make everyone happy all of the time. Instead, she developed a system in which, if someone complained about something, she would ask herself whether the responsibility was really hers. If not, she adopted new rules, such as "There's only so much I can do" and "I cannot be 100 percent responsible for anyone else's emotional state."

A final point about these examples is that the beliefs or rules that Carol and Ellen identified had consequences, not only for their emotions, but also for their behavior. Carol's rule about getting perfect grades led her to study hard and to get things as perfect as possible before handing in her assignments. This sometimes led to sleepless nights and a lot of anxiety about tests. These behaviors themselves were problematic, and the thought of having to get an assignment "just right" sometimes led Carol to avoid starting a project. It was as if each test or assignment became a test of her worth. Many people might put off a task if their performance was so closely tied to their sense of self-worth. Similarly, Ellen found that her beliefs about needing to make everyone happy led to a lot of behavior designed to do just that, make everyone happy. This pressure increased her investment in having people give her good feedback, and when they didn't do so, she was that much more disappointed and hurt. Behaviors that come as a result of emotional rules or beliefs are called *compensation strategies*. Compensation strategies are designed to ensure that we meet the standards set by our rules. Unfortunately, they also set us up for continuing to feel bad about ourselves and are usually self-defeating. Understanding and grappling with your own emotional rules also means looking at your behavior and making sure that what you do is in your best interest.

Sometimes it is much easier to recognize other people's emotional rules or beliefs than it is to see your own. However, examples like Carol's and Ellen's will help you get a good sense of the types of beliefs you will want to identify in yourself. Also, remember that when you are feeling well, these beliefs may not be as strong as when you are feeling depressed. That's because the negative emotions that come with depression seem to activate these rules and make them much more of a focus. One way to figure out your own rules is to consider what your thoughts are like when you are depressed. We've also included a blank belief worksheet to help you to identify your own beliefs. This worksheet contains a number of steps to help you challenge rules that may be getting in your way. Sample worksheet 6.5 provides a completed belief worksheet using Ellen's example. The first step in completing the belief worksheet is to simply transcribe a hot thought that appears regularly on your thought worksheets. As you'll see, Ellen recorded the hot thought, "The chili was horrible, and the party was a disaster."

In step 2, record the other situations in which similar thoughts have occurred. In some cases, the situations will be almost identical; in other cases they may share at least a few common elements. For example, in step 2, Ellen recorded that she has similar thoughts when her children complain about meals and when her husband is unhappy about the way she maintains the house.

In step 3, you are asked to consider the *meaning* of the hot thought. This process involves asking yourself one or more of the following questions: What if the hot thought is true? What might the consequence be? What's so bad about that thought coming true? For example, in step 3, Ellen recorded that the consequence of the chili actually being horrible would be the implication that she was a bad hostess and cook. Even writing that down, she recognized that she made similar criticisms of herself as a homemaker and social planner when her husband and kids complained about her work in the home.

In step 4, you have an opportunity to start putting all of this information together, to summarize the situations in which the thought occurs, and to identify the consequences of those kinds of thoughts. Ellen simply put together the information from steps 2 and 3, and then recognized just how often this happens to her.

In step 5, you have your first opportunity to write down the belief you identified. Writing it out as one simple sentence will sometimes lead you to see that you've got a handle on the belief or you may find that more work needs to be done. If you've identified a belief, don't be surprised if some negative emotions are stirred up. In this case, more emotions are an indication that you're on the right track. For example, Ellen wrote for her summary belief, "If I can't make everyone happy all the time, then I have failed completely." Immediately after writing this belief, she was struck by just how extreme this was, but she was also tearful because she recognized how much this belief was responsible for generating negative emotions.

The questions in step 6 are designed to help you to reflect on the rule you've identified; they should demonstrate clearly the unfairness in the rule, and may help you to recognize that this rule has many drawbacks and few advantages. Finally, in step 7, you are asked to write a more fair and balanced rule—one that you will try to adopt in the coming weeks. For Ellen, the new rule was "I can only do my best. If others are unhappy with that, I cannot hold myself responsible for all of their emotions."

The belief worksheet may take some time to get used to. We can't emphasize enough how important repeated practice is. You may have a few attempts that don't go anywhere at all, and that's fine. You should also be aware that sometimes when people struggle with these kinds of worksheets, they may inadvertently be activating some of their emotional rules like "I'm stupid if I can't get this" or "If I don't understand something right away, it means that I never will." If you believe those rules, they may prevent you from persevering and from getting the hang of the worksheets. So we encourage you to persevere and to be careful that your emotional rules don't prevent you from developing new skills, such as completing these worksheets. Also, remember that changing behaviors, in this case compensation strategies, may be harder than it looks. We know that people struggle even to change superficial behaviors, like their diet and their level of physical activity, so changing more subtle behaviors related to our emotional rules is not easy. For example, it may take many attempts to shift the need to always please others or the desire to create something "perfect." But each attempt you make toward changing your behavior is a step in the right direction. New habits of behavior don't always work the first time we try them, but each attempt brings us closer to adopting the new behavior for good.

You will also find that beliefs themselves are a little harder to change than automatic thoughts, and that's true for almost everyone. Beliefs are much more deeply engrained than we might expect and they can often go unnoticed. In fact, underlying most rules and beliefs are other layers that we call *core motivations*. In depression, core motivations include things like perfectionism and dependency—important enough topics in their own right that we have devoted separate chapters to them later on in the book, with special attention to how they may increase an individual's risk of experiencing a relapse or recurrence of depression.

Worksheet 6.5
Sample Belief Worksheet

Step 1. Referring to my thought worksheet, the hot thought I am interested in working on is:

The chili was horrible, and the party was a disaster.

Step 2. Write the situation in which the thought occurred. Has it ever occurred in other similar situations?

At the party, but also when the kids complain about meals and when my husband

says the house is messy.

Step 3. If the hot thought from step 1 is true, what does that say about me? What does that hot thought mean to me?

These thoughts mean I'm a bad hostess, and with the family it's that I've failed as

a mother, or wife, or social planner.

Step 4: Create an "if . . . then" statement with the situations from step 2 and the consequences from step 3.

If someone complains or tells me that things are not what they want, then I've

failed or it's something I did somehow.

Step 5: Rewrite the "if . . . then" statement from step 4 in a single sentence.

If I can't make everyone happy all the time, then I have failed completely.

Step 6: Ask yourself the following questions: Does this rule make sense? Is the rule fair to me? What are the most likely emotional consequences of this rule? Does the rule lead me to act in my own best interests? Would I recommend that people I care about adopt this rule?

Step 7: Write an alternative rule, keeping in mind the answers to the questions in step 6.

I can only do my best. If others are unhappy with that, I cannot hold myself

responsible for all of their emotions.

Worksheet 6.6
Belief Worksheet

Step 1. Referring to my thought worksheet, the hot thought I am interested in working on is:

_____

Step 2. Write the situation in which the thought occurred. Has it ever occurred in other similar situations?

_____

_____

Step 3. If the hot thought from step 1 is true, what does that say about me? What does that hot thought mean to me?

_____

_____

Step 4: Create an "if . . . then" statement with the situations from step 2 and the consequences from step 3.

If _____ ,

then _____

Step 5: Rewrite the "if . . . then" statement from step 4 in a single sentence.

_____ ,

Step 6: Ask yourself the following questions: Does this rule make sense? Is the rule fair to me? What are the most likely emotional consequences of this rule? Does the rule lead me to act in my own best interests? Would I recommend that people I care about adopt this rule?

Step 7: Write an alternative rule, keeping in mind the answers to the questions in step 6.

_____

_____

Summary

In this chapter, we described the ideas behind cognitive therapy, which has proven to be very useful for coping with depression. You've seen how, in depression, thoughts can become biased and distorted, how a person's self-confidence can be undermined, and how a range of negative emotions and problematic behaviors arise. We also described how cognitive therapy strategies can be useful for relapse prevention. We've tried to emphasize that it is important to catch mood shifts early on, when they first occur, well before they have a chance to start a depressive spiral. By tracking your thoughts carefully and by using a thought worksheet to monitor any negative emotions that appear to last for too long, you will be able to defuse many situations that might previously have led to more lasting emotional difficulties. We've also described another level of thinking, the beliefs or rules for living that sometimes set us up to experience mood shifts across a wide range of similar situations. By completing the belief worksheets, you will become more aware of emotional rules that are often difficult to detect and are typically not in your best interest.

As a reminder, just reading this chapter will not protect you from future depression unless the strategies discussed are integrated into your everyday life. We encourage you to practice these skills. We fully expect that people will need to reread this chapter as they work on these exercises. Remember, too, that if you have questions, a cognitive therapist in your area may be able to help you work out any obstacles in your practice of these strategies. In the appendix, we identify a number of resources to get you in touch with cognitive therapists, as well as other references to flesh out the techniques described in this chapter.

Summary Exercise

Record what you believe is the bottom line from this chapter, then record what practices, exercises, or worksheets you would adopt as part of your wellness plan.

Chapter 6, Realistic Thinking Each and Every Day, reviews CBT strategies to beat negative thinking. My bottom line in this chapter is:

_____

_____

The practices, exercises, or worksheets I will use from this chapter are:

_____

_____

Chapter 7

Having Fun and Living Healthy

In this chapter we consider another very important area for staying well, everyday activities and lifestyle choices. This might seem like a very nonpsychological, or perhaps even unimportant, area. What do daily routines have to do with depression? The answer is, a lot. In fact, one of the oldest models of treating depression rests on some very simple principles that are directly related to everyday activities. This model, called the *behavioral model,* goes back to the early 1970s (Fester 1973; Lewinsohn 1974) and is based on a simple but profound idea about depression. The behavioral model evolved from research with animals and how animals (and humans) learn behaviors. For that reason, behavioral approaches are also often called *learning theories.* Behavioral models say that we engage in behaviors because we have been *reinforced,* or rewarded, for those same behaviors in the past. The simplest example might be in a dog who has learned to sit for a treat offered by his owner. A behaviorist would say that the treat is positive reinforcement for sitting, and that the association between the command "sit," the behavior of sitting, and the delicious treat represents learning for an animal. They would also point out that no dog sits automatically when it sees a treat, but rather that repeated associations between the command, the proper behavior, and getting a tasty morsel is how the dog was taught to sit.

Behaviorists think humans learn in the same way. That is, we are offered positive rewards or *reinforcers* (for example, a paycheck) in exchange for a behavior (such as the work we do) and this is why we work or why we have learned to work. Similarly, behaviorists argue that we unlearn behavior when we are punished or we do not get a reward. That is, if we are given a *negative outcome* (something aversive) we tend to stop the behavior. A speeding ticket is a fine example; here the behavior (driving too fast) results in the consequence of a fine. The idea is that this learning experience results in driving more slowly, or one might say that fast driving has been unlearned because it led to punishment. Taking things a step further, even the anticipation of a reward or punishment can make us change our behavior. For example, we do not often get paid hourly or daily for our work, rather we anticipate the reward, which may come biweekly or monthly, and the behavior continues. Similarly, a punishment can be anticipated and can still change behavior. For example, signs that display hefty speeding fines have their influence on behavior because they are symbolic of the punishment of a real fine that could happen if we speed. Even the possibility of such a punishment can, and does, make us ease off the gas pedal. So we learn behaviors when they are associated with rewards, and we unlearn behaviors that do not lead to a reward or are punished.

We have explained these concepts only so as to help explain the behavioral model of depression, which focuses on an *absence of positive reinforcement* (or insufficient rewards for behavior) as the critical factor in depression. A behaviorist would say that a depressed person is not getting enough positive reinforcement from their life and this explains why they have withdrawn from their usual behaviors. In fact, when you look at the average depressed person's daily activities, this model often rings true. Depressed people frequently spend a great deal of time that is neither productive nor pleasant. For example, depressed people can spend a lot of time watching television, but having absolutely no connection with what is being presented on the television. Thus they are not entertained at all, and yet time goes by. Depressed people often spend more time than other people lying in bed but not sleeping. Thus, even though they are in bed, they are not getting the benefit of a good night of sleep. Many depressed people end up in a kind of "behavior limbo," where they are neither feeling productive, nor resting and relaxing. Clearly, this state of lack of positive behavior has tremendous potential to keep a person feeling depressed.

It is important to say that the behavioral model is probably not a very complete or total account of depression for a number of reasons, but mainly it is insufficient because it does not really explain the cause or the origin of depression (Blaney 1977; Clark, Beck, and Alford 1999). What the model does do well though is describe depression once it has started. Most people who are depressed tend to have a withdrawn, inactive lifestyle. After all, this is one of the critical diagnostic criteria. Furthermore, once people have stopped engaging in their normal routines and activities, they get into a negative cycle. They do very few things that might have positive consequences; and because they have so few positive rewards as a result of this withdrawal, they are unlikely to start new behaviors. The result is a kind of spiral in which disengagement from normal activities leads to even more of a sense of loss and malaise; these emotions further undermine the depressed person's motivations to do positive things.

To counter this downward spiral the behavioral model of treating depression suggests an approach generally called *behavioral activation*. This approach, which we describe in the next section, has been a component of a number of depression treatments and recently has been studied and compared to other established treatments in two important studies (Jacobson et al. 1996; Gortner et al. 1998). The first of these two studies showed that behavioral activation—which has been considered by some as too simple to be effective—was as useful as another well-established and more complex form of treatment for depression; that is, behavioral activation alone led to very substantial improvements in symptoms (Jacobson et al. 1996). The second study showed that behavioral activation made changes that were as lasting as another form of therapy; this suggests that the impact of behavioral activation was enduring and not simply a "Band-Aid" (Gortner et al. 1998). Thus, behavioral activation, at least in these two studies, looks like it is a valuable intervention. In the next section we consider this approach more closely, especially from the perspective of relapse prevention.

Behavioral Activation and Relapse Prevention

Remember that, basically, the behavioral model of depression says that depression is nothing more than the lack of adequate positive reinforcement or rewards. For someone interested in staying well or warding off depression, the goal then is to maintain enough rewards and reinforcement on a daily basis. Doing this every day is likely to be much easier when someone is not depressed and presumably has normal levels of energy and interest in activities, as compared to increasing reinforcement when someone is depressed. Because depressed people are, by definition, likely to be pessimistic and fatigued, the prospect of activities of almost any sort is almost frightening. Even for those with normal mood, it helps to consider the rationale for engaging in more rewarding activities even when their lives already seem full and busy enough. Next, we describe some things to keep in mind when considering adding new activities to your life.

Most people think of themselves as a kind of energy storage device, say a battery, that draws energy for various activities over the course of the day, and then by bedtime the charge is low, so we retire and recharge. There is some truth to this idea. Clearly, we do become tired by the end of the day and sleep certainly restores us. And yet there are also ways in which we are more like a generator; that is, a device that produces its own energy as needed. For example, in addition to sleeping to restore ourselves, we can gain energy by eating and drinking, and the body will tell us to do this when we place demands on ourselves. The bottom line is that, when called upon, our bodies produce more energy to meet the demand we set. A concrete and common example may help to illustrate these ideas. Jeff likes to exercise, but can only reasonably do so after work from about 5 P.M. to 6 P.M. By the end of most work days, he feels pretty worn out by the demands of his job as a manager. Because he feels so worn out, he frequently thinks about skipping his exercise and wants to go straight home. When he does go straight home, he often finds that the feeling of fatigue and lethargy continues until bedtime. However, when he goes to the gym, he finds that for the first ten minutes he is almost sleepwalking through the exercise routine, but by the end of his workout at 6 P.M. he feels more alert; he also discovers that his thoughts and feelings about work are much more manageable. Moreover, he finds that, in the hours from 6 P.M. until bedtime, he is much more content and able to enjoy other activities. What is most important for Jeff to remember when he is feeling worn-out is that all he has to do is get himself over to the gym, and then let that experience take care of itself. Exercise is perhaps the best example of the idea of doing something that you know will be positive, even when you do not feel like it's a good thing to do *at that moment*. A regular exercise routine generates more energy and long-term motivation by infusing energy into the mind, body, and spirit.

One important maxim for adding positive behaviors is to remember that they may not always *feel* positive at every moment you are doing them. Remember to assess the worth of behaviors in the long run, and not during every second you are doing the behavior. The other maxim in adding positive behaviors is balance. Many people easily get into a set of activity habits that can get overwhelming. The number of responsibilities they have to meet often becomes unacceptably high. This sets up a potentially stressful situation, since it is also very easy to fail at meeting all those high demands. In addition to meeting responsibilities, it is simply necessary to find time for yourself, to indulge your needs, to challenge your abilities. Living life is about reward, not just obligation. In the next section think about your own life and what you do on a daily basis. Important questions to keep in mind are: How balanced is my life? What can I do to increase that balance?

Defining Satisfaction

There are two basic elements or kinds of rewards in our lives that we balance—pleasure and mastery. Most people have no problem understanding the concept of pleasure; it is simply having fun or enjoying an activity moment-to-moment. Of course, what gives one person pleasure may often be another person's idea of a terrible time. For example, some people travel the world to ride on the very best and fastest roller coasters. Obviously, riding on these is a pleasure for such people. For others, being strapped into a roller coaster seems like a nightmare, and they would not enjoy a single second of that experience. This is an important point to keep in mind about pleasure: we all know what it means, but how we get it is unique to each of us.

The second component of reward is mastery, which people sometimes have trouble with at first. Mastery is simply a sense of accomplishment or satisfaction, usually at achieving some kind of goal. With mastery experiences, there may be less moment-to-moment enjoyment; in fact, some mastery activities are challenging enough that they are frustrating. But in the end, when we get it right, we get a strong sense of accomplishment. Mastery experiences also have a very wide range in practice. Washing the dishes is a mastery event; the dishes start off dirty and the goal is to have clean dishes. The hot soapy water and the scrubbing, rinsing, and drying process may not be wonderfully fun for most people, but after the dishes are done we can be satisfied that we have, indeed, cleaned up the dishes. A round of golf can be a mastery experience as well as pleasurable. During that round of golf, there may be frustrating moments when we wish we were somewhere else or had never picked up a club, but by the end of the round we have a certain satisfaction from making the good shots that makes us want to return for another round. The list of mastery experiences is impossibly long and also unique to each individual.

You may recognize by now that work can be a source of mastery experiences. Again, a person may not take immediate pleasure in every work day, but what keeps us doing it is a sense that we are attaining meaningful goals. The need to accomplish, or have mastery, seems like it is almost a built-in human drive. For example, even people who have all the financial means to fund a life of complete leisure, if they wish, typically look for things to do that they see as worthwhile, and often bind them to a schedule of responsibility. Retirees, when one looks closely, often have certain activities—a sport, gardening, or a serious hobby—that take the place of the sense of accomplishment they formerly got from their careers. Ironically enough, we are often presented with the idea that, if we had the means, the ideal thing would be to buy an island in the South Pacific and relax under a palm tree. However, few people ever do this because lying under a palm tree is going to be pleasant for a few hours or days at most. People need more challenge in their lives, or some kind of resistance to push against somehow.

Many of us struggle to balance rewards and challenge, and it is easy for us to get unbalanced by going too far in the direction of either pleasure or mastery. For example, Paul came to see one of us after struggling with repeated episodes of depression because he sensed that he was backsliding into yet another. Paul was the model of the successful businessman who had risen to the top of his profession and by the age of fifty had been able to make a series of brilliant deals that earned him enough money to retire. In fact, this had been Paul's plan since taking his business degree and he had done everything he could to work toward the goal of retiring at fifty with a great deal of money. But since his retirement, his propensity to get depressed had increased, which he found very paradoxical. When we examined Paul's life, it was focused exclusively on leisure. He traveled frequently, exercised, read, spent time with his wife and family, and actively avoided dealing with business matters. What Paul had done was create a life that was, for all intents and purposes, too unchallenging for him. He was a very bright man who was highly motivated, and yet he was idling away. The only times he was really passionate were when talking about his work life and the heyday of his deal making. Eventually, Paul decided that he would rebalance his life by returning, part-time, to the business world and trying his hand at what he was truly good at. He also planned to both teach business students and take courses to further develop his skills. Paul found it somewhat strange that the answer to his problems, going back to work, was exactly what he had been trying for most of his adult life to get away from. Paul's story is not unique at all, and it is very common for people who retire to have an unexpected depression in response to this dramatic life change.

Even more common than too much pleasure is an imbalance in mastery. This is especially true for people who are working and have family commitments at the same time. Their daily schedules often run at twelve hours plus of work, parenting, and household tasks. Here, there may be an abundance of mastery but an absence of pleasure. People in this situation look at the idea of adding balance with pleasure with an exasperated sense of "where will I find that time?" This is a very reasonable response and surely it is difficult to carve out blocks of time for yourself when work, family, and other responsibilities are tugging at your sleeve for attention. But then again, if all of their responsibilities put a person at risk for depression and generally wear them down to the point that they cannot take care of their responsibilities, the person really has no choice but to take preemptive action. Also, there are often "shoulds" and "musts" in people's lives that are not nearly as necessary as the person may believe. Most things that we do are, at some level, negotiable and can be changed. The bottom line is that engaging in pleasant events is not a luxury; pleasure is a necessity for all of us.

Rating Your Own Levels of Mastery and Pleasure

You may or may not have seen your own life reflected in these examples, but now it is time to apply these ideas to your own life. We have included a very simple worksheet that consists of a schedule grid with the days of the week and most of your waking hours. The idea for this worksheet is to record your activities for the next seven days in order to maintain or establish a greater balance. Rarely, people will find that they have an exactly right balance of mastery and pleasure, and that is fine. If the worksheet establishes that things are optimal, it is still well worth doing.

To complete the worksheet, simply write a couple of words about the activities you are doing each hour. Mostly, this will be one or two words, such as working, watching TV, reading book, at gym, with kids. It is okay to enter an activity once and then draw an arrow to indicate that the activity is going on for whatever length of time. Also, for each activity make two different ratings. First, rate the activity on a scale of 0 to 10 for how much pleasure it gives you, with 10 being the most pleasant thing imaginable and 0 being not all pleasant. Also, rate the level of mastery that an activity brings you, with 10 being the most mastery possible and 0 being no mastery at all. For example, your activity might be "reading novel," with a pleasure rating of 8 and a mastery rating of 2. This would suggest that you had a distinct sense of pleasure, but little sense of mastery, as a result of reading.

Once you have completed this worksheet, answer the following questions to help establish whether your current activities are balanced and contain enough mastery and pleasure.

Question 1: Looking at all the ratings for the week, how do your levels of mastery and pleasure compare to one another?

If you find that your mastery ratings, when added together, are higher than your pleasure ratings added together, this may mean that your activities are imbalanced in the direction of too much mastery and not enough pleasure. Similarly, if your pleasure ratings outweigh your mastery ratings, you may not be having enough mastery experiences.

Question 2: Can you clearly identify several activities that led to a high mastery rating (7 or more)?

If the answer to this is no, you may need to identify some experiences that are more purely mastery related and that lead to a sense of accomplishment.

Worksheet 7.1 Weekly Activity Schedule

Instructions: Record your activities for the week and rate your levels of pleasure and mastery for each on a scale of 0 to 10.

	Monday	Tuesday	Wednesday	Thursday	Friday	Saturday	Sunday
8:00 A.M.							
9:00 A.M.							
10:00 A.M.							
11:00 A.M.							
12:00 P.M.							
1:00 P.M.							
2:00 P.M.							
3:00 P.M.							
4:00 P.M.							
5:00 P.M.							
6:00 P.M.							
7:00 P.M.							
8:00 P.M.							
9:00 P.M.							
10:00 P.M.							
11:00 P.M.							
12:00 A.M.							

Question 3: Can you clearly identify several activities that led to a high pleasure rating (7 or more)?

Again, if the answer is no, you may need to identify some experiences that are more purely pleasurable and that simply lead to moment-to-moment enjoyment.

Question 4: If your best friend showed you this activity schedule with the same ratings of mastery and pleasure, what would you tell them to do differently?

This approach, the best-friend point of view, often leads to a profound perspective shift. Your answer might be "take more time for yourself" or "get out there and try some more things." This will be an important clue for you as to how to modify your own life.

Once you have answered these questions for yourself, it should be clear what kind of activities, mastery or pleasure needs to be added. Keep in mind that sometimes you may also have to think about what can be taken away. For example, if there is an activity you recorded that takes up a significant amount of time in your day, but has neither a high mastery nor pleasure rating, is there some way to reduce the amount of time you spend in that activity? Some neutral activities cannot be altered. For example, working at a job that leads to neither mastery nor pleasure may be necessary to pay the bills. However, in the long run, it is important to make sure that you focus as much as possible on filling your time with activities that offer some kind of reward.

Adding Mastery and Pleasure Activities

Most people do not have an ideal schedule when it comes to mastery and pleasure. The fact is, it is difficult to attain a schedule that is perfect when there are so many demands on your time and not enough time to go around. Nonetheless, this does not mean that nothing can be changed, and you may want to add some activities to increase your levels of mastery and pleasure. This is best done in three steps: (1) brainstorming for new activities to fill the mastery or pleasure need, (2) trying out the new activity, and (3) assessing the impact of the new activity.

Brainstorming New Activities

Having completed the ratings of mastery and pleasure in the section above, you should now have a fairly clear sense of what kinds of activities (mastery, pleasure, or both) you would like to add. Be creative as you come up with ideas about new activities. Remember, while brainstorming, no idea should be dismissed so that your creativity is not stifled. The biggest obstacle to this exercise is usually self-censoring—dismissing something as too ambitious, costly, or extravagant. If there is something you can imagine, even if it does not seem realistic, put it down on paper and reexamine it later. The best source of activities is probably your own mind. Ask yourself questions like, "What have I always wanted to do but didn't have the time, the resources, or the information I needed?" This question will often tap into people's dreams and aspirations, often forgotten in our day-to-day routine. One common pleasure activity that people describe is a wish to travel; and, no doubt, traveling is often a time when people feel like they are not only enjoying themselves, but mastering new experiences, languages, and places. Often the next thought is, "but I can't afford it," or "I have no time," or "it would be too short-lived."

This was very true for Sarah, whose first response to this exercise in therapy was a wish to study French in Paris—something she considered a frivolous dream. Like many people, Sarah often dismissed that thought on the grounds of its "irrationality and irresponsibility." Indeed, it was not possible for Sarah to just do this overnight. However, she and her therapist used the kernel of this idea for both mastery and pleasure. Sarah decided that she would pursue this goal in two years time and, in the meantime, would spend one evening per week doing the background research, reading Paris travel books, taking a basic French course, and looking on the Internet for places to see and stay. To Sarah's surprise, even the act of surfing the Web for language schools was the most pleasant thing she did in the next week. Having committed to fulfill her dream of actually going in two years time, she found that thinking about the trip and planning and replanning what she wanted to see and do was a bit like traveling to Paris for a few hours a week. Had Sarah dismissed the idea of Paris right at the beginning, she would not have discovered this source of positive reinforcement. We have seen many similar examples in which people identify what seem to them like unrealistic goals for mastery and pleasure, ranging from hobbies (such as building model railroads) to developing skills or talents (like learning to sing). Most of these goals are achievable with time and patience; and for most people, even taking a few steps in the right direction can add an element of enjoyment and meaning in their lives that they did not expect.

Another way to brainstorm for new pleasure and mastery activities is to look back on the past. For many reasons, as time goes by we often give up activities that used to give us pleasure. These can range from playing sports, to picking up a musical instrument, to hobbies long abandoned for whatever reason. Frequently the activities that really are fun and interesting fell away because other responsibilities got in the way, or the activity seemed, at the time, to belong in another phase of life. For many people, however, blowing the dust off their much used roller skates, old baseball glove, or saxophone can bring about a sense of rediscovery and fond memories of younger days. In many cases, people who have been depressed gave up things during their depression that were no longer fun or interesting (remember, losing interest in normal activities is one of the key features of depression). Sometimes, people in that situation believe that the activity will no longer be fun, because at the time they gave it up they were depressed. Tom was one such patient, who had been quite depressed when he sold his sailboat and resigned from the sailing club in which he had been a member. As he began to recover from his depression, Tom and his therapist devised a plan for Tom to stop by the sailing club and track his reaction and mood. To his surprise, Tom enjoyed even the simple act of walking on the shore and seeing the boats in their moorings. On another visit, he ran into some people he knew who invited him for a sail. Within a few weeks, he arranged to rent a small sailboat and had a wonderful time rediscovering his skills as a sailor. The lesson here is that things we enjoyed in the past are an excellent place to look for things we will enjoy in the present and future.

A final way to brainstorm activities is to look at outside resources, which can range from talking to friends about activities they enjoy, to browsing through a hobby shop, to reading through offerings for adult education at local recreation centers, fitness facilities, schools, and colleges. For almost every kind of activity that anyone has ever enjoyed, there is undoubtedly a Web site and a list of resources to help people get involved in that hobby, activity, or pastime.

Trying Out a New Activity

At the end of the brainstorming, all you need is a starting point. Perhaps the long-term goal you will choose is to adopt a new hobby. The first step might be buying a book or magazine that highlights this new interest, or perhaps you can attend a meeting of a club that pursues that hobby. Whatever activity you choose, remember that it should not be overwhelming. Trying to fit in many hours of new activities can be more stressful than it is helpful. Moreover, if your goal is too large, it's easy to feel like you are falling short. Make sure that you choose goals that can be accomplished within the time you have set aside. Above all, remember that what is to be enjoyed about these activities is the experience, not some grand and perfect goal.

Another thing that is very useful when starting a new activity is to choose a place and time in advance. We are all creatures of habit and, left to our automatic way of being, it's easy to forget the new plan or to reach the end of the week and then realize too late that you had intended to try your new activity. The best way to initiate something is to look at the activity schedule you completed previously. Where does the new activity fit best in your schedule? Keep in mind that you do not want to be unrealistic about how efficient you will be. Leave some room for error so that you will provide yourself enough free time to fit in the new activity. Remember also to track your mood and your sense of mastery and pleasure while doing the new activity.

Assessing the Impact of the New Activity

Once you have tried out the new activity, it's important to take some time to assess its impact. After all, what you are really doing here is a kind of experiment to discover whether you can make life more pleasant and interesting, and therefore more fulfilling. So you need to measure your success on those dimensions. To know whether the activity was successful in terms of the goal of improving your life, you may want to ask yourself:

- Did you enjoy the activity? Did it give you a sense of mastery and pleasure at the level you were looking for?

- Was there something about the activity that was surprising in a good way; that is, was it more fun or interesting than you expected? Were there benefits to the activity that you did not expect?

- Was there any downside to the activity? Was it less pleasant or interesting than you had hoped? Were there obstacles to doing the activity that you did not expect?

The answers to these questions should help you determine whether the new activity is something you would like to keep or enhance, or whether you need to look elsewhere. It is important to continue to experiment with adding and taking away activities. Keep in mind that you probably do not want to put yourself in a position where an activity feels like yet another "must" or "should." Keeping up healthy routines is important for wellness, but being flexible enough to sometimes forgo the usual routine is also an important part of staying well. People who are vulnerable to depression, especially those with perfectionistic traits (see chapter 11), often get caught up in the idea that they *should* accomplish everything they set out to do. Likewise, the very idea of having to do things "just right" is often what keeps people away from trying things out just for fun. In the end, a rewarding, regular but flexible routine is the goal.

Rewards in the Long Run

Up until now we have described techniques that involve adding new rewarding activities to your daily or weekly routine. Adding time for a new hobby, creating a time to enjoy a movie, or carving out time for regular exercise requires a bit of adjustment for most people. These kinds of changes, while meaningful, are probably not that radical to carry out. Sometimes though, a more rewarding daily routine involves more changes that stretch out over more time.

We mentioned earlier that it is important to also consider removing things from your life that bring neither pleasure or mastery. This seems like a simple idea, but it can have big implications. For example, many people, on paying careful attention, discover that the jobs they do bring them a sense of neither mastery nor pleasure. However, when someone discovers this, he or she is rarely going to be in a position to quit that job and find something more rewarding the next week. Similarly, sometimes after completing this process a person finds that something to which they have committed is not as rewarding as they had anticipated. Again, it may not be possible to change this in the next days or weeks. At the same time, if these things are identified as underrewarding, it makes sense to also make a long-term plan for change. Work that is understimulating is one of the most common themes people with depression identify and one of the most difficult to change. However, this is a good example of thinking and planning for the long term. If a person's work is not satisfying them, what can they do? The options are actually quite numerous. For example, the simplest path may be to alter the kind of roles the person has at their current job; in other words, can their actual duties be made different in a way that would provide more interest? If that is not possible with the current employer, are there other kinds of work the person is interested in and qualified for? If qualifications are needed, can these be achieved while remaining in the current job? None of these approaches will be immediate. Nonetheless, given the number of hours that most of us spend at a job, working on finding the right kind of job should be a priority.

In addition to making long-term plans that have to do with changing one's life, some activities that people choose to add can take time and need to be considered as long-term goals. Some pursuits require a commitment to achieve; for example, learning a martial art, becoming a ballroom dancer, building radio-controlled airplanes, or growing vegetables in a garden (the list is endless). With these kinds of activities that take time, it will be useful to do two things. First, in order to keep the activity enjoyable, it is important to not become overly ambitious and feel like things ought to be moving faster. This is sometimes difficult when we are exposed to people who have already mastered the activity or craft. At the first ballroom dance lesson, you may see people who look like they ought to be featured on television. It is difficult to not use these "experts" as a comparison or benchmark, but of course those people have probably had years of experience and thousands of hours of practice. When we are new at something, making comparisons is something to be cautious of. The only person one probably wants to compare against is oneself at an earlier point in time. That is, it is fair to ask, "Am I better at this now than when I started?" That is the only benchmark that counts. So the main thing to remember when taking on a new challenge is that it will need time. The point is to enjoy the journey of learning, not just the destination. At the same time, when learning something as involved as ballroom dancing, it may make sense to develop a plan for how this can happen. This plan should take into account your ultimate goal. One person may have a goal that says, "I'd like to be able to dance at social gatherings comfortably." Another person may have a goal that says, "I'd like to be at the point where I enter local amateur competitions." Obviously, the amount of time the people with these two goals put into the activity will be quite different. So when it comes to long-term plans, consider what you would like to get out of the activity and plan accordingly.

In this section, we have moved from considering simple rewards and getting enough reinforcement to establishing long-terms goals and building on your interests. Next, we consider two areas of daily activity that are crucial in depression and relapse prevention—sleep and exercise.

Essential Daily Routines: Sleep and Exercise

Mastery and pleasure are defined differently for each individual, and establishing a balance is a matter of subjective judgement. However, sleep and exercise are two daily activities that should not be left to chance if you are vulnerable to depression. The reason for our focus on these two areas is not incidental and has to do with research that links these areas to the occurrence of depression and to treatments for depression that have been shown to work (Bootzin and Rider 1997; Tkachuk and Martin 1999). Sleep routines and exercise are of course part of our daily lives, and should be explicitly included in a weekly activity schedule just as any other event. Sleep especially is something that gets nibbled away at; we tend to go to bed later than we should and squeeze more into our day by getting up earlier than we should. Exercise is too often optional, or is sacrificed when things get too busy. Do not leave either of these areas to chance.

Sleeping Soundly

Sleep is a very important area in depression. Disturbed sleep—either too much or too little—is a key symptom for making a diagnosis of depression. In fact, some researchers believe that disturbances found in the sleep of people who are depressed may point the way to finding the ultimate cause of depression (Ware and Morin 1997). Some scientists even believe that depression is a sleep disorder, or at least a disorder based on problems in the person's biological rhythm (Reynolds and Kupfer 1988). While this is only one perspective on sleep and depression, it is pretty clear that the presence of depression profoundly affects sleep. Likewise, changing people's sleeping affects their mood and emotions. Depression mainly disrupts the REM (rapid eye movement) stage of sleep, and depressed people have less REM sleep. (Many people are familiar with REM sleep because they know that this is the stage of sleep in which people dream.) Also, depressed people enter the REM stage of sleep more quickly than nondepressed people (Rehm, Wagner, and Ivens-Tyndal 2001).

Researchers have also looked at sleep in another way by taking people with otherwise normal moods and having them sleep in a laboratory where they are gently roused just before they enter REM sleep. People in these studies will sleep all night, but they will not go through any of the normal REM stages. When people are deprived of REM sleep, they seem to be compromised in some ways, especially in their ability to cope with stress and frustration (McGrath and Cohen 1978; Ware and Morin 1997). While they may feel rested, their emotions are somewhat brittle. This has led researchers to conclude that REM sleep helps us cope with stressors, perhaps allowing the brain to sort through emotional thoughts and memories. In addition to the emotional impact of disturbed REM sleep, sleep deprivation more generally leads to irritability, greater sensitivity to pain, and memory problems (Ware and Morin 1997).

The implications for someone who may be vulnerable to relapse of depression is to make sure that their sleep rhythm is as regular and as restful as possible. Importantly, many of the best known antidepressant medications seem to help normalize sleep patterns, so maintenance medications for relapse prevention may have the benefit of keeping sleep regular (Ware and Morin 1997). But the idea of keeping sleep regular also has implications for your own behavior, some of which are obvious and some that are perhaps less obvious. The most obvious change is to leave room in your daily schedule for enough sleep. Most people seem to be at their best after around eight hours of sleep, though some will require less and others more. If you are a person who requires more, it is important to leave time for this rather than to try to cut yourself down to something less than what you need. Similarly, if you need less than eight hours, your body will probably not allow you to sleep for more than you need. There are several less obvious things that you can do to sleep as well as possible, and this is sometimes known as *sleep hygiene*.

Sleep Hygiene: Rules for a Good Night's Rest

Sleep hygiene has a number of rules or maxims (Bootzin and Rider 1997). First, it is best to go to bed at the same time every day and try to get up at the same time every day, especially if sleep has been a problem for you in the past. Having sleep that starts and ends at a regular time is likely to be the easiest on your body's daily rhythm and the internal clocks we have. Many people who keep a regular schedule do not need alarm clocks to wake, or any particular aids, such as sleep masks or ear plugs, to fall asleep. It is as if the body knows when to rest and when to awaken. Of course the problem with sleeping and waking at the same time every day often has to do with the idea that, on weekends or days off, it is fun to sleep in (especially if the night before has been a late one). Sleep hygiene should not spoil all of one's fun; there is probably no problem with occasional late nights because of a party, movie, or other pleasurable event. Nonetheless, it may be wise to at least get up at the usual time and try to reestablish your regular routine as quickly as possible.

Another problem, one that is harder to work around, has to do with changing sleep schedules due to shift work. Again, the general idea is to be on a specific rhythm as much as possible. If sleep is a real problem, however, to the point that the person is having many sleepless nights or sleep that is not restful, that person might consider whether they can find work that does not require shift changes. This may seem a drastic step, but if such disturbances in sleep make the person vulnerable to depression, changes are needed and justified.

A second rule in sleep hygiene has to do with substances like alcohol and caffeine. These need to be looked at very closely indeed. Some people get into the habit of using caffeine to wake up and alcohol to help them sleep. Other people use caffeine throughout the day, to the point that when they retire to bed the caffeine is still in their system. Both alcohol and caffeine have important effects on our brain and do influence our sleep cycles. A detailed discussion of these effects is beyond the scope of this book, but the central point is that these substances should not to be used as a crutch, or as aids to sleep. We recommend that alcohol and caffeine be restricted to no more than one dose per day, that is, one cup of coffee or one alcoholic drink. Obviously, we do not recommend any alcohol for a person who has struggled with substance abuse. Furthermore, it is probably wise to not drink alcohol or take caffeine around the time of trying to fall asleep or trying to wake up. These substances only distort your natural rhythm and can result in problems in the long run like *tolerance* (needing to take more of a drug for the same effect) and *withdrawal* (uncomfortable symptoms and sensations when the substance is not in the bloodstream).

Another important maxim in sleep hygiene is that beds are for sleeping. That is, if you are awake in your bed for more than about ten minutes, it is wise to get up and do something. Your bed should be associated with sleeping, as opposed to eating, watching television, doing your taxes, etc. Even worse, some people, when trying to fall asleep in their beds, often have numerous worries that interfere with sleep. Lying in bed worrying will result in an association between worrying and your bed. It is as if the bed has become the place to worry, rather than the place to sleep. Many patients we have worked with have spent hundreds, even thousands, of hours lying awake in bed, ruminating or worrying. The person should get up if they cannot fall asleep after ten minutes, even just to sit in a chair in the bedroom to read a book; this results in important changes. First, reading is always better than worrying, especially in bed where there is no opportunity whatsoever to solve the issue that the person is worrying about. Second, once the person is reading in a chair, they often find their eyelids getting heavy and may well fall asleep quite naturally. Moving back to bed once the person is nodding off is perfectly acceptable. The same is true when waking up. Many people tend to stay in bed after waking up, especially if they have awoken early. Again, the tendency is to lie awake and have negative thoughts and worries that you cannot do anything about. It is far better to simply get up and start the day as normally as possible.

Another maxim for sleep hygiene is to avoid any kind of emotional or physical stimulation before bedtime. So it is probably unwise to exercise just before going to bed, or to work on a difficult task before trying to sleep. Also, it is probably a good idea to avoid very strong emotions before trying to sleep. For example, a confrontation with someone or an upsetting conversation that happens before bedtime is likely to interfere with sleep. Ideally, the hour or two before bedtime is spent in a relaxed state doing something enjoyable.

One rule of sleep hygiene that is simple, but easy to overlook sometimes, is that the sleeping environment ought to be comfortable in all respects. This includes the bed itself, having a quiet environment, and darkness. People's tastes in what is a comfortable bed are wide ranging, but the main thing is to make sure that the bed you have is as comfortable for you as possible. People often compromise in their sleeping arrangements; that is, they try to tolerate the noisy furnace that wakes them up every hour, they do not feel justified in buying that new mattress to replace the lumpy one they have, or they let their pets or kids into the bed even though their own sleep is ruined. These compromises ought to be avoided. Sleep is a precious commodity and deserves to be protected.

The final sleep hygiene rule is the simplest of all: no napping! It is a very difficult rule to keep in place, especially when you have not gotten a good night's sleep. In some ways, a nap in the middle of the day is the body's natural compensation strategy for not being well rested enough. At the same time, a nap, especially if it's for any longer than twenty minutes, can actually trigger a whole new sleep cycle, as if it is nighttime. When traveling across time zones, all of us have had the experience of jet lag. Often, this means falling asleep during the day at our new destination and sleeping very soundly to the point that when we wake up we feel groggy and may not even know whether it is day or night. Having a long nap can be very similar to this experience, and may have a similar effect on your body's internal clock. Remember, the nap itself may be enjoyable, but later that night you will have that much more trouble falling asleep. Disturbing the sleep routine and napping to catch up can quickly become a vicious cycle. If you do find that during the middle of the day you have a natural lull, paradoxically, the best thing you can do is stay on the move. People are often surprised at how, if they keep busy during those nappish moments, within a few minutes they will have forgotten that they were feeling sleepy at all.

The sleep hygiene ideas above are all fairly simple strategies to try to get enough regular and restful sleep. Unfortunately, the rest of the world sometimes conspires to make sleep more difficult than it should be. In a fascinating book, Stan Coren (1996) has made the argument that Western culture has turned sleep into a dispensable activity. Coren describes many of the societal factors that can disturb our sleeping time, such as moving our clocks back and forth in fall and spring, imposing of shift work, and equating the need for sleep with a kind of moral weakness. Coren suggests that sleep problems may be responsible for everything from feelings of stress to fatal car accidents, and argues that more should be done to protect our need for sleep.

The sleep hygiene principles we have described should help. However, if these behavioral strategies are not sufficient for you, there are medications that effectively aid sleep. Many of the newer medications are much better than the sleeping pill of years ago. For example, some of the newer medications do not result in tolerance effects or withdrawal. Then again, as with most medications, there is the possibility of side effects or *rebound*. Rebound means that once the medication is removed, it is often more difficult for the person to sleep naturally. Weighing these trade-offs is something that is best done carefully with your doctor. Finally, like all the other strategies in this book, staying well rested is just another small but important way to ward off depression. In the final section of this chapter, we take a quick look at the protective benefits, both physical and psychological, of exercise.

The Joys and Benefits of Exercise

Aside from regular, restful sleep, exercise is another activity that deserves a place in everyone's routine. For most of us, exercise is a combination of mastery and pleasure. Most people do take pleasure in some of the sensations of exercise, or perhaps the environment (for example, jogging on a scenic path). And yet a good, long workout or a jog of several miles is not always fun. At the end, we realize we have done something significant and not easy, hence that sense of mastery. But exercise is more than pleasure and mastery; it also has effects on our physical and mental state that are far-reaching. Done right, exercise is one of the few things in life that has no downside.

The physical benefits of exercise for our bodies and medical health are obvious. People who exercise regularly live longer, are more physically capable, and are better equipped to deal with medical illnesses. Regular exercise is a standard recommendation made by all manner of health organizations from the World Health Organization to the American Medical Association. Our interest in exercise is more in what it does for depression. And indeed, it seems that exercise does lead to improvements in symptoms, especially in mild to moderate depression, when compared to placebo or no treatment (Tkachuk and Martin 1999). This is especially important for relapse prevention, since presumably most depressions start slowly, with some small increases in symptoms that become more and more noticeable. If exercise can help alleviate these mild symptoms and prevent them from becoming worse, it should be an important consideration in your plan for wellness.

How Much Exercise and When?

One of surprising things about exercise and depression is that you do not need to run marathons or become a bodybuilder to get the desired effects. It seems that three times a week of moderate exercise (brisk walking or slow jogging) that lasts between twenty and sixty minutes is sufficient to benefit mood (Tkachuck and Martin 1999). Of course, the exercise must be maintained over the long term to get lasting benefits for your mood, and the more you exercise, the better it seems to work (Greist 1987). Exactly why exercise should be so helpful is still difficult to say. Exercise certainly does have many positive effects on the brain: it improves learning and memory, protects the brain from injury, and results in having more of the chemicals that actually help build and maintain neurons (Cotman and Berchtold 2002; Sime 1996). At the same time, people who exercise also experience an increase in self-esteem. The net effect is, prior to exercising, you may be thinking and feeling a certain way, perhaps preoccupied with some worry or problem. After exercise, your perspective on that worry or problem may change so that it seems more manageable. One clear example of a shift to a feeling of wellness is the so-called "runner's high," which is probably what, at some level, each of us experiences during and after exercise. This psychological and physical change in our brains as a result of exercise is a truly remarkable phenomenon that researchers are continuing to study to better understand.

Before You Start

It is always wise to get medical clearance before starting to exercise. Check with your doctor regarding your routine. Then start slowly and make the exercise as simple as possible. Sometimes people are tempted to join a very posh gym or buy expensive gear before really knowing whether this is something they are interested in and want to maintain. Start any exercise very slowly so as to make sure you have a positive experience each time. If you want to start jogging, jog around the block on the first day. This may seem too short a distance, or too easy. But if you start the first day trying to do a couple of miles, you may exhaust yourself, pull a muscle, or generally have a miserable time. Starting slow and increasing the activity in five-minute increments each time you go will build up your capacity quite quickly without being overwhelming.

Also, if possible, find an exercise buddy. Another person can help motivate you on days that you don't feel like doing the exercising. And, committing to something publicly, or agreeing to do something with your companion, means that you are far more likely to stick to it. Look for an activity that has some other benefits, such as jogging or walking at a place where there is nice scenery. Some experts recommend that exercise be functional or serve a purpose; for example, walking to work or using stairs instead of an elevator to incorporate exercise into your daily routine. The idea behind this is that if exercise is tied into something else that is important to do, you are much more likely to keep it up. Finally, building an exercise habit is likely to be something that takes time, so be prepared for little setbacks like a sore knee or muscle stiffness. The important thing is not whether you exercise on any given day, but that you will be exercising more over a week, a month, or a year and that physical activity becomes part of who you are and how you live.

Summary

In this chapter we have considered the impact of positive reinforcement and rewarding activities in maintaining wellness. By focusing on your levels of mastery and pleasure, and making efforts to balance these, you will be doing your best to stay well. Sometimes, these ideas about rewards and daily activities are regarded as overly simplistic; that is, people may think these approaches do not go deep enough or are not psychologically profound enough. And yet the evidence concerning behavioral activation, sleep, and exercise is very convincing. In the end, these ideas also contain a lot of common sense, and since work and play are such basic human needs, it is not really that surprising that work and play also influence depression. Having a satisfying, enriching, and evolving daily routine is clearly a goal worth working for, and one that is likely to offer important protection against the return of depression.

Summary Exercise

Record what you believe is the bottom line from this chapter, then record what practices, exercises, or worksheets you would adopt as part of your wellness plan.

Chapter 7, Having Fun and Living Healthy, looks at daily routines and fulfilling activities. My bottom line in this chapter is:

_____

_____

The practices, exercises, or actions I will take from this chapter are:

_____

_____

Chapter 8

Mindfulness Meditation for Preventing Relapse

In this chapter, we describe a form of treatment, *mindfulness meditation,* that has been shown in carefully conducted research to actually reduce relapse risk in people who have previously been depressed (Segal, Williams, and Teasdale 2002). Mindfulness-based cognitive therapy (MBCT) is one of the first interventions that has been specifically designed to keep people well. Previously, people relied on maintenance treatments like ongoing medication and booster psychotherapy to prevent relapse (chapters 4 and 5), but MBCT is designed as a novel treatment. Unlike maintenance approaches which suggest that a person should continue with the treatment that made them well, MBCT can be taken up at any time by someone who wants to reduce their probability of relapse. The fact that research has shown that mindfulness, as a stand-alone strategy, prevents relapse makes it rather unique. Therefore, we have devoted an entire chapter to it. We will begin by explaining what mindfulness meditation is and what it is not. We then present a brief overview of mindfulness techniques, strategies, and hands-on exercises, and look at some of the reasons why mindfulness may be a good strategy for you to use in your wellness plan.

Mindfulness meditation is different from many of the other techniques we discuss because it is sometimes misperceived as having a spiritual, or even religious, connotation. Most of us are familiar with some forms of meditation practice that seem to require people to wear robes, do without modern technology, and believe in a certain kind of higher power. We want to start by dispensing with those ideas when it comes to MBCT.

Mindfulness meditation, in this context, is not about spirituality, traveling to Tibet, or giving away your earthly possessions. Rather, depression researchers have found an incidental, and very fortunate, link between the practice of mindfulness and the cognitive model of depression we described in chapter 6. Also, mindfulness meditation has been used in well-known institutions around North America for many years to help people with stress (Kabat-Zinn 1990). As a result, mindfulness has been adapted to a mainstream framework that does not ask people to give up or change their spiritual beliefs, values, or anything else, but does help people to work on specific skills that they can practice to reduce stress and stay well.

Before getting into exactly what mindfulness is and what it does, we will start with a very quick definition. "Mindfulness means paying attention in a particular way: on purpose, in the present moment, and nonjudgmentally" (Kabat-Zinn 1994, 4). This simple definition has profound consequences, especially when we look at the cognitive model and techniques discussed in chapter 6. A group of depression experts in the United Kingdom and Canada were the first to identify exactly how mindfulness is related to cognitive therapy, and much of what is described here is based on this recent and cutting-edge research (Segal, Williams, and Teasdale 2002). You may recall from chapter 6 that thinking and depression are closely linked, and that people who have recovered from depression may feel completely well, but may still be vulnerable to certain patterns of negative thinking. We also described some techniques to challenge negative thinking. Mindfulness complements this process in a rather unique way. First, practicing paying attention to and accepting what is going through your mind in a *nonjudgmental* way will take some of the sting out of your negative thoughts, take energy away from your negative moods, and help you to pay attention to simpler things, such as taking a breath. Also, mindfulness, or accepting your thoughts and feelings, may make you more aware of changes in your thinking; this can act as a kind of early warning system (Segal, Williams, and Teasdale 2002). Finally, we have found that using mindfulness with our patients allows them to focus on healthy and useful things that they are doing, rather than having their attention be distracted by events over which they have little control or thoughts that are not healthy. This often helps our patients to be more productive and spend less time on doing things that are harmful to themselves in the long run.

Based on these connections between cognitive therapy and mindfulness, Dr. Segal and colleagues conducted the first large-scale study of mindfulness for relapse prevention. A total of 145 people participated in their study. They were assigned randomly to receive either eight sessions of mindfulness treatment or "treatment as usual" (whatever regular appointments and remedies they would normally receive in the "real world"). The study had many interesting findings, but perhaps the most important finding was this: for people who had three or more past episodes of depression, the risk of relapse over a sixty-week period was reduced from 66 percent in the "treatment as usual" group to 37 percent in the mindfulness group, a very large reduction in risk (Teasdale et al. 2000). The researchers don't know for sure why the risk was reduced only for people who had three or more episodes, and to some extent that finding is counter to what one might expect. Researchers usually find that the more episodes of depression one has had, the more likely it is that depression will return again. It seems that mindfulness actually works better in people who have more risk of becoming depressed again, which is good news! Of course, this study will have to be repeated with other groups of people and in other clinics to verify the results, but risk reductions this large are unlikely to happen by chance alone. Mindfulness seems to work, and probably anyone who has been depressed should examine very carefully what mindfulness has to offer.

Learning Mindfulness

We have aimed to provide an overview of mindfulness and some techniques to get you started. However, mindfulness is difficult to describe completely in a single chapter, so our purpose here is really to whet your appetite. Once you have read this chapter, you may want more information. There are many, many books on mindfulness that give a more complete description of what is involved. For example, Jon Kabat-Zinn has written two excellent books, *Full Catastrophe Living* (1990) and *Wherever You Go, There You Are* (1994), that contain a lot of background and specific exercises on mindfulness. Dr. Segal and colleagues have written about their work in *Mindfulness-Based Cognitive Therapy for Depression* (2002); although written for professionals, this has a lot of useful information for the layperson about teaching and learning mindfulness. Books like this can provide much more detailed information than we can provide in one chapter. Also, mindfulness is something that can, and should, be shared with other people who practice this form of meditation. Teachers of mindfulness, regardless of their level of experience and expertise, commonly attend sessions or workshops in which they refine their techniques and learn from others. Obviously, if you are starting out with mindfulness, you may want to find other people who can help you learn and support your practice. Larger cities are likely to have various places where people meet to meditate and talk about their practice of mindfulness. Some of these places may have a more spiritual emphasis than others, so you may want to shop around and find a place that is comfortable for you.

What Is Mindful?

Mindful is just paying attention in a certain way. Simple enough, right? And yet that brief description isn't adequate. In our own reading and practice of mindfulness, we've discovered that a complete definition of mindfulness cannot be written down, no matter how many words are used. The musician Elvis Costello once said, "Writing about music is like dancing about architecture." Writing about mindfulness proves to be just as elusive and challenging. It is like trying to describe, using words, what is meant by the term "orange." How would we do this? You might start by saying that orange is a color, one that is a bit like red and yellow mixed together, and by pointing out examples of orange, like a sunset. But what would be the best way to describe "orange?" When we read the term orange, we see the color in our minds (proof that a picture is worth a thousand words). It's very simple for all of us to picture the color orange, and yet hard to capture orange in words. When writing about mindfulness, the best we can do is to talk around it. The way to understand it completely is to do it and to keep doing it and refining your experiences. There is no substitute for seeing the color orange. If you haven't seen it, you don't know it. Similarly, if you haven't practiced mindfulness, it is difficult to describe. Luckily, there are exercises and ways to introduce mindfulness into our lives that are much easier to describe than mindfulness itself. The results of doing these exercises can be profound.

In their work on mindfulness, depression researchers have suggested that the most important skill to take from mindfulness practice is the ability to "recognize and disengage" from patterns of negative thinking that are the first signs of relapse (Segal, Williams, and Teasdale 2002, 75). At the end of this chapter we will return to this central skill, but for now, we will describe more general exercises that are aimed at doing several things to help you get on the path toward greater mindfulness. At the start, these exercises help you to recognize what is called *automatic pilot,* the state we often find ourselves in as we go through our days. "Automatic pilot" really means that we are doing things but not really experiencing them. We may be eating our dinner, but doing so mechanically while at the same time thinking about something problematic that happened at work, a bill we need to pay, or even daydreaming about our next vacation. Automatic pilot is also a mode in which we do a lot of judging and evaluating. If you pay close attention to your normal stream of consciousness, you will find that it is filled with evaluations—evaluations of yourself as good or bad, that things around you are going your way or not, that the room you are in is too cold or too warm, that the food you are eating tastes good or bad, that the television show you are watching is funny or not funny, and so on. These appraisals are not bad, because evaluating is part of being human. At the same time, these kinds of evaluations pull our emotions in different directions. What mindfulness asks of us is to have these thoughts and feelings and to accept them, but to treat them as experiences that may or may not mean something. Instead of paying attention to these evaluations and how important they seem to be, mindfulness asks us to pay attention to something that is not evaluated, like breathing. Mindfulness involves moment-to-moment experiencing of yourself, your body, and your surroundings without evaluating those experiences as good or bad.

The Attitude of Mindfulness

The first exercise we will describe is not something specific, but rather a set of attitudes to reflect on as you plan to do the exercises. These attitudes, like any new behavior or thought, need to be cultivated rather than adopted. As you'll soon see, trying too hard to be a certain way is actually counter to the practice of mindfulness. Remember that no one is mindful 100 percent of the time. Even people who've practiced mindfulness for years evolve in their practice. The four attitudes associated with mindfulness are (1) nonjudging, (2) patience and nonstriving, (3) acceptance, and (4) letting go. Since these are not necessarily familiar terms, we define each one a little more in this section.

Nonjudging

The first attitude to approach these exercises with is *nonjudging*. Kabat-Zinn (1990) describes nonjudging as being an impartial witness to your own experience. That is, if you practice a breath exercise and notice that there is a draft in the room, you may say to yourself, "I'm going to get too cold." This example may seem odd, but it's actually common for physical sensations to become quite noticeable when sitting quietly in mindfulness exercises. Once you've judged the draft as too cold, you've labeled it as a problem and you may go on to think, "I should turn up the heat, close a window, or get a sweater." You may even find it hard to resist getting up and doing one of these things. In this instance, you have judged something (the draft) to be a problem, and your attention is now drawn to that problem in order to find a way to fix it. If you were able to cultivate the attitude of nonjudging, you may say to yourself, "I feel a cool breeze, a draft perhaps; it's making my skin react in certain ways." Instead of focusing on what that draft means, you refocus on breathing or whatever the exercise is. By not judging, your emotions and your impulses to act (such as getting a sweater) will be quite different. Not that you shouldn't get a sweater or close a window if you're cold—sometimes action is the thing to do. However, even if you do decide to take action, nonjudging is a very useful and often calming attitude to take, especially in what is normally an uncomfortable situation like being anxious or having physical needs. You observe yourself in that state, but don't get pulled into it as completely, and even your actions are more intentional and mindful. The result of a nonjudging attitude is a certain calmness that is different from being in a relaxed state—it's a calmness that comes with mindfulness.

Patience and Nonstriving

The second attitude to work toward in mindfulness practice is *patience and nonstriving*. This is an attitude that, at first glance, makes a lot of sense; while trying to meditate, a person ought to be patient and is, by definition, not striving for something external. But this attitude goes one step further and says that we must also strive to not be mindful—that is, we ought not to strive for an internal state of mindfulness. At this point, you may be wondering how this can be, how can we devote ourselves to being mindful but not strive to be mindful? The answer is that just about anytime you have a thought that goes something like, "This is my forty-five minutes to be mindful, so I better be focusing," it is doubtful that you are, indeed, in a mindful state. When we try too hard to strive for mindfulness, it tends to get further and further from our grasp. You may notice your attention wandering from place to place and you may wonder whether you are indeed doing things right. When that happens, it is all right to notice this going on, so long as you gently bring your focus back to the exercise at hand. In short, the less preoccupied you are with trying to be mindful, the better your chances of getting there. Remember, the goal in mindfulness is not to do anything or be anything, or even to have a peaceful state of mind (Kabat-Zinn 1990).

Acceptance

The third attitude to cultivate in mindfulness is *acceptance*. Whatever happens during an exercise is what happens during that exercise. Often, people learning about mindfulness for the first time believe they have been successful when they have no negative thoughts and emotions. That may not be a bad thing, but the absence of a negative feelings or thoughts is not the barometer of success in mindfulness. Rather, attending to a negative feeling state, noticing it is there, and returning your focus to the exercise is the mark of mindfulness. Also, in chapter 6 we spent a lot of time on the issue of examining negative thoughts for evidence and distortions, and these are useful techniques to be sure. However, in mindfulness the aim is a little different. In mindfulness we don't take apart these negative thoughts to test them out. We instead accept them as thoughts or ideas, but not as gospel truths. A common saying in mindfulness is "you are not your thoughts." Mindfulness, like cognitive therapy, says that thoughts are mental events that happen, but that thoughts are not an ultimate truth. Accepting thoughts as no more than ideas actually can have the affect of diminishing their importance. In all of the mindfulness exercises we describe, do not try to suppress or hold back negative feelings or to banish negative thoughts from your mind. This actually takes up much more energy than acknowledging the thoughts and then refocusing attention on the exercise.

Letting Go

The final attitude, and one that is related to the other three, is *letting go*. Letting go really speaks to the bigger issue of not trying too hard to be or do anything and being very patient with the exercises. Letting go is also about its opposite, holding tight or not letting go, and how this can be problematic. This attitude of letting go is best illustrated with examples. Athletics makes for good examples, because an athlete's best performance is often accompanied by a very mindful state. For example, a great basketball player does not *think* about every movement on the court, the position of his or her hands or feet, or how to follow through with a wrist action. In fact, if an athlete does have a thought about those things, it can all go wrong. Talented players can make mistakes when under pressure, as when playing in major tournaments or playoffs when there is a lot at stake that might interfere with them letting go. Of course, it makes sense that during those pressure moments what is on their mind is the circumstance (for example, "If I don't make this shot, we're not in the playoffs. I have to focus on getting it just right"). That thought, which speaks to just how motivated the person is, can actually cause more harm than good by interfering with what comes naturally. In ice hockey, when a talented goal scorer is not playing up to his potential, there is a saying that he is "holding the stick too tight." Thinking about his scoring slump and how important it would be for him to score can make the player lose the necessary looseness and fluidness that makes him so capable. As a result, he grips the hockey stick in a way that is too rigid or rehearsed and the puck ends up in the wrong places. Similarly, certain situations in life work better when we let go. Imagine getting a ring that normally fits you stuck on your finger. The worst thing you can do at that moment is try too hard. By wrenching on the ring, it is likely to angle or twist, and get tighter. Your finger is likely to turn red and swell, and you may have thoughts like, "They'll have to cut it off, how painful and costly." The way to deal with the situation is to first let go, to work gently, and to almost stop paying attention to the ring. Soon enough the ring will come loose, and the problem is solved. Mindfulness is the same way—the first time you get there it will be because you gave up trying to get there.

In addition to these four attitudes, keeping up consistency in your practice is probably the most important thing you can do to become more mindful. Most advocates of mindfulness suggest that you practice it every day. By practice, we do not mean that doing mindfulness should be a chore, rather that it is an activity like exercise, leisure, or eating that brings something positive to your life. If you want to have the benefits, it is important to find a place for mindfulness in your life and to protect that time for your practice. The exercises we describe next are really vehicles or supports to get you started, but you'll find that as you practice you will develop some of your own approaches to being mindful. For now, we'll describe some specific things you can do to get started.

The Raisin Exercise

Many mindfulness-based treatments start with this simple exercise to help people experience, often for the first time, what mindfulness is like. This exercise is also very straightforward as it requires only a few raisins and a quiet place to sit where you won't be interrupted for a half hour or so. Start by thinking about the way you normally eat raisins. If you love raisins and eat them by the handful, that's fine. If you hate raisins and never eat them spontaneously, that's fine too. Either way, your goal for this exercise is to eat mindfully. Take the first raisin you have and focus your attention on it, then spend several minutes doing the next steps of the exercise. Simply look it over, perhaps getting close to it. Notice its color, its texture. Does the raisin have a smell of any kind, and what is that smell like? Spend a couple of minutes looking at the raisin, and then pick it up and put in the palm of your hand. Now focus on the tactile aspects of the raisin. What does it feel like? Is it hard or soft? What does the surface feel like? Chances are you have never looked at a raisin quite like this, and that's the point. You will notice things about a raisin that you have never noticed—its complexity, its variations in color, its ridges. Next, place the raisin next to your ear, roll it in your fingers, and listen. Then put the raisin against your lips, but don't put it in your mouth just yet. Do you notice any new physical sensations? Your mouth may be filling with saliva in preparation. If you don't like raisins, you may feel other kinds of sensations. Just take notice of the sensations, don't try to judge them. Whether you like raisins or not, pay attention to the object itself and just what you are sensing about it. Now, place the raisin in your mouth and focus on the first bite. What is the sensation of biting into the raisin like? What do you taste? Is the raisin sweet, or sour, or both? Again, you may notice more saliva forming in your mouth, and you'll soon notice the urge to go ahead and swallow. Focus on that urge and what it is like, but don't swallow the raisin just yet. The point is to simply be aware of what is happening as you chew. Then, after a minute or so of chewing, go ahead and swallow the raisin while paying attention to the action in your mouth and throat, and any aftertaste. This eating of a raisin should take about five minutes, which is a long time for eating one raisin. That's the point!

People react very differently to this exercise, but tend to agree on one thing. Eating a raisin like this bears very little resemblance to the way they eat raisins in everyday life. For some people, the raisin tastes much better and more complete in this exercise. Most people find it hard to believe that a single raisin can offer such a complete dining experience. Even people who don't like raisins seem to be able to eat one in this exercise, and they may find at least something they appreciate about the experience. By approaching the raisin in a nonjudging way, people are able to eat the raisin without many of their usual negative responses. Other people take away from the experience how fascinating a raisin is physically, for example, its colors, the sound it makes next to the ear, its textures, forms, and shapes. It really is a little world unto itself and people often reflect on where raisins come from.

In a small but significant way, this raisin exercise encourages some of the attitudes we described earlier. By observing the raisin in this new way, we are practicing nonjudging. You may have started this exercise with a pretty firm opinion on raisins. Chances are, by eating a raisin mindfully, you've come to a different perspective on it. Some people, before the exercise, will even tell you that they find raisins "ugly." By focusing on the raisin itself and not one's evaluation of the raisin, a new perspective develops. You also practiced patience and nonstriving. Eating a raisin is not particularly difficult, and really one might say that the goal of the exercise has nothing to do with the notion of eating a raisin. If that had been the goal, you would have done it in less than a second. Instead, you patiently went with the experience. The exercise also teaches you about acceptance and not necessarily following through on an impulse. You accepted your like or dislike of the raisin, but you did not allow that to dictate your behavior. Even the impulse to swallow, which is pretty hard-wired in the brain, was something that you could observe and yet you did not *have to* swallow just then. Finally, you were able to let go of each thought, impulse, and physical sensation. Many people, after the exercise, say something about how they never would have believed they could spend this much time eating a raisin. By letting go of our usual raisin-eating behavior, an entirely new experience is created.

This small exercise can be carried out in other domains and fairly easily with other foods. One thing it should make clear is how much of the time we pay very little attention to what we are eating, how it tastes, and the experience of eating. Our busy lives often make eating more like filling a car with gas; something that happens quickly and efficiently, and serves the purpose of keeping us moving. Eating is one of those things that, when done mindfully, enhances our experience. Some people are never the same after doing the raisin exercise, but in a good way. These people often use the occasion of eating as a kind of memory jog. They remind themselves, as they prepare to eat, to recall the attitudes to mindfulness and to eat mindfully as much of the time as possible. This is an excellent way to make mindfulness part of their routine and to practice frequently. You also may want to try eating other kinds of foods mindfully. Better still, you may want to think of other activities you do where you would like to cultivate mindfulness, whether this is at your work, with other people, or in your leisure activities. The following exercises will help you to further develop mindfulness in your life.

Breathing Room

You don't need to rely on having raisins around to practice mindfulness; you can do it without any props whatsoever. What is useful, especially at first, is to have something on which you focus your attention. The raisin nicely serves that purpose in the first exercise, because it's a tangible object and this helps people when they are starting out. For this next exercise you'll need nothing but a quiet place to sit for up to forty-five minutes, though it is sometimes recommended that you start with ten minutes the first time and gradually increase to forty-five minutes. What you do in this exercise is focus on something that is noticeable and readily available; that thing is your breathing. We breathe several times per minute and, of course, we are usually entirely unaware of this fact. When we are exercising, or if the air we are breathing is not clean, we often become very aware of our breathing. In this exercise, we want to consciously bring our focus to our breathing. This is what we will concentrate on, and when our attention starts to wander we will always bring it gently back to the breathing.

To start this exercise, focus on one of two areas—either your *diaphragm* (the muscle that helps you breathe, located just below the point where your ribs join) or your nostrils. The diaphragm rises and falls in a noticeable way when we breathe, and for some people it's easy to focus their attention on the diaphragm. The nostrils are also a good spot to notice breathing because you can feel the air moving in and out of your nostrils as you breathe. There is no preferred way for everyone; in time you'll discover which is easier for you to focus on. The rest of the exercise is fairly simple. Sit in a comfortable, reasonably quiet spot and bring your attention to your breathing. You may want to close your eyes, but you don't have to if you don't want to. It may help you to look at one spot in the room and keep your eyes there, especially if you find that closing your eyes takes you closer to sleep. In a way that reflects nonstriving, keep your attention on your breath, at either the diaphragm or the nostrils, for the next forty-five minutes.

Of course, an important aspect of the exercise is that this is hard (and perhaps impossible) to do perfectly. You will find your mind wandering about, and that's a normal part of the exercise. Accept the places your mind goes and do not judge this experience. Most people are amazed to discover that their mind wanders, again and again, away from the breath. However, once you've noticed whatever thought or emotion you've encountered, bring your focus back to the breath. Try to be patient with yourself and remember that bringing your attention back to the breath is the thing to do. You'll probably notice that your mind is full of things; indeed, it's very hard to have no thoughts. Focusing on your breathing gives your mind a spot to center on, and you'll find yourself returning again and again to that breathing center. After the allotted time is up, open your eyes and slowly move from the position you were in to proceed with whatever your day brings. As in all mindfulness exercises, it is important to try not to snap out of the state you are in too quickly at the end of the exercise. A good example of the snapping-out approach is in hypnosis, where you may have seen a hypnotist count to ten and then instruct the person to "wake up, refreshed, as if nothing had happened." In mindfulness, the transition between doing an exercise and regular life should be gentle because the whole point is to bring a state of mindfulness to your activities and your life. As you practice, you'll feel your mindful state lingering for longer and longer.

The breathing exercise is not that complex, and yet the first time you do it those ten minutes will probably seem much longer than ten minutes does under normal circumstances. That's a testament to how much of the time we are on automatic pilot and times goes by without us noticing. Most people report that after the first time they did the breathing exercise, their mind went to many places, a "whirlwind tour" of their lives, so to speak. In fact, the variety of thoughts that pop into consciousness over a ten-minute period is what often surprises people. Again, by simply accepting the experience, and then returning to a focus on breathing, we've expanded our awareness of what's on going on in our minds. Also, it is during the breathing exercise that people will sometimes notice negative thoughts, like the kind we discussed in chapter 6. These negative thoughts may be evaluations of yourself, other people, or your situation. They can also be worries or fears. That is very much a part of this process and proves that mindfulness can work as an early warning of negative emotions and thoughts. You may not have been aware that these thoughts and feelings were brewing, but now you will be aware and in a position to do something about them. Of course, you also help yourself in the breathing exercise by simply accepting and then letting go each thought. Under normal circumstances, you might tend to dwell on a negative thought; it is as if the thought gets stuck in your mind and you wonder about what it means and what you should do, and ultimately you end up having cascading negative thoughts.

During the breathing exercise, you simply say to yourself, "I am aware I am having this thought" and most importantly remind yourself that, "I am not my thoughts," and then return your attention to your breath. That notion of having thoughts, but being able to recognize that your thoughts are not the same thing as you is very important. Thoughts are mental but also physical events; thoughts are, after all, only neurons firing in the brain. This, in many ways, makes thoughts like any other physical event, such as respiration, the heart beating, or perceptions from our eyes, ears, or taste buds, and yet we often believe that thoughts are facts and have some very special qualities. The ability to disentangle your thoughts from yourself as a person is enhanced as you practice this and other mindfulness techniques.

The breathing exercise is something that you can continue to do regularly, and it may form one of the mainstays of your own mindfulness practice. However, as you will see later, the breathing exercise can be adapted to another use, one that is much shorter and may allow you to use mindfulness even as you work or spend leisure time. As you will see, breathing will continue to be an aspect of other mindfulness techniques. Nothing is as basic as breathing, so it's no mystery that mindfulness starts and ends with a focus on the breath.

The Body Scan Exercise

The body scan is another well known and very useful exercise in mindfulness. It too requires few props, though in our experience it helps to follow a specific, consistent set of guidelines. For example, Jon Kabat-Zinn has an excellent series of audiotapes that walk you through the body scan (see Additional Resources). The purpose of the body scan is to notice the feelings and sensations in the body and in some ways help to reconnect our minds with our bodies. Kabat-Zinn (1990) has pointed out that we tend to have a very ambivalent relationship with our bodies; that is, we tend to see our bodies as objects. Moreover, we often aren't happy with some part of ourselves, and may wish that we were thinner, toned, or in shape. These are all goals that tend to be imposed upon us by society, and the net result is that we aren't always comfortable with and don't accept ourselves. People interested in mindfulness for prevention and relapse of depression point out that negative emotions are often manifested in our bodies, in our posture, in muscular tension, or in feelings of heaviness (Segal, Williams, and Teasdale 2002). The body scan is designed to help identify those feelings and, just like the breathing exercise, to bring them to awareness, and allow us to then let go of or accept those experiences.

To begin a body scan, simply start by lying down on a comfortable surface, like a mat, sofa, or bed. Use some of the breathing focus initially to allow your attention to become centered and focused on the sensations of lying down, like the contact of your body with the surface below and the force of gravity acting on you. The next step is to bring your attention to a certain part of your body. We'll start with the toes of your left foot. Focus on the feelings and sensations in those toes—their temperature, whatever the toes are touching, whatever it is that you feel. Once this is done (it may take a few minutes), take a breath in, and then, as you breathe out, imagine the air moving down through your leg, into your foot, and out through your toes. This idea of breathing out through your toes often seems a bit odd the first time you try. The idea is to visualize, but also try to feel the breath moving out of that part of the body. Also, if you notice tension in any particular part of the body, breathing out through that part of the body may be useful in noticing, accepting, and then letting that part of the body relax. Once you have tried several exhalations through the toes of your left foot, you can move on to do the same thing with the rest of your left foot. Then you carry on, scanning each part of the body. There is no perfect way to divide the body up, but we provide a potential ordered list below. In each case, bring attention to that part of the body, feel whatever sensations, tensions, or even thoughts come from that part of the body, and then breathe those feelings out of the body.

1. Toes of left foot

2. Rest of left foot

3. Left calf

4. Left thigh

5. Toes of right foot

6. Rest of right foot

7. Right calf

8. Right thigh

9. Lower abdomen

10. Chest

11. Left shoulder

12. Left bicep

13. Left forearm

14. Left hand, including breathing out through the fingers

15. Right shoulder

16. Right bicep

17. Right forearm

18. Right hand, including breathing out through the fingers

19. Neck

20. Mouth and jaw

21. Eyes and forehead

22. Top of the head

At the end of the body scan the idea is to visualize and feel yourself breathing through the top of your head. Kabat-Zinn (1990) describes this as being like a whale breathing through its blowhole. The breath comes into the lungs and on each exhalation the air flows freely through your whole body and then out. You will want to spend a few minutes doing this before the exercise is over.

The body scan, of all the mindfulness exercises, is the one that most people associate with relaxation training. Indeed, it does share some elements with the well-known technique called *progressive muscle relaxation* (PMR), which also relies on a step-by-step scan of the body. The difference is that in PMR many of the muscles in the body are flexed or tensed on purpose, followed by directed attempts to relax those muscles. Mindfulness does not include the tension exercises and does not set relaxation as a goal, although when we are in a mindful state in a body scan there is some overlap with the state of relaxation. The point is that you may do a body scan sometime and not feel relaxed. This is fine; it is just another part of the process of practicing mindfulness. However, you will now be aware of that tension and will be much more in tune with the signals your body is giving you. Finally, the body scan is probably the one exercise we describe in which using a tape or following verbal instructions can be very useful. Again, this is a situation in which identifying other mindfulness practitioners or other resources will be helpful. The body scan, like breathing meditation, is a backbone of mindfulness practice. You will find that it will vary each time you try it, and that it can have a different outcome when you follow a different set of instructions using different images or metaphors. The body scan, ultimately, will help to get past the artificial distinction we often make between the mind and the body. Mind and body are one system and mindfulness can help us to synchronize that system to increase awareness and sensitivity.

Instant Mindfulness: The Three-Minute Breathing Space

Breathing meditation and the body scan, once fully developed, take about forty-five minutes to do. Consistent practice will be critical for maintaining a mindful state outside of this practice. But what should you do if you experience a sudden stressor, or what if you would like to be more mindful at some point in the day, but don't have forty-five minutes you can set aside? The three-minute breathing space (Segal, Williams, and Teasdale 2002) addresses precisely this challenge. We have found that people learning mindfulness as a component of their treatment also begin to recognize the trouble spots, difficult or negative situations they encounter, or the kinds of stresses that put them at risk (chapter 9). Maybe it's stress at work, such as too much to do, a difficult set of relationships with colleagues, or a hectic pace. For others, their trouble spot is in a relationship they are in; perhaps it is a relationship that is conflicted somehow. In these cases, being able to become mindful relatively quickly can help people to acknowledge, accept, and let go of some of their negative thoughts, feelings, and physical sensations. Perhaps most importantly, it can keep people focused on their goals and on what is most healthy for them to be doing. This point is often difficult for people to grasp at first because they think that mindfulness is some ideal state in which you do nothing but meditate. Remember that ultimately mindfulness is not supposed to be an altered state, or an "either-or state" (such as either you are mindful or you are working, either you are mindful or you are an attentive father, mother, or spouse). Instead, the goal is to be a mindful worker, or a mindful parent or spouse. Practicing mindfulness, by increasing your awareness, focus, and sensitivity, should make you better at what you are doing in the moment. Nonetheless, being mindful in moments of stress is a challenge, and that's where the three-minute breathing space is designed to help. There are three steps in the exercise and each step takes one minute to do. First is *awareness,* followed by *gathering,* and finally *expanding* (Segal, Williams, and Teasdale 2002).

In *awareness,* the aim is to bring yourself into the present moment. If you are doing a three-minute breathing space exercise because you are facing a stressor or your mind and body are signaling that something negative is happening the awareness minute is designed to help you take an inventory of what is happening. You may want to ask, "What emotions am I experiencing right now?" Focus on these emotions and also allow whatever thoughts are associated with them to enter your awareness. You may also want to ask, "Do these thoughts relate to the emotions and do those emotions connect to any physical sensation?" Remember, in this case we are expecting that something about this situation is unwanted or not ideal, so in some ways you will probably have a more negative focus to your thoughts, feelings, and physical sensations here, than when doing a breathing exercise or body scan. At the end of the awareness minute, you will have a clear understanding of why you are feeling troubled.

In the second minute, *gathering,* the aim is to redirect your full attention to the breath. Focus on either the diaphragm or the nostrils as you would do in a breathing meditation, and bring your mind back to the inhalation and exhalation after acknowledging whatever thoughts and feelings occur. It is very important to also let go each of these thoughts and feelings and to remember that, because of the nature of the three-minute breathing space, more of these thoughts and feelings will be negative now. One important point to emphasize here goes back to the idea that you are not your thoughts; recognize that these thoughts are part of your experience right now, and then let them go. This will create some useful distance between these potentially negative thoughts and yourself.

In the final minute, *expanding,* bring your awareness to your whole body, including your breathing. You may want to quickly scan your body, the way you are sitting or standing, for any troubling physical sensations. Here too, it is important to be aware of those sensations, but also to let go of them. In the end, the larger aim of a three-minute breathing space is to be present in the moment (Segal, Williams, and Teasdale 2002).

Putting all this together—awareness, gathering, and expanding—will help you to be mindful when you can benefit from it most. You will notice that this exercise cannot really be said to be a problem-solving exercise, and sometimes this confuses people. When hearing or reading about it for the first time, people often think that the three-minute breathing space must be designed to help them cope with a problem situation. That is both true and untrue at the same time. The three-minute breathing space is not a tool that will dismantle a problem, sort it all out, and then take the problem away, although there is certainly room for problem-solving in preventing relapse of depression, as we will describe in chapter 9. Mindfulness, and especially the three-minute breathing space, is designed to help you become more aware and to be less drawn into or pulled around by negative thoughts, feelings, and sensations. It is always important to acknowledge the limitations of these techniques, and mindfulness alone cannot solve all problems. Rather, we would say that adding mindfulness to active problem solving or other coping strategies will make a difficult situation that much easier to experience and recover from. In our own practice, we have found that mindfulness brings a certain stillness to coping with problems we encounter. To put it simply, a mindful person is less perturbed by whatever swirls around them without sacrificing sensitivity to everyday situations.

Summary

Mindfulness practice is a very useful way of being if our goal is to prevent relapse in depression. At the beginning of this chapter, you may have imagined mindfulness or meditation as a very mysterious set of spiritual practices. Alternatively, you may have seen mindfulness as a set of skills that you could put in your personal toolkit to prevent relapse.

Hopefully, we have demystified mindfulness by taking away some of the spiritual trappings that sometimes come attached to the notion of meditation. We also hope we've made the point that mindfulness is more than a set of skills—it's more like a way of living. In writing this chapter, we faced the task of having to pare down our description of mindfulness and pick exercises that would be useful and easy to understand in a written format. There are many, many more exercises to try. Among them are mindful stretching, mindful yoga, mindful walking, and mindful reading (Kabat-Zinn 1990; Kabat-Zinn 1994; Segal, Williams, and Teasdale 2002). There are also hundreds of useful metaphors and artistic renderings associated with mindfulness that try to, as much as possible, express in "picture-words" what mindfulness is like (Hanh 1987; Hanh 1976). Each of these exercises and experiences adds a new wrinkle to the experience of mindfulness and we certainly encourage you to consult these other sources and to make contact with people who also pursue or teach mindfulness practice where you live. Sharing your practice with others and having them share with you will add significantly to your experiences.

Finally, we want to emphasize one more time that mindfulness-based techniques have actually been shown to prevent relapse, and we are not aware of any other stand-alone treatment program that has shown this ability. Many factors have been clearly associated with risk of relapse, and indeed much of this book is based on the research that links various factors with relapse. Nonetheless, mindfulness stands out for researchers because it is an approach that has been directly tested and shown to work. Practitioners of mindfulness will also tell you that, although its impact on their lives is hard to measure scientifically, the benefits are profound and difficult to overstate.

Summary Exercise

Record what you believe is the bottom line from this chapter, then record what practices or exercises you would adopt as part of your wellness plan.

Chapter 8, Mindfulness Meditation for Preventing Relapse, examines mindfulness-based practices that have been shown to prevent relapse. My bottom line in this chapter is:

_____

_____

The practices, exercises, or actions I will take from this chapter are:

_____

_____

Chapter 9

Better Coping during Stressful Times

If you were to ask the average person on the street, "What kinds of things cause depression?" surely one of the most common answers you would get is "stress." And that answer would be correct. Dozens of studies have confirmed that a stressful life event often precedes the onset of a depressive episode, which is exactly why we are writing about stress in a book about relapse prevention. Like some of the other factors we have described in this book, the idea that stress can lead to depression is something that was scoffed at by experts before the 1980s. Prior to some landmark studies, mental health experts tended to believe that depression was related either to biological mechanisms that had little to do with life events, or to factors from early childhood that also had very little to do with everyday stresses. But as a result of some careful studies, it emerged that people who had experienced a depressive episode often had more stressors in the year before that episode compared to people who did not have a depressive episode (Billings, Cronkite, and Moos 1983; Brown and Harris 1978). In fact, it seems that people who have an episode of depression have often had *three times* as many stressors in the time leading up to that episode compared to other people. Clearly, there is something important about the relationship between stress and depression and this needs to be incorporated into any wellness plan. In this chapter, we describe the relationship between stress and depression, what it may mean for you, and the implications for staying well.

The Stress-Depression Connection

Despite the very clear finding that stress can lead to depression, researchers are not yet clear on exactly why this should be. Of course, it is obvious to all of us that when something goes wrong, like losing a job or having a loved one fall ill, there is a certain amount of emotional distress. However, this straightforward relationship is not as simple as it might seem. In fact, even defining what we mean by the term "stressful life events" is somewhat controversial in the field (Monroe and Simons 1991). Some researchers believe that we should restrict the term "stressful life events" to very clearly identified events that most people would consider stressful. These include such events as the death of a loved one, the loss of a job, being diagnosed with a serious illness, getting into legal trouble, and getting divorced. In fact, the number of really big stresses that can happen to us are not all that large; some lists of stressful life events used in research list fewer than a dozen specific events that are truly stressors.

Other researchers take a different perspective, essentially arguing that stress is in the eye of the beholder. These scientists would still say that stressors are events that happen to us, but they would also say that what determines stress is what the event means to the individual.

Both sides in this debate have some good points. For example, it would clearly be upsetting to have one's uncle suddenly diagnosed with a terminal disease. But it would be especially upsetting if you were very close to your uncle, saw him almost every day, and considered him to be both a family member and a friend. In contrast, the news might be more manageable if your uncle lived in another country and if you had only met him once, many years ago. Obviously, these two scenarios would lead to very different feelings. So it does seem that the context and personal meaning of a stressful event are important. At the same time, defining stressful life events *entirely* based on the eye of the beholder can be problematic, in that almost anything can then be considered a stressor, including missing the bus in the morning or not having enough change to buy coffee. For the purposes of this chapter, we define stress as an external, negative event that is somewhat unusual or unexpected and an event that has a lot of personal meaning for the individual. Next, we consider why stress sometimes results in depression.

Why Stress Results in Depression

Although the relationship between stress and depression is well-established, many experts have pointed out that not every stressful life event leads to depression and that not everyone who experiences life stressors gets depressed. Clearly then, if we want to explain the relationship between stress and depression, we need another link in the chain. One factor that may explain why stress does not always lead to depression is an individual's *diathesis,* which simply means his or her level of vulnerability (Billings, Cronkite, and Moos 1983; Cronkite and Moos 1995). An individual with a diathesis for developing depression is a person who has an underlying vulnerability or predisposition to become depressed given the right circumstances. This vulnerability could be biological (for example, one's genetic makeup) or psychological (for example, a negative thinking style), and it may be that the vulnerability itself, in the absence of a negative event, is not really a problem on its own. Rather, the vulnerability may become triggered only when a life event occurs that puts undue pressure on that vulnerability.

For example, in chapter 12 we discuss the notion of interpersonal dependency and its relationship to depression. Dependency can be said to be the diathesis or vulnerability, and the life event that puts extra pressure on that diathesis could be the ending of a relationship. When an overly dependent person loses a relationship, he or she is likely to have a much stronger emotional reaction than someone who is not especially dependent. So when there is a match between a person's particular vulnerability and the negative life event that he or she experiences, a stress-related depression could be triggered. Unfortunately, we do not yet know enough about all the possible vulnerabilities people might have to make an exhaustive list. However, the idea of a specific vulnerability, perhaps one that is unique to each person, would explain why some do not get depressed after a stressor (the person may not have that vulnerability) and why not every stressor triggers depression (the event the person experienced did not match their vulnerability).

There are also several explanations of the link between stress and depression that are more biologically based (Post 1992; Rehm, Wagner, and Tyndal 2001). These theories have to do with the way stress affects the brain and many of these ideas have actually been tested in animals. Stress does appear to put a kind of a load on our bodies, on both the nervous system and the organs. Stress, especially when it accumulates, may wear down our physical capacities in numerous areas, and when some critical point is reached, a depression may be triggered. These models also suggest that, over time, it may take smaller and smaller stresses to trigger depression (Post 1992). Like more psychological theories, these biological theories would also explain why stress sometimes triggers depression and why the relationship between stress and depression is not a perfect 1 to 1 relationship. Next, we consider whether there is something about the relationship between stress and depression that we can control.

Stress and Depression: Is It All Just Accidental?

Sometimes the literature on stress and depression can make people feel a little helpless, and perhaps fatalistic. After all, there doesn't seem to be a lot one can do about losing a job, having a family member fall ill, or getting into a serious car accident. These are things that we do not anticipate and usually have no control over. In many instances, events such as car accidents or the loss of one's job are not, statistically speaking, uncommon over the course of one's lifetime, so it might seem that someone who is vulnerable to depression is doomed by chance alone. But in the last ten years a new idea has emerged in the literature on stress that does point the way toward something that can be done.

The early studies on stress and depression tended to focus on events that happened to people. This perspective, which we will call the *fateful* perspective, sees the individual as someone who goes through life and, somewhat randomly, either experiences stressors or does not. However, the fateful perspective is not a terribly accurate representation of life. It is certainly true that in some instances we have little power over what happens in our lives. For example, any of us could be struck by lightning or be the victim of a crime, and those things would not be under our control. But in a larger way, we play an important role in constructing our lives; that is, in part, we create our environment and therefore perhaps also our fate. For example, losing your job, a fairly obvious stressor, can come about in different ways. To demonstrate this, we will provide a couple of case examples.

Bob was an accountant for a very prestigious business enterprise. Bob worked hard, was well respected, and had every expectation that his work life would continue to go as well in the future as it had in the past. But Bob worked for a corporation that had a few problems, in fact, the board and the CEO had been involved in a number of questionable deals and transactions. As news of this spread, the company's stock plummeted and Bob, being a well-paid accountant at company headquarters, was one of the first to received a notice of termination as the company dissolved in bankruptcy.

George was also an accountant at a prestigious company, but George had recently begun to struggle at work. He was often late, and this had been noted on several performance appraisals. He met with his boss, who told George that his work was good, that he was well liked, but that lateness could not be tolerated because everyone had to play by the same rules. Over the next year, George received several warnings but did not change his ways. He just could not seem to arrive at the office before 9 A.M. One morning when George was late yet again, his boss greeted him with a termination notice.

Bob and George both recently experienced the stress of losing their jobs. But there are some very big differences between them. Bob's stress was fateful. He knew nothing about what the CEO and the board were up to and could not have anticipated what would happen. George has, on the surface, experienced the exact same stressor, losing a job. But it could be argued that the person most responsible for George's stress is none other than George himself. The point is that some stress is fateful and other stress is *self-generated*.

Of course, some stressors fall right in between, with aspects that are fateful and aspects that are self-generated. Let us go back to the earlier examples of being struck by lightning and being the victim of a crime. These seem like fateful consequences. But what if you knew that the person struck by lightning had been playing golf during a thunderstorm and had not heeded repeated warnings from the marshals to leave the course and seek safe shelter? What if, in the second fateful example, the person had been on their way to buy some marijuana in a crime-riddled part of the city and had been hit over the head for the contents of their wallet? These are, granted, rather extreme examples that may not be representative of typical stressors, and in no way are we saying that the people in these examples "deserve" what happened. The point is to show that even in apparently fateful stress, it may be important to look at the person's role in creating that stress.

Researchers have indeed examined whether people with depression play some role in creating stress in their lives. For example, psychologist Constance Hammen and her colleagues have done many studies looking at depression and stressors in relationships (Hammen 1991; Hammen 2000). According to Hammen, problematic interpersonal relationships are particularly likely to be stressors for people vulnerable to depression, and of course these relationships are, in part, created and maintained by the depressed person. Hammen believes that these stressors are "created" for two reasons. First, people (her studies actually focus mainly on women) may choose partners who are not a good match or do not meet basic physical and emotional needs. Second, people prone to depression may not solve relationship problems as effectively as they could. More recent evidence from large-scale studies of twins also supports the idea that self-generated stress is a bigger contributor to depression than fateful stress (Kendler, Karkowski, and Prescott 1999; Kendler, Thornton, and Gardner 2000). Kendler and his colleagues assessed fifteen classes of life events and the triggering of a major depression in a one-year period. The life events were also rated on the extent to which the event was dependent on the person, that is, to what extent the life event could be said to have been generated, at least in part, by the person him- or herself. The researchers found that depression was much more likely to be triggered by the dependent, or self-generated, stressors (Kendler, Karkowski, and Prescott 1999; Kendler, Thornton, and Gardner 2000). Kendler and colleagues concluded that people who are predisposed to depression might be selectively putting themselves into high-risk environments. Again, this suggests that people who are vulnerable to depression may be constructing a life that is prone to stress. Next, we examine why this might be the case.

Stress Generation: Coping Strategies and Problem Solving

The studies we have described so far already hint at some possible explanations for why people who are depressed and those who are vulnerable to depression have more stress. In one of the first studies of the stress-depression link, it was found that people who had more stress and who ended up depressed tended to use more "emotion-focused" coping (Billings, Cronkite, and Moos 1983). The term "coping" refers to the way in which a person tries to handle, defuse, or deal with a threat or stress. In fact, there is a whole distinct area of research on stress and coping that looks at all the ways people behave, think, and feel under stress. *Emotion-focused coping* involves strategies such as talking about the problem with other people, thinking about how it makes you feel, and expressing your emotions about a problem. This might not seem like it is a bad thing; after all, it is usually a good thing to talk about problems and to freely express emotions, but perhaps this is best done in moderation. In addition to using more emotion-focused coping, researchers have found that depressed people use more emotional support seeking (for example, talking over a problem with others) and less problem-solving coping (Cronkite and Moos 1995). Also, people who are depressed tend to overuse *escape coping* (such as trying to distract themselves too much or pretending that the problem does not exist). In fact, there is some evidence that using escape or *avoidance coping* makes episodes of depression last longer than they normally would (Cronkite and Moos 1995).

Clearly then, emotion-focused coping and escape coping are problematic if they are done too much. In the first case, devoting too much emotional energy to a problem could spark more and more negative thinking and negative emotions. One might say that the emotion-focused coping sets the person up for ever more negative thoughts and emotions. In the second case, avoiding thinking about a problem is in no way going to actually solve a real problem. For example, if someone lost his or her job and responded only by avoiding the thoughts and feelings related to this loss, the real issue (such as the need to find another job) would never be dealt with. No doubt, expressing sad feelings about losing one's job or talking through other job possibilities with a loved one is going to be helpful, but only if it is equally balanced by active problem solving, that is, seeking and pursuing other job prospects. To maintain wellness, it seems that emotion-focused coping and avoidance strategies should be used very selectively and balanced with other strategies that include attempts to resolve the problem. We address this in more detail in the next section on using better coping and problem-solving strategies.

We have mentioned the notion of problem-solving several times. Like too much emotion-focused and avoidance coping, poor problem-solving has been identified as a probable cause of some stress that leads to depression (Davila et al. 1995). In fact, poor problem solving has been described as a core determinant of depression (D'Zurilla and Goldfried 1971; Nezu 1987) and several studies have shown problem-solving deficits in people who are depressed or who are vulnerable to depression. For example, Joanne Davila and her colleagues have shown that women vulnerable to depression are less able to solve problems that come up in their intimate relationships. Elisabeth Marx and colleagues have found that depressed people produce less effective solutions to problems than do other people (Marx, Williams, and Claridge 1992). In these sorts of studies, problem-solving skills are usually assessed by looking at the various problem-solving components. These include being able to state and explain the problem, coming up with a set of workable solutions to that problem, being able to anticipate and plan for roadblocks related to the different solutions, and having the ability to carry out those solutions. To date, it is not entirely clear which of these problem-solving components is most compromised by depression, but there are several possibilities. For example, someone who is vulnerable to depression and is relying on emotion-focused coping may not have the mental resources to sit down and analyze the problem more logically. It may be that negative emotions limit the number of options people can come up with and the number of problems they can foresee with those solutions. It is also possible that, once negative moods have begun, it becomes harder for the person to carry out the problem-solving strategies in the way they had planned. What is clear is that people who are well (or not depressed) may rely on better coping and effective problem-solving. Thus, in the next section of this chapter we present some effective coping strategies and problem-solving skills.

Coping and Problem Solving

In the first part of this chapter, we presented a good news/bad news scenario. The bad news is that stressful life events can lead to depression. The good news is that these stressors may be more controllable than one might at first believe. It is becoming clear that the way a person constructs and directs his or her life may have as much an impact on triggering stressful events as does random chance or bad luck. This takes at least some of the power away from fate and puts it back in your hands. We begin this section by looking at coping strategies, with an emphasis on ways of handling stress that occurs despite your best efforts. As you will see, there are many different potential coping strategies, and almost all of them are useful for certain types of stressors. The trick is to know which strategy to use for which situation. After discussing strategies for coping with stress, we will present an overview of strategies for solving problems effectively and early, before they become big stresses.

Coping Strategies and When to Use Them

It may surprise you to learn that after at least two decades of careful research on coping with stress, we still don't have a very clear picture of how many different coping strategies there are. This is not the fault of hard-working researchers, but has more to do with the fact that people confront so many different types of stressful situations, each of which can be coped with in unique ways. Therefore, our understanding of coping strategies is not as clear as we'd like. Some researchers have argued that it is best to consider separately each way in which people cope with stress, whereas others argue that these individual strategies can be grouped into larger categories. For the purpose of this chapter, we will describe three different types of coping, each of which includes many specific behaviors, emotions, and thoughts.

Distraction-Avoidance Coping

We will call the first type of coping *distraction-avoidance coping*. This type of coping essentially involves trying to ignore the problem and doing something else to change your thoughts and feelings. Some examples of distraction-avoidance coping in response to a stressor include

- going to see a movie or watching television

- eating a meal or a snack

- sleeping or napping

- having a drink

- playing a video game or surfing the Internet

- talking to other people about everything but the stressor

- going to a party and trying to have fun

- leaving town to visit another place

Distraction-avoidance coping reduces the sense of distress a person has about a problem by giving him or her something else to do.

Action-Oriented Coping

The second kind of coping strategy we will be talking about is *action-oriented coping*. In action-oriented coping, you attempt to reduce stress by trying to come to grips with the core of the problem and taking it out at its source. This may involve getting more information about the problem, coming up with alternative ways to fix the problem, and acting on those strategies. Action-oriented coping in response to a stressor might include things like

- trying to find out more about the situation

- getting professional advice or consulting other sources of information

- talking to others who have had the problem to see what they did about it

- taking steps to resolve the problem

- making a list of things that could be done about the problem

- contacting someone who could take action to help you

- working on the most logical solution to the problem

Action-oriented coping involves problem solving, to which we devote a whole section later in this chapter. Action-oriented coping tends to involve more behavior, logic, and information gathering compared to other kinds of coping.

Emotion-Focused Coping

Finally, there is *emotion-focused coping*, which we described earlier. Emotion-focused coping in response to a stressor includes strategies such as

- having a good cry about the problem

- sharing with someone else the way the problem makes you feel

- exploring the basis for your feelings about the problem

- disclosing the problem to people around you

Emotion-focused coping is motivated by the belief that, by talking, thinking, and expressing feelings about a problem, things will become more clear or will seem more manageable.

We want to emphasize that each of these strategies has a function and each has its place. A person who uses only one of these categories of coping strategies may not be as happy or may not function as well as someone who uses the right strategy for the right situation.

How do you know which strategy will be best? It is important to keep in mind what each type of strategy can and cannot do. For example, distraction-avoidance coping may actually be useful when someone is facing a stressor that he or she cannot prepare for and one that cannot be put off. For example, imagine that tomorrow you are undergoing a somewhat uncomfortable, though not dangerous, medical procedure. Obviously, you cannot study for the medical procedure, and let us imagine that you have already informed yourself about what the procedure involves. Since there is nothing you can do to affect the outcome, the best thing you can do is probably to distract yourself. Perhaps the night before the procedure you rent your favorite movie or have an enjoyable meal. Distracting yourself with activities such as these will reduce the amount of time you spend in distress and really has no downside. On the other hand, in a situation for which you have more control and more you need to do (for example, working on a project with a deadline), distraction coping will not be useful and could even be harmful. Distraction may pull your attention off the task and make you feel momentarily better; however, used in the long run, distraction will undermine your ability to solve the problem by getting the project done.

Action-oriented coping is most helpful when there is a clear problem that can be solved, and this is probably the coping strategy that should get the most use for this reason. Whenever there is something that you have some control over and what you do has an important consequence for you, action-oriented coping should be a big part of what you do. However, the benefits of action-oriented coping have their limits. In the earlier example of undergoing the medical procedure, how much action can really be taken? Other than learning about the procedure, there is little else you can do to affect what happens.

Also, it's important to fully appreciate a problem before you take action. Some people always prefer to leap in and solve a problem, without perhaps appreciating all of the nuances of the situation. To fully understand a problem and your place in that problem, emotion-focused coping is useful. Emotion-focused coping helps to establish the true nature of the problem. For example, if a relationship ends, it is probably best to take some time to come to grips with your feelings about that ending, to reflect on what the relationship meant to you, and to consider what you learned about yourself. This would be far better than not trying to understand your feelings and simply taking action to find a new partner. Turning immediately to action-oriented coping may result in repeating a pattern that is less than ideal. Also, by understanding your feelings and clarifying your thoughts, you will be able to determine whether something is a truly big problem and what kind of priority this issue ought to have in your life. However, as we described earlier, too much emotion-focused coping may start a spiral of negative thoughts and feelings. It also does not actually make your situation any different. If all you do is clarify your feelings and thoughts, you may not be taking enough action to be moving in the right direction. For example, after a relationship has ended and you have had some time to clarify emotions, it will be important to pursue other relationships. Once emotion-focused coping is completed, action is the next step. After all, understanding and insight about the ending of the last relationship will, in the end, be a poor substitute for a new partner.

To help sort out the use of coping strategies in different problem situations, we have included a sample coping worksheet. This is followed by a blank coping worksheet. The sample worksheet uses an example involving the loss of a job in step 1, where you record the problem with which you need to cope. Large problems, like losing a job, will probably require all three types of coping strategies in different doses. In steps 2 through 4, the worksheet describes the three types of coping strategies, and asks you to record to what extent each of these strategies will be useful in this situation. In the example, emotion-focused coping is used to clarify feelings to take the time to grieve a little, but also to establish what the person wants to do in the future. Action-oriented coping is used to actually pursue job options and careers, and distraction coping is used to make sure that the person is not preoccupied twenty-four hours a day with the job loss.

The worksheet also prompts you to consider what each of the coping behaviors is supposed to do, and in the example each strategy has a different goal. This is probably the most important step. If you are thinking of using a coping behavior but you cannot specify what the goal of that behavior is, you may be better off selecting another behavior, or a different strategy altogether. The worksheet also asks you to record what the limits to the three types of coping strategies are for this situation. In the example, the person recognizes that neither emotion-focused nor distraction-avoidance coping will actually help in finding a new job. However, action-oriented coping alone would find the person a job, but not necessarily a job with an ideal fit, given the individual's abilities and desires. After working on problems using this worksheet, you may wish to look at the sheet again from time to time and make adjustments to optimize your coping. Remember that coping is your best defense against stressors.

Worksheet 9.1
Sample Coping Worksheet

STEP 1. The problem I am trying to cope with is: (describe the problem you are dealing with)

Losing my job and figuring out what to do next.

Step 2. Emotion-Focused Coping

To what extent can I use emotion-focused coping and what strategies will help me to do that? (Brainstorm to come up with one or more emotion-focused strategies for coping with the problem.)

I need to understand how I feel about the loss of my job, so I will talk out those feelings.

What am I trying to accomplish in using the emotion-focused coping strategies? (Describe the goal of the emotion-focused coping strategy. Will it really achieve what you hope?)

I would like to clarify my feelings about my work and my work identity, and to

figure out what other work I might like to try.

What are the limits of emotion-focused coping in this situation? (What about the problem cannot be handled or dealt with by emotion-focused coping?)

I could get caught up in trying to find a perfect job or dwelling on my feelings of

rejection, which could get in the way of my trying something new.

Step 3. Action-Oriented Coping

To what extent can I use action-oriented coping and what would the action behaviors be? (Brainstorm to come up with one or more active steps to solve the problem.)

I need to gather information, work with a job counselor, sharpen my résumé, and

do some networking.

What am I trying to accomplish by using the action-oriented coping strategies? (Describe the goal of the action-oriented coping. Will it really be able to do what you hope?)

This will give me some options and actually get me working to support myself.

What are the limits of action-oriented coping in this situation? (What about the problem cannot be handled or dealt with by action-oriented coping?)

I don't want to just find any job, that would be easy. I need to make sure the work I

do is fulfilling and is something I'm suited to do.

Step 4. Distraction-avoidance Coping

To what extent can I use distraction-avoidance coping and what strategies would help me do that? (Brainstorm to come up with one or more distraction-avoidance strategies for coping with the problem)

Dealing with this situation could preoccupy me too much; I need to take time off

from the job search and have some fun.

What am I trying to accomplish by using the distraction-avoidance coping strategies? (Describe the goal of the distraction-avoidance coping. Will it really be able to do what you hope?)

This would help me to see myself as a regular person, not someone who's

unemployed and miserable.

What are the limits of distraction-avoidance coping in this situation? (What about the problem cannot be handled or dealt with by distraction-avoidance coping?)

On its own, distraction wouldn't help me find a job or help me to figure out what I want.

Worksheet 9.2
Coping

Step 1. The problem I am trying to cope with is: (describe the problem you are dealing with)

_____

_____

Step 2. Emotion-Focused Coping

To what extent can I use emotion-focused coping and what strategies will help me to do that? (Brainstorm to come up with one or more emotion-focused strategies for coping with the problem.)

_____

_____

What am I trying to accomplish in using the emotion-focused coping strategies? (Describe the goal of the emotion-focused coping strategy. Will it really achieve what you hope?)

_____

_____

What are the limits of emotion-focused coping in this situation? (What about the problem cannot be handled or dealt with by emotion-focused coping?)

_____

_____

Step 3. Action-Oriented Coping

To what extent can I use action-oriented coping and what would the action behaviors be? (Brainstorm to come up with one or more active steps to solve the problem.)

_____

_____

What am I trying to accomplish by using the action-oriented coping strategies? (Describe the goal of the action-oriented coping. Will it really be able to do what you hope?)

_____

_____

What are the limits of action-oriented coping in this situation? (What about the problem cannot be handled or dealt with by action-oriented coping?)

_____

_____

Step 4. Distraction-Avoidance Coping

To what extent can I use distraction-avoidance coping and what strategies would help me do that? (Brainstorm to come up with one or more distraction-avoidance strategies for coping with the problem.)

_____

_____

What am I trying to accomplish by using the distraction-avoidance coping strategies? (Describe the goal of the distraction-avoidance coping. Will it really be able to do what you hope?)

_____

_____

What are the limits of distraction-avoidance coping in this situation? (What about the problem cannot be handled or dealt with by distraction-avoidance coping?)

_____

_____

Problem Solving

Problem solving is related to coping strategies, particularly action-oriented coping. However, the term "problem solving" refers to a particular set of skills that can be used to define a problem, come up with possible solutions to that problem, and help you to achieve a positive outcome. One of the important benefits of problem solving is that it can actually help you to avoid big stressors. We have already seen that stressful life events can trigger depression and that we often play some role in the stressors we experience. But what if a person was able to detect and solve a problem before it got out of hand? For example, if someone who is married realizes that the relationship is in trouble and is able to improve the relationship, he or she could potentially avoid the stress of a separation or divorce. Or if someone who has received negative feedback about his or her job performance is able to correct the problem and get a good job evaluation, the prospect of getting fired may be avoided. By resolving a stressor before it happens, effective problem solving may help to prevent relapse and recurrence of depression.

Problem solving is a set of skills that can be taught and learned, and as we mentioned earlier, some depression experts believe that people who are vulnerable to depression may need to make sure that their problem-solving skills are used to their fullest potential. Particularly when things are not going well and some amount of sad mood has already been triggered, a person looking to stay well should ensure that the best possible approach to problem solving is being used. In this section, we present a step-by-step approach to problem solving and include worksheets to help you with the process.

The Steps to Problem Solving

The process of problem solving is best broken down into several steps (D'Zurilla and Goldfried 1971; Mueser 1998). First, the problem needs to be assessed, defined, and understood. Second, potential solutions need to be generated and each possibility evaluated for how useful and realistic it is. Third, some decisions need to be made to identify the best of the solutions and the practical steps needed to implement the solutions. Finally, the outcome or result of these problem-solving steps needs to be considered.

This idea of breaking down the process into steps is very important. Unless you have defined the problem first, no amount of action will help, since the action could be aimed in the wrong direction. Similarly, no really useful action can be taken if a critical piece of information about the problem is missing. It is important to take only one step at a time and to take those steps in the order they are presented here. In the next section, we describe each of the four steps in more detail, and we have included several worksheets to help you work on problems that are unique to you.

Step 1: Defining the Problem

This is the critical first step to solving any problem and involves the basic question, "What is the problem?" At first you may only be aware of the problem in a vague way, as an area of your life which is causing tension or distress. In this first step you'll need to translate those feelings into words and specific issues that seem to be related to the sense of distress. For example, if you believe there is a problem in a relationship, it needs to be defined very specifically, otherwise you will not know what your role is, what your partner's role is, or what either of you can do about it. Is this a problem about physical intimacy, emotional intimacy, not feeling understood, or not spending enough time together? Without knowing this, the action you take may not fit the problem. For example, if you try to solve a relationship problem by spending more time with your partner, but the problem is actually that your partner doesn't feel understood, your solution may not solve the problem on its own.

Of course, many problems are problems precisely because we are not able to get a handle on them. To identify the nature of the problem, there are other questions you can ask yourself: Why is it a problem? What is involved in the problem? Who is involved in the problem? Is this someone else's problem that has become my problem? Each of these questions may put a different perspective on what is at stake and what it means to you and your life. Sometimes the problem can become too large or complex, involving too many other people or things that are not in your immediate control. In that case, start small by examining one specific aspect of the problem—the one that relates mainly to you. The typical areas that people have problems in are hard to list exhaustively, but they often have to do with relationships, work, health, finances, family, and home life.

The next step in defining the problem is actually defining the opposite of the problem, namely the goal or how you would like things to be, compared to where they are now. Perhaps there is some ideal state you wish to achieve in the future. Or, perhaps you would like things to be the way they used to be. Of course, some amount of realistic thinking also has to be part of the goal. What can you actually achieve with respect to this problem? What is realistic? Notice that these questions are heavily oriented toward what you want, because the solution to a problem needs first and foremost to be satisfactory to you. In worksheet 9.3, there are some questions to first orient you to the problem, and then, in step 2, to help you spell out the problem and your goal.

Worksheet 9.3
Defining the Problem

Step 1: Get a handle on the problem by asking the following questions:

In what area or life domain is the problem that I am trying to work on (for example, work, relationships, etc.)? _____

_____

Who are the people involved in the problem? _____

_____

How did the problem come about? _____

_____

How would I want things to be in the future with respect to this problem? _____

_____

What is a realistic goal with respect to this problem? _____

_____

Step 2: Use the answers to the questions in step 1 to describe the problem.

The problem I am going to work on is: _____

_____

My goal in working on this problem is: _____

_____

Step 2: Brainstorming Solutions and Evaluating the Options

The next step is divided into two parts. The first part involves brainstorming—coming up with as many possible solutions as you can. In this part, the aim is to be as creative and uncritical as possible. The second part involves looking at all the solutions with a more rational and logical approach and figuring out which solutions are most practical and which will work best given your goals.

Brainstorming Worksheet

Brainstorming has some rules, and the first rule is there are no rules! In other words, any idea is fair game and no solution should be judged as good or bad. The more outlandish and creative the ideas the better, and the more options you create the better. There will be plenty of time later to narrow down the choices and make decisions among the options, but the point of brainstorming is to think about the problem in new ways. One way to unleash some creativity is to strip away your assumptions about a problem. Imagine you have just arrived here from another place or country (or planet if you like), and try to see the problem as if for the first time through a brand new pair of eyes. You may need to put the past out of your mind and to disregard the traditional ways of thinking about a problem. Sometimes it is helpful to think that you are someone else, a best friend, or a colleague you respect, who is looking at the problem without all the baggage of your own history with that problem. Write down all of the ideas and give yourself lots of time and space to do this. Worksheet 9.4 lists the guidelines for brainstorming and leaves lots of room for you to generate ideas and solutions. The rest is up to your creativity!

Worksheet 9.4
Brainstorming

- ◆ The rules: There are no rules

- ◆ Be open-minded

- ◆ Be creative

- ◆ Anything is an option

_____

_____

_____

_____

_____

_____

_____

_____

_____

_____

_____

_____

_____

_____

_____

_____

Consider Your Options

Once you have a nice long list of options, there is an important transition to make. This involves taking off the creative hat and putting on your logical, rational hat. Look again at the options you created and consider several things. First, how feasible, or doable, is each one of these options? Could that option actually be carried out? Think carefully about what the consequences of each option would be. If you proceeded with option "X," what would happen? What are the advantages of using that particular option? What are the drawbacks or disadvantages of that option? The goal of this process is to answer three questions about each solution you have listed while brainstorming: (1) how realistic is the option? (2) how many advantages does the option have? and (3) how many disadvantages does the option have? All three ratings are important. At the end of all this, the option that should go to the top of the list would be the one that has the highest feasibility rating, the most advantages, and the fewest disadvantages. Worksheet 9.5 has spaces to write out the options, rate their feasibility, and then list both advantages and disadvantages of each option. You can use as many copies of the worksheet as you need to evaluate the options you created with brainstorming.

Worksheet 9.5
Evaluating the Options

Solution Option 1 is: _____

How feasible is this option (0 = not at all, 10 = extremely feasible)? _____

What are the advantages of this option? _____

_____

Number of advantages: _____

What are the drawbacks or disadvantages of this option? _____

_____

Number of disadvantages: _____

Solution Option 2 is: _____

How feasible is this option (0 = not at all, 10 = extremely feasible)? _____

What are the advantages of this option? _____

_____

Number of advantages: _____

What are the drawbacks or disadvantages of this option? _____

_____

Number of disadvantages: _____

Solution Option 3 is: _____

How feasible is this option (0 = not at all, 10 = extremely feasible)? _____

What are the advantages of this option? _____

_____

Number of advantages: _____

What are the drawbacks or disadvantages of this option?_____

_____

Number of disadvantages: _____

Step 3: Commitment and Follow-Through

By this time you will have developed a list of options, and perhaps have a front-runner based on feasibility, advantages, and a relative lack of disadvantages. Now is the time to commit to one option. Sometimes, especially under stress, we doubt ourselves, try different paths, and ultimately do not carry through with any comprehensive plan. By committing yourself, you are declaring that you will follow this particular plan and see where it leads before switching to another plan. Commitment also involves focusing on the nitty-gritty of what actions need to be taken, by whom, and when. Problem solving plans often involve gathering more information, lining up resources that may assist you, and sometimes asking others for help. Just like when committing to lifestyle plans like exercise and pleasurable events (chapter 7), it is important to pick out a time and place and to be specific about what you are going to do. Writing it down will also increase the chances of following up. Remember to take things up in the most logical order. Most problem solving is best done in a specific sequence where the first action sets the stage for the second action, and so on. Worksheet 9.6 asks you to record the option you have chosen and to specify each step. There are also spaces to record what kinds of information and help you will need and when you will take each step. The worksheet lists five steps, but you can carry on with another sheet if the solution has more than five steps.

Another aspect of problem solving that is important in the commitment and follow-through stage has to do with obstacles you might face in following your plan. Problems are problems exactly because they are so often complicated, and so any plan to deal with a difficult problem may face some hurdles or roadblocks. Not every hurdle can be anticipated, but many obstacles can be planned for in advance. Getting around obstacles is very much like micro–problem solving. You first try to understand the obstacle, brainstorm ways to beat it, pick a strategy that should work, and then implement the plan. The follow-through portion of problem solving is probably what will take the longest and require the most perseverance. But it is also the step in which problems become solutions.

Worksheet 9.6
Problem-Solving Follow-Through

The option I am following up on is: _____

Specify Each Step

Step 1 is: _____

Who is involved in this step? _____

What I need to carry out this step is: _____

I will do this step on (date and time): _____

Step 2 is: _____

Who is involved in this step? _____

What I need to carry out this step is: _____

I will do this step on (date and time): _____

Step 3 is: _____

Who is involved in this step? _____

What I need to carry out this step is: _____

I will do this step on (date and time): _____

Step 4 is: _____

Who is involved in this step? _____

What I need to carry out this step is: _____

I will do this step on (date and time): _____

Step 5 is: _____

Who is involved in this step? _____

What I need to carry out this step is: _____

I will do this step on (date and time): _____

Step 4: Evaluating the Outcome

This step is one that is sometimes forgotten once people have swung into action. Forgetting this part can be a problem because this is the point when you really figure out whether the solution has worked. Start this step by looking back at your problem definition and then take stock. Does the problem you had still exist? Ideally, by the end of problem solving, the issue has been resolved. If the problem is gone, pat yourself on the back and give yourself credit for a big success.

In many cases though, the problem will not be totally gone. Sometimes problem solving requires that more than one option be used. Perhaps the problem is too complex to have been solved in one try. Or perhaps the option you picked has worked somewhat, but has not completely eliminated the problem. Some of your actions may have had consequences but you did not expect, or some things you thought would have one consequence in reality had another. Evaluating your problem solving is a little bit like debugging or troubleshooting (Mueser 1998). It may be useful to go over your plan backward to see where the plan did not work as you expected. Also, review all of the other solutions you developed during brainstorming. It may be that one of those options, with the benefit of hindsight, now looks like it could have been a better choice. This can be somewhat disappointing, but trying to improve our lives is often what is called an *iterative* process. Iterative simply means that something is repeated, but the repetition takes into account what happened the first time we did something. Learning any skill is really an iterative process. If you are trying to learn to hit a golf ball, you try it one way and then, based on the result, you make a correction and try again. As time goes by, the swing looks better and better and becomes more reliable. Working on the problems in our lives is an iterative process for all of us.

Looking at the outcome of problem solving is vital for knowing what to do next, and what to do when facing a similar problem in the future. When you evaluate the outcome it is also a time to learn from what happened. Knowing the outcome now, what would you do differently? Completing this step is very much like building wisdom and making sure you have valuable information you can use when facing a similar problem in the future. Worksheet 9.7 will help you to record the outcome of your problem-solving attempts. It also will allow you to compare what you got with what you wanted, helping you to spot unintended consequences and to focus on what you learned from your attempt at solving the problem.

Worksheet 9.7
Evaluating the Results

Step 1: The problem I was working on was: _____

_____

Step 2: The goal for this problem was: _____

_____

Step 3: Rate to what extent the problem solving has resulted in reaching the goal (0 = not at all close to the goal, 10 = goal completely attained)? _____

Step 4: Looking back on the option I chose, what went well was: _____

_____

Step 5: Looking back on the option I chose, what did not go as intended was: ____

_____

Step 6: Looking at the problem and my attempts to solve it, what still needs to be accomplished is: _____

_____

Step 7: The lesson I learned from working on this problem using this solution is:

_____

Step 8: Keeping in mind what still needs to be accomplished and what my previous action achieved, my next step is to: _____

_____

Summary

In this chapter we examined the critical link between stressful life events and depression. We have seen that stress is a very important trigger for some episodes of depression, and therefore dealing with stress needs to be part of any relapse prevention plan. Of course, some stressors are difficult to predict or to plan for. These kinds of fateful stresses, like having someone you love fall ill or having to move to a different city for a new job, are part of everyone's life at some point. Also, these kinds of stressors will always cause some emotional disruptions, which are an entirely normal part of adapting to new circumstances. But we also pointed out that when someone is vulnerable, stressful disruptions may lead to too much emotion-focused coping and may increase the risk of having a full-blown depression relapse. To counter this, we have tried to provide you with some useful information about how to cope with these kinds of stressors, and we included a worksheet for developing and using the best possible coping strategies. This will not prevent all negative moods, but using a good variety of coping strategies should really help you to curtail the downward mood spiraling that could lead to relapse. We also introduced the idea that not all stress is due to bad luck or fate, and that, when it comes to depression, there is evidence that people who are vulnerable may play a role in creating stressful circumstances. The very specific problem-solving skills we presented here are designed to help you solve problems before they truly become stressors. By carefully defining the problem, putting together options, following up, and evaluating how things have turned out, you will be taking the most responsibility and control over your life that is possible. Taking action to solve problems and to cope effectively with stress will be one of your best defenses against relapse.

Summary Exercise

Record what you believe is the bottom line from this chapter, then record what practices, exercises, or worksheets you would adopt as part of your wellness plan.

Chapter 9, Better Coping During Stressful Times, examines the relationship between stress, coping, and relapse. My bottom line in this chapter is:

_____

_____

The practices, exercises, or worksheets I will use from this chapter are:

_____

_____

Chapter 10

Depression and Other Health Issues: Anxiety Disorders, Alcohol Use, Chronic Pain, and Other Medical Issues

In this chapter we consider other types of problems that often lead to, or are associated with, depression. The technical term for this linkage between depression and other sorts of problems is *comorbidity*. "Comorbidity" means that two different conditions are occurring in the same individual. Sometimes the two conditions occur together by chance, with independent causes. For example, someone who is depressed might break a bone in his or her arm. In that case, the timing would be unfortunate, but the two health problems would probably have occurred together only by chance (depression doesn't normally cause broken bones). Other times, the two or more conditions that happen to occur together are linked. For example, someone who is diagnosed with a very serious illness like cancer may develop clinical depression after finding out that he or she has cancer. In this case, while we cannot say for sure that the cancer diagnosis caused the depression, it is likely that the two problems are related and that the depression might not have occurred if the cancer had not been diagnosed. The reason comorbidity is important to discuss is that, in the end, there are numerous health conditions that can make you much more vulnerable to depression. Understanding these links between depression and other health issues should be an important part of your wellness plan.

Beating Anxiety and Depression

Anxiety disorders are among the most common problems to overlap with depression. Like depression, anxiety disorders are classified as psychiatric disorders, but in the anxiety disorders, the most important features include fear, worry, symptoms of physical arousal (such as racing heart), and avoidance of feared objects and situations. More often than not, people who suffer from depression also experience problems with anxiety at some point in their lives (Brown et al. 2001b). In fact, it appears that having an anxiety disorder might put a person at increased risk for developing a subsequent episode of depression (Brown et al. 2001b). At times, depression can also come before an anxiety disorder develops. When depression occurs together with anxiety, psychiatric guidelines suggest different approaches to treatment (Enns et al. 2001). Thus, in your plan for wellness it is important to appreciate the impact of anxiety disorders, and how these are treated when they occur together with depression.

A number of anxiety disorders are known to co-occur frequently with depression, including panic disorder, social phobia (or social anxiety disorder), post-traumatic stress disorder, obsessive-compulsive disorder, and generalized anxiety disorder. We describe each of these below. Additional recommended readings on each of these conditions are provided in this book under Additional Resources.

Panic Disorder with and without Agoraphobia

The most important feature of *panic disorder* is the presence of unexpected panic attacks occurring out of the blue, without any obvious trigger or cause. A *panic attack* is a sudden rush of fear that peaks very quickly and is associated with a number of physical arousal symptoms, such as dizziness, breathlessness, sweating, and racing heart. People with panic disorder are often very frightened by their panic attacks and are concerned that they may be having a heart attack, losing control, going "crazy," or experiencing some other catastrophe. As a result, they often start to avoid situations where their panic attacks are particularly frightening, such as crowds, driving, enclosed places, being alone, and situations from which escape might be difficult. In extreme cases, people with *panic disorder with agoraphobia* may be unable to leave the house alone.

Social Phobia

Social phobia is a problem in which people are extremely anxious in social and performance situations where they might be judged by other people. Examples of commonly feared situations in social phobia include parties, meetings, dating, conversations, public speaking, and being the center of attention. In social phobia, the fear is severe enough that it causes significant distress and interference and affects the person's work, relationships, and other areas of functioning.

Post-Traumatic Stress Disorder

Post-traumatic stress disorder (PTSD) is an anxiety disorder in which an individual has an unusually strong reaction to a trauma in which he, she, or someone else was exposed to some kind of physical threat, such as a rape, assault, accident, fire, or combat. Some of the common features of PTSD include intrusive dreams, memories, or flashbacks that make it difficult to stop thinking about the trauma; a tendency to avoid people, situations, and thoughts that remind the person of the trauma; feelings of emotional detachment and a lack of interest; and symptoms of high arousal, including poor sleep, impaired concentration, and a tendency to be easily startled.

Obsessive Compulsive Disorder

People with *obsessive-compulsive disorder* (OCD) tend to have repetitive intrusive thoughts that are often frightening or bothersome to the individual (these are called *obsessions*) as well as repetitive behaviors that they engage in to reduce their anxiety and prevent unwanted consequences from occurring (these are called *compulsions*). Common obsessions include fears of contamination from germs or poisons, unwanted aggressive thoughts, and doubts about whether tasks have been completed correctly. Common compulsions include washing and cleaning, excessive checking, counting, and repeating actions. The obsessions and compulsions tend to be very time-consuming and cause considerable impairment in the person's life.

Generalized Anxiety Disorder

The main feature of *generalized anxiety disorder* (GAD) is frequent and excessive worry about a number of different topics, including work, finances, family, health, and day-to-day hassles. In fact, people with GAD will often report worrying too much about everything. Some of the other features of GAD include difficulty controlling the worry, difficulty sleeping, poor concentration, muscle tension, feeling keyed up or on edge, fatigue, and irritability. GAD symptoms are common in people who feel depressed, but to get a separate diagnosis of GAD, the anxiety symptoms have to be present even when the person is not feeling depressed.

Treatment of Anxiety Disorder and Depression

Many of the treatments that are useful for depression are also useful for treating anxiety disorders. For example, all of the anxiety disorders described in this chapter respond well to certain antidepressant medications, even if the individual is not feeling depressed (chapter 4). Psychological treatments are also effective for combating anxiety. For example, cognitive therapy (chapter 6) is often included in the treatment of panic disorder, PTSD, GAD, and social phobia. Anxiety disorders also respond well to exposure-based treatments. Essentially, exposure involves confronting a feared situation repeatedly until it no longer triggers fear. In the case of social phobia, exposure might involve interacting with other people at parties or at work until these situations become easier. Exposure is typically used in the treatment of social phobia, panic disorder, OCD, and PTSD. Finally, relaxation-based treatments, such as muscle relaxation exercises, are useful for treating anxiety, particularly in the case of GAD. For a detailed discussion of these treatments, check out some of the recommended readings in the Additional Resources section.

Alcohol Abuse and Depression

As with anxiety disorders, it seems that alcohol abuse and depression occur together in people much more often than one would expect by chance alone. Exactly why this should be the case is still unclear, and the reasons for the association between depression and alcohol abuse may be different from one individual to the next. For example, in some cases the same genes that make people vulnerable to depression may also make them vulnerable to alcohol abuse. Or it may be that overuse of alcohol, and the impact of the abuse on the brain and on the person's life, results in an increased chance of becoming depressed. Likewise, if a person becomes depressed, he or she may use alcohol to self-medicate and therefore be at an increased risk for becoming dependent on the alcohol. Although we don't completely understand the reasons for the association between excessive drinking and depression, it is clear that when these two conditions occur together, successful treatment and recovery are less likely than when these conditions occur alone (Brown and Ramsey 2000; Brown et al. 1997). Thus, the use of alcohol in anyone who is vulnerable to depression is potentially problematic, and these facts need to be considered in any wellness plan.

Defining What Is "Too Much" Alcohol

Many people drink alcohol in ways that are not problematic. For example, some people, having read that a daily glass of red wine may ward off heart disease, may go out of their way to have a glass of wine with dinner. Other people may have a beer after they mow the lawn, share a round of drinks while out with friends, or have a bottle of champagne to toast some happy occasion. This pattern of alcohol use is probably fine for most people. However, if you are vulnerable to depression, and particularly if you are also taking antidepressant medication, it may be wise to minimize your intake of alcohol as much as possible. But just when does alcohol use become a real problem?

The *Diagnostic and Statistical Manual of Mental Disorders (DSM-IV)* defines two broad types of problem drinking (American Psychiatric Association 2000). The first is *alcohol abuse,* in which a person, during a twelve-month period, has repeatedly used alcohol in a way that might lead to problems with family relationships or work, legal problems, or an increased risk of harm to oneself or others (such as driving while intoxicated). When problem drinking becomes even more severe, criteria for *substance dependence* may be met. As is the case for alcohol abuse, substance dependence is associated with significant problems stemming from the drinking. In addition, substance dependence is often associated with a need to drink more and more alcohol over time to get the same effects (known as *tolerance*) and a tendency to experience uncomfortable physical feelings upon stopping drinking (known as *withdrawal*). In addition to tolerance and withdrawal, other features of dependence include repeated, unsuccessful attempts to stop drinking or to cut down, and spending significant amounts of time in an intoxicated state.

If, after reading these descriptions, you get a sense that these descriptions may fit your own pattern of drinking, and if you have not sought help in the past, this may be the time to seek help. Next, we describe some of the treatments that have been used for alcohol problems in people who also struggle with depression.

Treatment for Alcohol Problems and Depression

Antidepressant medications have frequently been studied in people who have both alcohol problems and depression. However, the results from these studies are not terribly clear (Brown and Ramsey 2000; Litten and Allen 1995). In some studies, antidepressants seem to help both the symptoms of depression and help the person reduce their intake of alcohol, but in other studies this is not the case. It is also important to note that when a person takes antidepressants and drinks alcohol, several complications can occur. First, the alcohol can, with some medications, reduce the level of antidepressants in the bloodstream (Litten and Allen 1995). Also, people who abuse alcohol have much more trouble sticking to their medication regimen; that is, they do not take their antidepressants as they should. Therefore, when depression and alcohol problems occur together, the recommendation is that antidepressants be combined with an intervention designed specifically for the alcohol use. We look at these interventions next.

One of the treatments we have previously described for depression, cognitive behavioral therapy (CBT), also seems to be very useful for people who have alcohol problems and depression (Brown and Ramsey 2000; Brown et al. 1997). The CBT, in this case, can really be used in two ways. First, it can help a person to deal better with the pessimistic and negative thoughts that come from the depression. Second, CBT can help a person to look at the kinds of situations and thoughts that lead him or her to overuse alcohol. In addition to CBT, other treatment approaches for alcohol problems have shown themselves to be useful. Not all of these approaches even require an expert. For example, Alcoholics Anonymous (AA) has been shown to be a quite effective treatment for many people, as have approaches that involve family interventions and other kinds of psychotherapy (Mack, Franklin, and Frances 2001; Project MATCH Research Group 1998). The advantage of AA is that it is accessible no matter where you live, costs nothing, and people at AA will be able to provide a lot of information about other treatment options in your area. What is still unclear though is which kind of treatment works best for which kind of person, and it is difficult to predict what any one individual's chances are of succeeding in a particular attempt to quit drinking (Project MATCH Research Group 1998). So, to some extent, finding what works best for you may be a matter of trial and error. Keep in mind that if a particular treatment approach does not work, this does not mean nothing will work. Many people who struggle with alcohol make numerous attempts to quit before finding the way that works best for them.

What does seem to be important for determining the outcome of treatment for alcoholism is having a good therapeutic alliance; that is, a strong, trusting, empathic, and empowering professional relationship between the client and therapist (Carroll, Nich, and Rounsaville 1997; Connors et al. 1997). Also, people who stick with the therapy, attend the treatment sessions, and follow the instructions and procedures seem to do better (Mattson et al. 1998). No matter what treatment is used, what is important is that the alcohol user acknowledges that he or she has a problem and is motivated to take action to solve that problem.

A Final Word on Alcohol

Use of alcohol is the norm in our society; alcohol has been around for so many centuries that it has woven itself into the fabric of our lives. Alcohol is in evidence in almost all social occasions and important cultural events—even those that are religious or family-oriented. Many people believe that society's tolerance and even encouragement of alcohol use is extremely hypocritical when one considers the emphasis placed on the "War on Drugs." Make no mistake, alcohol is a very potent drug with well-established effects on the brain and harmful effects on other organs when it is overused. And alcohol causes considerable damage in our society. In the United States alone, alcohol abuse costs the country an estimated $85 billion dollars annually (Brown and Ramsey 2000). This is before considering the personal toll, such as deaths from alcohol overuse and deaths of innocent people killed by drunk drivers. We write this not to frighten you or even to make the point that you should reject alcohol on principle. Rather, we want to point out that alcohol is, in many ways, no different from an illegal drug, and yet it is around us all the time. If you have ever, for any reason, decided you were not going to have a drink at a wedding, party, or celebratory gathering, you may have experienced subtle or not-so-subtle social pressure to go along and have a drink like everyone else. But when you are vulnerable to depression, you do have a very good reason to not drink at all.

Chronic Pain and Depression: Breaking the Cycle

On the surface, it may not be obvious how physical pain and depression might be related, though these two problems often occur together. By "pain," we are not so much talking about the acute pain of everyday incidents like stubbing a toe or getting a paper cut. Instead, we are referring to recurrent and longer-lasting conditions of pain, such as chronic headaches, back pain, or pain from an illness like arthritis. In these kinds of chronic conditions, level of depression seems to be one of the most important predictors of how much pain a person perceives (Gatchel 1999). Also, chronic pain and depression seem to lead to a kind of vicious cycle: people with chronic pain become vulnerable to depression and the experience of depression seems to result in more pain (Robinson and Riley 1999). Therefore, people who suffer from chronic pain need to consider how that condition might influence their vulnerability to depression.

Many people have some difficulty understanding how an emotion, like depression, can actually influence how much physical pain they feel. After all, depression is an emotional state, whereas pain is a physical state, stemming from nerves near the site of the pain (back, head, wrist, and so forth). The answer is that all pain is actually experienced, not in your back, head or wrist, but in your brain. Of course, the brain also supplies you the information about where the problem is, so you experience the pain as located in a particular part of the body.

In addition, pain is usually a signal that one is doing something that may be injuring the body. Pain really is telling you to stop and check out that you're not injured or injuring yourself. But the experience of pain is more complex than that. Almost four decades ago, Melzack and Wall (1965) proposed the *gate control theory* of pain, in which they suggested that the connection between pain sensations and the brain involved a kind of gate that could be opened, closed, or left somewhere in between. They created this theory to account for some unusual aspects of pain experiences that were hard to ignore. For example, there are many instances of athletes sustaining quite severe injuries (even broken bones) who described no pain and a desire to continue playing in whatever game or competition they were in. Also, there were common reports of soldiers who had been horrifically wounded on the battlefield requiring seemingly little pain medication (far less, it seemed, than civilian patients with much less severe injuries). Melzack and Wall explained that, in these cases, the gate for pain experience was closed by other parts of the brain. In the athletic situation, presumably the gate was closed because the person was entirely focused on winning the game. In the example of soldiers, the explanation appeared to be that, despite the grave injuries, the soldiers were pleased to be alive at all and happy that they were being removed from the front lines in order to recuperate.

The gate control theory of pain led eventually to a *biopsychosocial model* of pain. That is, pain experiences are now looked at not just as a physical or biological problem, but also in the context of the person who has the condition—his or her psychological state and surroundings. All of these factors have been linked to how much pain people report and, even more importantly, how well they function in everyday life. Next we describe some ways in which pain and depression seem to interact to put a person at risk of experiencing even more depression, and more pain.

The Pain and Depression Cycle

Depression seems to influence the experience of pain in numerous ways, but mainly depression seems to open the gate to pain. In fact, when people are in a sad mood, they seem to be much more likely to interpret a given stimulus as painful, and may even describe their depression in terms of pain (Dworkin, Wilson, and Masson 1994). This process, sometimes called *somatization* (Robinson and Riley 1999), seems to amplify uncomfortable physical sensations and then categorize them as pain. People who are *somatizing* are constantly scanning their bodies looking for signs of pain or some physical problem, and when they find something, that sensation tends to intensify. A second way depression influences pain experiences is in *catastrophizing* (Robinson and Riley 1999). People who are depressed and experience pain seem to see their pain as dangerous and as an indication of future problems. As we described earlier, pain is usually a signal that the body is in some kind of danger, but in chronic pain conditions (such as lower back pain), the pain is usually not a sign of imminent catastrophe or something being injured further. A depressed person who interprets back pain as indicative of a serious physical injury may picture themselves doing more damage to their spine, for example, imagining discs in their back as grinding together. People may also carry the image further, envisaging themselves in a wheelchair or unable to move at all. Naturally, this horrible consequence leads them to avoid movement and exercise, which only further weakens their muscles and makes them even more sensitive to pain.

Finally, pain also seems to be greater when people have a sense that their life is not under their control and their interpersonal relationships are perceived as unsupportive. People who see the pain condition as limiting what they can achieve do actually end up feeling even more pain (Robinson and Riley 1999). Also, people who have troubled relationships with others, or who lack good social support systems, tend to report greater levels of pain. Next we consider some ways to help with these problems.

Treating Pain: Treating the Person

The treatment of pain has evolved considerably in the last two decades, and most pain treatment programs take into account the physical causes of pain, the context in which the condition occurs, and the person who has the condition. First and foremost, it is important that if you have a pain condition, it needs to be properly investigated by the appropriate medical specialist. This will help to establish the medical diagnosis, and what the options are for treating the underlying pain condition. Not all pain conditions are easy to specify. For example, lower back pain seems to have so many potential causes that many people never get a clear answer to exactly why it is they have back pain. Nonetheless, getting properly diagnosed is important because it will tell you what medical options you have. For many people, going to specialists helps them determine whether what they have is stable versus deteriorating, and whether there are any risks to continuing to try to function (for example, continuing to move a joint that hurts or continuing to walk if walking hurts their back). Also, for many conditions that lead to pain, there is no absolute cure, only treatments that can make the pain less severe and help to increase functioning.

The treatments for pain itself fall into two categories, passive and active (Gatchel and Turk 1999). Passive treatments are things like taking analgesic medication, electrical stimulation, and temperature manipulation (hot and cold packs). These passive treatments are usually recommended for temporary pain states, but may have some use in more chronic conditions. The second group of pain treatments are active treatments and involve carefully monitored physical movement (physiotherapy), stretching, and increased physical activities. The active treatments help to build up a person's general physical condition and their muscle strength in the affected areas.

In addition to direct treatment of the pain, it is equally important to find a treatment program that focuses on emotions around pain and their interpretations of pain. Many pain clinics now have interdisciplinary treatment teams. If you were to seek out such a clinic, you would be seen by not only a physician, but any number of physical rehabilitation specialists and mental health professionals. These professionals, working as a team, would then put together an individualized treatment package designed to work on all the aspects of your pain problem. Some pain clinics may offer a group treatment, often a modified version of CBT that looks at how pain triggers negative thoughts and how certain emotions and thoughts lead to pain experiences. The evidence from treatment studies suggests that these treatments are effective (Gatchel and Turk 1999). Although the treatment of pain and depression is a complex area, and one that is hard to summarize in a few sentences, there are a few themes that seem to run through these kinds of treatments.

The first theme has to do with reframing the meaning of pain experiences. Rather than viewing pain as a sign of a dangerous injury and further damage, individuals are encouraged to view their chronic pain as an unpleasant, but not dangerous, sensation that can be dealt with using a number of coping strategies. The second theme in these treatments is to make sure a person stays active, and that pain is no longer perceived as a signal to stop or withdraw from an activity. Instead, the person learns that activity is likely to strengthen the body and, over time, reduce pain sensations. The final theme in these treatments is that the kinds of things one relies on to deal with acute pain (such as a sprained ankle or a headache), like rest and using analgesic medications, may be counterproductive when they are overused, especially when pain becomes chronic. When people rely on rest and medications to cope with pain, it is more likely that their body will become deconditioned from lack of activity and that they will need more medications to control their pain. People who are vulnerable to depression and who have a chronic pain condition face many challenges, but in this case, seeking multidisciplinary treatment for the pain condition should, as the saying goes, kill two birds with one stone.

Other Medical Illnesses and Depression: Staying Well in All Ways

Like many of the other conditions we have described, the relationship between depression and medical illnesses like cancer, cardiovascular conditions (such as heart disease), endocrine disorders (such as diabetes), and progressive central nervous system diseases (such as multiple sclerosis or Parkinson's disease) is very complicated. In time, researchers will probably find out much more about the links between these medical disorders and depression. In some conditions, it may be that the same genes that account for the occurrence of depression are also responsible for the other medical disorders. In some cases, including certain types of cancer (like pancreatic cancer), the cancer itself may affect areas of the brain and trigger depression (Stevens, Merikangas, and Merikangas 1995). In addition, some researchers believe that depression is a risk factor for developing other disorders, such as high blood pressure. Finally, it seems that in some cases, the diagnosis of a serious medical condition can result in depression. For example, depression rates in cancer patients can be as high as 85 percent (Stevens, Merikangas, and Merikangas 1995). In many cases, it may be that depression occurs as a reaction to news of a disease that may be life-threatening. Obviously, with all the possible links between depression and other medical illnesses, it is difficult to give clear-cut advice to cover all situations. Nonetheless, we have outlined several general areas to pay attention to that are important for preventing relapse in depression. The suggestions we make will be most applicable when your mood is relatively stable, but you have been diagnosed with a medical condition that may complicate your life and make you vulnerable to depression.

Medical Illness and Antidepressants

A number of medical problems can make medication treatment for depression more complex. For example, the tricyclic antidepressants discussed in chapter 4 can cause some cardiac anomalies and would not be appropriate for someone who has had a heart attack (Stevens, Merikangas, and Merikangas 1995). However, the SSRI antidepressants, also discussed in chapter 4, seem to cause fewer cardiac complications and may even have some additional benefits for people who have had a heart attack (Kilbourn, Saab, and Schneiderman 2000). Also, some drugs given for hypertension (high blood pressure) seem to cause symptoms of depression and some antidepressants seem to interfere with drugs used to control blood pressure (Stevens, Merikangus, and Merikangus 1995). In any case, when a medical condition is newly diagnosed and treatment is started, it makes sense to discuss with your doctor possible interactions between the treatment being used for your medical condition and the treatment being used for preventing the recurrence of your depression. In most cases, the complications or interactions between medications will probably be relatively minor. What may be needed is simply careful monitoring to make sure that all of the medications work well enough together.

Medical Conditions That Cause Depression

Certain physical illnesses can directly cause depression because their impacts on biological systems result in depression. Under the criteria set out in the *Diagnostic and Statistical Manual of Mental Disorders (DSM-IV)*, these conditions are not actually diagnosed as a mood disorder such as major depressive disorder. Instead, such a condition would typically be referred to as *depression due to a general medical condition* (American Psychiatric Association 2000). It is difficult to construct a comprehensive list of medical disorders that can directly cause depression. Examples include certain degenerative neurological conditions, such as Parkinson's disease or Huntington's disease; cerebrovascular disease, like a stroke; metabolic conditions, like a vitamin B12 deficiency; endocrine conditions, such as problems with glands like hyperthyroidism or hypothyrodism; autoimmune disorders, like lupus; or viral infections, such as HIV or hepatitis (American Psychiatric Association 2000).

It is not always straightforward to distinguish major depressive disorder from depression caused by a general medical condition. Certainly, one important factor has to do with timing. If the disease started a short time *before* the depression started, it makes it more likely that the disease caused the depression. If you have a relapse of depression symptoms and suspect the episode is related to a new, undiagnosed medical condition, you need to see your doctor immediately. If this turns out to be the case, the most useful thing may be to treat the underlying medical illness which should, in most cases, also resolve the depression caused by that medical illness.

Medical Conditions That Increase Vulnerability for Depression

Clearly, the diagnosis of a major medical condition is an important event in someone's life. Whether the problem is cancer, a cardiovascular problem, or a degenerative disease, the implications are huge. At worst, these kinds of conditions can lead to an early death, but even at best such conditions may limit a person's physical capabilities. Moreover, the treatment regimens associated with these problems are often intense and difficult. For example, chemotherapy for cancer and dialysis treatment for kidney disease are difficult for patients to tolerate. These treatments entail some degree of pain and discomfort, and spending a lot of time around medical facilities—time that cannot be spent in other more enjoyable ways. Some negative emotions are likely to occur for anyone who has to endure these circumstances. For someone who has been depressed in the past, a serious medical illness will definitely increase their vulnerability to becoming depressed again. Next, we talk about reducing this vulnerability by making sure your depression is recognized early.

Getting the Best Possible Care

One of the biggest obstacles that gets in the way of good treatment for depression and other medical disorders is the failure of health care professionals to recognize depression in people with medical illnesses (Kilbourn, Saab, and Schneiderman 2000; Stevens, Merikangus, and Merikangus 1995). This may be because these professionals are still not familiar with depression as an illness; it may even be that some doctors think becoming clinically depressed after a having a serious medical problem is normal. However, regardless of how a depression is triggered, it needs to be recognized and treated. The best possible advocate you have is yourself. Knowing that you are vulnerable to depression and addressing the topic with your medical specialist are the best things you can do. This will put your problem on the table and you will have a better sense of how familiar your doctor is with treating these two conditions together. If your doctor seems to be ignoring the depression issue even after you raise it, consider getting a second opinion.

Once the issue of the medical illness and depression has been raised, sit down with your doctor and other health care professionals, and together come up with a treatment plan that takes into account your vulnerability to relapse. This may mean having to adjust either your antidepressant medication or the treatment regimen for the medical disorder. There will probably be trade-offs to making these adjustments, and it is important to consider the advantages and disadvantages to all the options. Doctors are very familiar with helping patients decide among different treatment options by looking at the pros and cons of each choice. By including the issue of relapse, you simply add another important consideration to what the best treatment choice is for you.

Also, with many medical conditions, you may have to make certain adjustments to your life. This is particularly true when the treatment for the problem is intense and has the potential to interfere with your daily routine, your ability to work, or your ability to meet other obligations. For example, kidney dialysis takes many, many hours over the course of the week. Sometimes the medical disorder itself means that you will no longer be able to work or do things that are important to you. Also, many degenerative illnesses may not be life threatening, but may interfere with physical movement. In these cases, the illness has brought about an unwanted role transition (this will be discussed in chapter 13). In this case, you may have to deal with giving up a part of your daily routine or stopping activities that previously were an important part of your identity. These changes should also be discussed with your doctor and other health care providers as soon as they come up. As in other fields of medicine, most clinics for medical disorders now have multidisciplinary teams. Instead of focusing just on the physical aspects of the illness, these clinics can offer other services, from finding help in the community for people with disabilities to counseling around the losses caused by physical illness. Finding such a clinic and getting the supports to help with illness will be important protection from depression relapse.

Summary

In this chapter we have looked at a wide range of health issues associated with depression, including anxiety disorders, alcohol use, pain conditions, and other medical illnesses. We hope that this chapter helps to broaden the way you think about depression and vulnerability to depression. In many ways this chapter is a good example of the multiple ways that depression can affect people, and how the illness has many different tentacles that reach across areas of health and functioning. In fact, there really are no areas of medical disease or dysfunction where the issue of depression is irrelevant. Most of the factors that have an impact on your physical health and well-being are also important to consider in your wellness plan to prevent relapse of depression. Depression can be triggered in so many ways from such different directions, some of which you might expect and others you may not have thought of. The best thing you can do is to evaluate where the risks are for you and to be prepared should those risks arise.

Summary Exercise

Record what you believe is the bottom line from this chapter, then record what practices or exercises you would adopt as part of your wellness plan.

Chapter 10, Depression and Other Health Issues: Anxiety Disorders, Alcohol Use, Chronic Pain, and Other Medical Issues, examines problems often associated with depression that need to be attended to. My bottom line in this chapter is:

_____

_____

The practices, exercises or actions I will take from this chapter are:

_____

_____

Chapter 11

You Don't Need to Be Perfect: Changing Perfectionism and Self-Criticism

What's wrong with being a perfectionist? On the surface, perfectionism may seem like a good thing. After all, without setting high standards, people would not be able to reach their peak levels of performance. Athletes would not train as hard, musicians would not bother rehearsing, and companies would not bother striving to be successful. In chapter 7, we discussed how increasing activities that provide a sense of accomplishment or mastery may help an individual to stay free of depression. You might think that setting high standards increases your sense of accomplishment. If that's so, wouldn't striving to be perfect be a positive thing? Not necessarily.

As you will see throughout this chapter, a tendency to set high standards can be a double-edged sword. On the one hand, setting one's sights high can help a person to achieve at a much higher level. On the other hand, perfectionism has been found to be related to a number of different problems, including depression, anxiety, and eating disorders (Antony and Swinson 1998; Flett and Hewitt 2002). The key to whether having high standards is useful has to do with how high a person's standards are, how rigid they are, and how a person responds when his or her particular goals are not reached.

What Is Perfectionism?

The Merriam-Webster's Collegiate Dictionary (1993) defines perfectionism as "a disposition to regard anything short of perfection as unacceptable." Psychological researchers who study perfectionism have tended to define the term in more detail, in an effort to distinguish perfectionism from a healthy desire to achieve high standards. For example, psychiatrist David Burns defined perfectionists as people "whose standards are high beyond reach or reason" and "who strain compulsively and unremittingly toward impossible goals and who measure their own worth entirely in terms of productivity and accomplishment. (1980, 34)"

More recently, psychologists have proposed multidimensional definitions of perfectionism, with the assumption that there are different types of perfectionism. For example, Flett and Hewitt (2002) define three different types of perfectionism: self-oriented perfectionism, other-oriented perfectionism, and socially prescribed perfectionism. Each of these is defined below.

Self-oriented perfectionism: This is a tendency to have standards for oneself that are so unrealistically high that they are impossible to attain. Self-oriented perfectionism is associated with a tendency to be very critical of oneself and to be intolerant of one's own mistakes and faults. High levels of self-oriented perfectionism have been found to be associated with depression.

Other-oriented perfectionism: This is a tendency to expect others to meet one's excessively high demands and expectations. People who have excessively high standards for others are at risk for being disappointed frequently, as others continually let them down. This can lead to stress in the workplace, in relationships, and in various day-to-day interactions with others. The constant disappointment can also increase a person's risk for developing problems with anger or depression.

Socially prescribed perfectionism: This involves having an exaggerated belief that others expect perfection. People who are high in this type of perfectionism feel extreme pressure from others to meet unreasonably high standards, even though others may not actually be exerting such extreme pressure. As a result, socially prescribed perfectionism is associated with a tendency to be very anxious about making mistakes, disappointing others, and not doing a good job. Not surprisingly, this type of perfectionism also puts people at risk for developing problems with depression, as well as anxiety and feelings of resentment toward others.

Although there are a number of different definitions of perfectionism, almost all share a number of key elements, as reviewed by Antony and Swinson (1998). Having high standards may be helpful; however, perfectionism is associated with having standards that are so high that they are no longer useful. In such cases, perfectionism can actually interfere with performance by causing people to avoid challenges, procrastinate, or become easily overwhelmed. Perfectionism is generally thought to be a risk factor for developing depression, which is why we have devoted an entire chapter to perfectionism in this book.

Perfectionism and Self-Criticism

Self-criticism is a concept from the psychological literature that is very much related to perfectionism (Blatt 1995). Self-criticism involves a tendency to view oneself as unworthy and inferior, a loser or a failure. People who are self-critical tend to be overly critical of themselves and always fear being disapproved of, criticized, or rejected by others. As a result, they may be very competitive and hardworking. In fact, they may be very accomplished, achieving a great amount of success in their work, but they are rarely satisfied with their achievements. People who are self-critical constantly feel as though they need to accomplish more in order to meet their own standards, as well as the standards of others. Not surprisingly, people who are depressed are often extremely self-critical as well (Blatt 1995).

Costs and Benefits of Perfectionism and Self-Criticism

In moderation, perfectionism and self-criticism are not necessarily a bad thing. As discussed earlier, having high standards can help a person to achieve particular goals, and the resulting sense of accomplishment may actually protect a person from becoming depressed. Similarly, realistic criticism of one's own performance may help to motivate an individual to work harder and achieve more. However, perfectionism and self-criticism can become a problem when they are excessive.

But how are we to distinguish between a high standard that is helpful and one that is excessive? Unfortunately, it can be very difficult to evaluate whether one's own standards are too high; as reviewed in chapter 6, our natural tendency is to assume that our own thoughts are true. For example, a person who is on a first date may have the thought, "It is important that I make a good impression." Is this a perfectionistic belief or just an appropriate belief that leads to a greater likelihood of getting a second date? As reviewed by Antony and Swinson (1998), whether such a belief should be considered perfectionistic depends on several factors:

- the *excessiveness* of the standard (in other words, can my goal be met?)

- the *accuracy* of the belief (for example, is it true that the standard *must* be met?)

- the *costs and benefits* of imposing the standard (for example, is it helpful for me to have the belief or standard?)

- the *flexibility* of the standard or belief (in other words, can I adjust my standards easily and change my beliefs when necessary?).

Standards that are realistic, accurate, helpful, and flexible are probably much less likely to be problematic than those that are unattainable, exaggerated, harmful, and inflexible. In the next section, we review some of the features of perfectionism, with the goal of helping you to determine whether perfectionism is a problem for you.

Perfectionism and Thinking

Chapter 6 describes in detail the notion that our emotions are very much tied to the types of beliefs and assumptions that we hold. In the case of depression, it is negative thinking that is particularly problematic, and often the types of negative thinking that contribute to depression have themes related to perfectionism and self-criticism. Examples of how this type of thinking can contribute to negative moods include

- If I lose my temper even once with my children, I am a bad parent.

- If I don't get an A+ on my exam, I should drop the course.

- I need to be the top performer in my sales department, or I will have let myself down.

- If my grades are not high enough to get into Harvard Law School, then I will have failed.

- I need to be a perfect spouse, or my partner will leave me.

- It is very important not to make mistakes so that others will approve of me.

- It would be absolutely terrible if I did not make this deadline.

- I should always be able to anticipate trouble before it happens.

Perfectionism and Behavior

According to Antony and Swinson (1998), perfectionism is often associated with two particular types of behaviors. The first type includes behaviors designed to help an individual meet his or her unreasonably high standards. Examples include constantly checking and seeking reassurance to make sure that one's standards are being met or that others approve; spending much too much time on tasks in order to make sure they are done perfectly; overpreparing for stressful situations; constantly comparing oneself to others to ensure that one's own performance is adequate; and doing excessive research before making decisions.

A second type of perfectionistic behavior includes avoidance of situations that might require an individual to live up to his or her perfectionistic standards. Examples include procrastination (for example, putting off starting a task because one's need for perfection makes the task difficult and unenjoyable); giving up on tasks prematurely because perfectionistic standards are unlikely to be met; and avoiding social situations for fear that others will be critical or judgmental. In the short term, these perfectionistic behaviors help an individual to feel more comfortable. In the long term, however, these strategies have the effect of reinforcing excessively high standards and maintaining perfectionistic thinking, therefore interfering with performance, getting in the way of having a balanced life, and increasing one's levels of depression and anxiety.

A Perfectionism Self-Assessment

In order to decide whether perfectionism is a problem for you, it is important to consider the impact of your high standards. In other words, are they helpful, or do they lead to problems? Here are six questions to ask yourself (Antony and Swinson 1998):

1. Are my standards higher than those of other people?

2. Am I able to meet my standards?

3. Are other people able to meet my standards?

4. Do my standards help me to achieve my goals or do they get in the way (for example, by making me overly disappointed or angry when my standards are not met, or by making me get less work done)?

5. What would be the costs of relaxing a particular standard or ignoring a rule that I have?

6. What would be the benefits of relaxing a particular standard or ignoring a rule that I have?

Answering these questions should help you to decide whether perfectionism is an issue for you. If you are unsure of the answer to one or more of these questions, consider asking for the opinion of someone who knows you well. Perfectionism may be a problem for you if your standards for yourself or others are higher than those of most people and are almost impossible to attain, and if those standards are interfering with your work, relationships, or enjoyment of life.

How to Overcome Perfectionism and Self-Criticism Once and for All

The strategies discussed in this section have been shown to be effective with a wide range of problems that are associated with perfectionism, including depression, anxiety, anger control problems, and eating disorders. Although there have been no studies examining the treatment of perfectionism specifically, the fact that these techniques are useful for dealing with related problems provides good reason to think that these strategies will help you to keep your standards and expectations in check, and ultimately help you keep your negative moods in check. A more detailed description of strategies for overcoming perfectionism is provided in the book *When Perfect Isn't Good Enough: Strategies for Coping with Perfectionism* (Antony and Swinson, 1998).

This section is divided into several parts. First, we discuss the importance of considering the costs and benefits of making particular changes. Next, we discuss methods of changing perfectionistic thoughts and behaviors. We conclude with a review of strategies for long-term change. After all, the goal of this book is to help you to prevent your depression from returning.

Assessing the Costs and Benefits of Making Changes

If perfectionism is a factor in your depression, chances are that the high standards you hold for yourself or others are long-standing and very ingrained. You may also be ambivalent about giving up these standards. Although you may acknowledge that perfectionism and self-criticism are a problem at times, it may be difficult for you to determine which beliefs are overly perfectionistic and which standards are appropriate. You may also be concerned that things will fall apart if you allow your standards to be lowered. After all, what if you were to mistakenly lower the wrong standards? You may be reluctant to lower your standards at all if you believe that your performance will suffer, or that there will be other negative consequences.

In most cases, there will be both costs and benefits to relaxing your standards. For example, if you spend an unusually large amount of time checking and rechecking your work to make sure it is perfect, a cost of spending less time is that you will likely make a few more mistakes. However, a benefit of spending less time checking is that you will potentially get more work done, or have time to do other things. In this example, the key is finding an equilibrium that allows you to balance work with other activities (such as hobbies or relationships), to be relatively productive, and to make relatively few mistakes.

Before deciding whether to change a particular standard, a first step is to evaluate the potential costs and benefits of making the change. In addition to listing the possible costs and benefits, it can be useful to consider the likelihood of those costs and benefits coming true. For example, a possible cost of doing a less-than-perfect job on a particular task at work is that you will be fired. However, although that outcome is possible, it is probably very unlikely. Ideally, you will want to make changes that lead to benefits, such as increased productivity or increased enjoyment in life, without having to suffer significant consequences.

Stop Thinking like a Perfectionist

As discussed in chapter 6, one of the most effective ways of improving your mood is to change the patterns of negative thinking that contribute to depressed mood. In this section, we review a number of techniques that can be useful for changing the self-critical thoughts that are characteristic of perfectionism. The goal of these strategies is to help you consider alternatives to the perfectionistic standards that are currently causing you difficulties. Also, if you need a refresher, we recommend that you take another look at chapter 6 for a more detailed description of how to change negative patterns of thinking.

Perspective-Taking

Perspective-taking involves trying to consider how someone who isn't a perfectionist might view a situation. This process involves asking yourself questions such as

- How might someone else (for example, a close friend) view this situation?

- Are there other ways to look at this?

- What might I tell a close friend who was having similar thoughts?

For example, if you are convinced that you are a bad parent because you find it difficult to work full-time, keep your home spotless, cook gourmet meals each evening, and still have the time and energy to spend hours each day playing with your children, you may want to ask yourself, "What might a close friend of mine tell me right now?" Chances are that a close friend would raise the question of whether your expectations are realistic. Is it even possible to meet all of those demands perfectly? Trying to take another person's perspective is often a useful way of shifting one's own perfectionistic thinking.

Compromising with Yourself and Others

Perfectionistic thinking is sometimes referred to as "all-or-nothing thinking." A characteristic of this style of thinking is a tendency to see things in terms of "black-and-white" or "right and wrong." An example of black-and-white thinking is the belief, "If I make a mistake during a presentation, I will make a fool of myself." In reality, there are a lot of different levels of performance between the extremes of a perfect performance and one in which the presenter comes across as completely incompetent. Although nobody wants to come across as completely incompetent, it is probably not essential for each and every presentation to be outstanding either. In fact, insisting that every presentation is perfect will be costly, in terms of the time necessary to achieve such a performance, as well as the emotional price that one pays if that expectation isn't met. The question to ask yourself here is, "How good is good enough?" The key is to recognize that nobody can be good at everything and to allow some areas of your functioning to be average or even below average. Remember, in any particular dimension (including intelligence, athletic ability, sense of humor, height, or attractiveness), half of us are below average!

Shifting Your Standards

The comedian George Carlin has a routine in which he criticizes people who constantly complain about "not having their needs met" in relationships. His response to them is, "Well, lose some of your needs!" One of the problems with perfectionism is the tendency for standards to be inflexible. This is fine if your standards are realistic and useful. If not, the inflexibility may be costing you. Sometimes, it is excessively important for people to come across to others as consistent. In fact, some individuals would rather people disagreed with them than have others view them as wishy-washy or indecisive. We see this in politics all the time. Politicians can pay a big price for having an unpopular policy or view. However, they also pay a big price for changing their policies or views, because their opponents are quick to criticize inconsistencies. In reality, there is nothing wrong with changing your standards if you discover that they were inappropriate in the first place, or that they are no longer appropriate. Changing one's views in light of new information is often a good thing, even if some people are quick to be critical. Remember that changing one's standards can have both costs and benefits; the goal should be to make changes in which the benefits outweigh the costs.

Looking at the Big Picture

Perfectionism is often associated with a tendency to get bogged down in the details of day-to-day life. For example, someone who is excessively self-critical may dwell for days on the fact that a friend didn't phone as promised on a particular day. One way of learning to live with not having your expectations met is to step back and ask the questions: Does this really matter? What are the consequences of this situation? Will this still matter tomorrow? How about next week? Next year? When you look at the larger picture instead of focusing on the immediate consequences of a negative event, the situation will suddenly seem more manageable.

Learning to Tolerate Uncertainty

A sense of vulnerability and helplessness is a consistent feature of depression. In the face of uncertainty, people often attempt to control aspects of their lives to minimize the uncertainty, and ultimately to decrease their sense of vulnerability. Perfectionistic behaviors are examples of ways in which people sometimes try to reduce their uncertainty about the world. For example, a person who is worried about what might come of his or her children if they don't get perfect grades in school may try to maximize the children's likelihood of doing well by insisting that all of their time be spent studying. Of course, controlling one's children in this way does not really increase the chances that they will be healthy and happy. In fact, it may not even lead to an improvement in their grades. Part of overcoming perfectionism, particularly when it is associated with a fear of uncertainty, is learning to identify those situations that can be controlled and those that cannot. Once that distinction has been made, it is much easier to divert one's efforts to improving those situations that can be improved, and learning to tolerate the uncertainty created by circumstances that cannot be predicted and controlled as easily.

One strategy for coping with uncertainty is to imagine a number of various outcomes and to consider ways in which you might cope with each if it were to occur. For example, if you are paralyzed by the thought of having to apply for a job because you may not get it, one strategy for dealing with your apprehension is to imagine that you don't get the job and how you might deal with that. Going through this exercise might help you to recognize that the situation would be manageable and that you have little to lose by trying. In fact, by avoiding applying for the job, you are guaranteed not to get it!

The Origins of Perfectionistic Thinking

What so many of these cognitive strategies for perfectionism have in common is that they ask you to think through what perfectionism really does for you. Perhaps equally important is to think about where your perfectionism comes from. When people start to really look at what the perfectionism does for them and how self-defeating it is, they often wonder, "How did I get this way?" There is not usually going to be a complete answer to that question. But like other beliefs and motivations we carry around, perfectionism probably stems from early experiences. For example, some people with perfectionism problems were encouraged by their parents to be perfect. In other cases, people observed others striving for perfection and took on the same challenges. The central point is that looking at the past may sometimes explain how you got to be this way.

Once you have such an explanation, it may help to unpack the ideas underlying perfectionism. In other words, there is no absolute need to be perfect, but there may be some good reasons why you became a perfectionist. Having some understanding about the origins of your perfectionism may become important as you try to change. People who struggle to become less perfectionistic often have to remind themselves how they got this way and why are they are working so hard to change. Making such profound changes in yourself is never easy. It may even seem unnatural at first to try to think differently, but remember to reflect on the long-term goal of warding off relapse. The next section, which focuses more on perfectionism behaviors, will also help you maintain your momentum as you change.

Stop Behaving like a Perfectionist

In the previous sections, we reviewed some strategies for changing perfectionistic and self-critical patterns of thinking. Just as important, however, are strategies for changing behaviors that may be designed either to ensure that you do things perfectly, or to help you avoid having to confront situations in which you might do a less-than-perfect job. Stopping your perfectionistic behaviors and learning that the consequences are minimal will help you to recognize that these behaviors were not necessary in the first place and that sometimes it is okay not to meet one's expectations. Below are some specific strategies for stopping perfectionistic behaviors.

Allow Yourself to Make Mistakes

One of the most powerful ways to challenge the belief that your performance has to be perfect is to conduct behavioral experiments in which you test out whether perfectionistic thoughts are reasonable. For example, if you are convinced that it would be terrible to make some sort of mistake (such as leaving out an ingredient when cooking dinner, putting a stamp on an envelope upside down, misspelling a word in a report, folding your shirt inside out, or arriving a few minutes late for an appointment), you could try making the mistake to see what happens. In all likelihood, the consequences will be minimal and you will learn that at least some of the effort you put into trying to be perfect is unnecessary.

Of course, you want to choose exercises that are relevant to your own perfectionistic thoughts. For example, if you are not overly concerned about getting places early, there is no reason for you to purposely practice being late for appointments. Also, you should use good judgment when designing behavioral experiments. Do not select experiments that have a very good chance of backfiring and therefore leading to serious negative consequences. For example, if your flight to Europe is leaving at 7:00 P.M., it would be a mistake to arrive at the airport at 7:00 P.M. just to see what happens!

Confront Anxiety-Provoking Situations

One of the most effective ways of reducing anxiety is through exposure to anxiety-provoking situations. Exposure is based on the premise that people can get used to almost any feared situation if they are given the opportunity. Essentially, by exposing yourself to the situations you fear, you will learn that your negative predictions do not come to pass, and eventually your anxiety will decrease. For example, if you feel overwhelmed with anxiety in social situations, such as job interviews, dating, and going to parties, repeated exposure to those situations will help to reduce your anxiety.

Initially, we recommend that you develop a list of situations that you fear, and then order them by rank from easiest (at the bottom) to most difficult (at the top). The next step is to begin practicing the various items on your hierarchical list. You don't need to start with the most frightening situation you can think of. Instead, start with an anxiety-provoking situation that is more manageable. Then work your way up to the more difficult situations on your list. For example, if dating makes you very anxious, you might start by practicing talking to potential dates over the telephone or via e-mail. Once that becomes easier, the next step might be to respond to personal ads in an effort to meet new people. Eventually, you might end up trying to date people from other areas of your life (for example, asking a person in your night school class out for dinner).

If you are afraid of being judged by others, exposures would involve purposely doing things to look foolish, or at least to draw attention to yourself. Examples might include purposely showing up for a haircut a few days before your scheduled appointment, answering a question incorrectly, or forgetting your ticket when you pick up your dry cleaning. With repeated practice, these situations will become less anxiety provoking. If the thought of having a job interview is overwhelming, we suggest applying for lots of jobs, even jobs you are not interested in getting. If you have less invested in the outcome of the interview, you will experience less pressure. With practice, your anxiety during the interviews will decrease, and eventually you will be less concerned about making a perfect impression on the interviewer.

To maximize the effectiveness of exposure, there are a few guidelines to keep in mind:

- Plan exposures in advance. Choose situations that are somewhat predictable and under your control, if possible.

- Expect to feel anxious and uncomfortable, especially early in the process.

- Stay in the situation until your fear has decreased. For example, don't leave a party early just because you are beginning to feel overwhelmed. The feeling will likely pass.

- Practice frequently (schedule exposures close together). For exposure to be most effective, practicing several times per week is recommended.

- Don't rely on subtle avoidance strategies and overprotective techniques. For example, don't spend an excessive amount of time preparing for the situation, having a few drinks to get relaxed, or distracting yourself to decrease your anxiety. These methods are all examples of avoidance and they may prevent you from learning that the situation is not as dangerous as it feels.

- Don't fight your anxiety. The more you try to fight the anxious feelings, the worse they are likely to get. Just let the feelings happen.

Set Priorities

Perfectionism is sometimes associated with a tendency to want to be perfect at everything. Of course, this is not possible. The most successful people in business, sports, or entertainment often pay a price in other areas of their lives. You can't be good at everything. To be a superstar at work, your family life may suffer. Parents who spend a lot of time with their children may find that they have to give up some of the hobbies and interests that they enjoyed in the past (such as traveling around the world). One strategy for dealing with perfectionism is to accept the notion that you cannot do it all; instead, you must set priorities. Are there particular areas in your life in which you can afford to do an average job? Are there areas where you can afford to be below average? Setting priorities means deciding in which areas you are going to focus your efforts and which areas you can afford to let slip.

Overcome Procrastination

People procrastinate for many different reasons, but sometimes a tendency to put off important tasks stems from a problem with perfectionism. This is particularly the case for individuals who procrastinate because they are fearful of not being able to complete the task well, they are afraid that completing the task will lead to negative consequences, or they get overwhelmed with the magnitude of the task and have no idea where to start. The best way to deal with procrastination is to break a large task down into many smaller tasks.

For example, the task of developing a résumé could be broken down into the following steps, each of which may not seem as overwhelming in isolation:

1. Search the Internet or skim a book from the library for some sample résumés.

2. Type the main headings for the résumé (name, address, education, job experience, interests, references, and so forth).

3. Brainstorm ideas for what might go under each heading.

4. Discuss your thoughts about the content with your spouse and a close friend.

5. Revise the content based on the advice you received.

6. Type up the résumé on your computer.

7. Have several people read the résumé and suggest changes.

8. Revise the résumé.

9. Purchase nice paper.

10. Print out your résumé.

Strategies for Long-Term Change

Although depression might come and go, perfectionism and self-critical thinking may be more resistant to change over time. Nevertheless, working on changing these patterns can pay off over the long term because they are thought to increase a person's risk of becoming depressed. In addition to the strategies discussed throughout this chapter, this section highlights some additional points to keep in mind in an effort to facilitate long-term change.

Set Specific Goals

Without defining the problem and setting goals, you can never know whether things have actually improved. Therefore, if you have decided to work on becoming less self-critical, less perfectionistic and more accepting, a first step is to set some goals. These goals should be realistic—beware, perfectionists are often tempted to set unrealistic goals, even for their therapy. In addition, your goals should be specific. For example, the goal of "being less critical of my spouse" may not be specific enough to allow you to change the appropriate behaviors. In contrast, the goal of "being more tolerant of my spouse's weight problem and not making negative comments about it" is more specific and would be helpful for developing strategies for meeting that goal. Another thing to keep in mind when setting goals is the period during which you want to achieve your goals. We recommend that you develop both short-term goals (for example, changes that you would like to make during the coming month) as well as longer term goals (for example, changes that you would like to make over the coming year, as well as over the next five years).

Practice, Practice, Practice

Simply reading this chapter on overcoming perfectionism will not help you to become less self-critical and perfectionistic, any more than reading a book on physical exercise will get you physically fit. Rather, it is essential that the strategies be used on a day-to-day basis. Of course, this suggestion applies to all of the strategies discussed in this book, not just those pertaining to perfectionism. We recommend that you practice the methods discussed in this book on a regular basis and that you occasionally reread relevant sections.

One way of increasing the likelihood that you will practice the strategies discussed in this chapter is to involve others in the practices. It may be helpful to ask your spouse to read this chapter and to participate in some of the exercises. For example, if you tend to be impatient with your spouse when he or she makes certain types of mistakes, you could ask your partner to purposely make those mistakes. As an illustration, if you insist that your laundry be folded a certain way, your partner could be encouraged to purposely fold it the wrong way. Eventually, your belief that there is only one way to fold laundry will begin to shift. Involving others in your practices increases the likelihood that you will continue to do the practices over the long term, just as having a friend join you to work out at the gym often makes it easier to follow through with regular exercise.

Anticipate and Overcome Obstacles

Overcoming perfectionism and self-critical thinking is unlikely to be easy. There may be hurdles and obstacles that get in the way. There may also be factors that reinforce your negative thinking. For example, if you work in an environment where your boss is extremely critical and perfectionistic, his or her behavior may feed into your belief that you need to be perfect. If this is the case, it will be important to find new ways of coping with the boss's behavior, find ways of changing your reactions to the boss's comments, or perhaps find a new job.

Summary

This chapter began with a description of perfectionism and self-criticism, providing definitions of each term and a discussion of how they relate to depression. This was followed by a review of how perfectionism is different from a more healthy tendency to set high standards for oneself. The cognitive and behavioral features of perfectionism were described, and several questions were provided to help you to determine whether perfectionism is a problem for you. Finally, the remainder of the chapter discussed specific techniques that can be used to reduce perfectionism, including changing perfectionistic patterns of thinking, stopping perfectionistic behaviors, and planning for healthy long-term change.

Summary Exercise

Record what you believe is the bottom line from this chapter, then record what practices or exercises you would adopt as part of your wellness plan.

Chapter 11, You Don't Need to Be Perfect: Changing Perfectionism and Self-Criticism, examines the role of perfectionism in vulnerability to depression and addresses how to become less perfectionistic. My bottom line in this chapter is:

_____

_____

The practices, exercises, or actions I will take from this chapter are:

_____

_____

Chapter 12

Dealing with Dependency

In chapter 11 you learned about self-critical perfectionism, how perfectionism can lead to depression and how you can change this core motivation. A second type of core motivation that often drives depression is called dependency. The idea that being overly dependent on others can result in depression has been around for a very long time. In fact, one of the reasons we included it in this book is because this idea has evolved from many different approaches and theories of depression, over a number of decades, and has been written about by many prominent depression researchers (Beck 1983; Blatt 1974; Blatt and Zuroff 1992). We will start by defining dependency and then go on to describe how it impacts, or even triggers, episodes of depression. Then we will help you to assess whether dependency is a problem for you. In the final section, we help you to make a plan for changing your level of dependency and thereby reduce your risk of relapse.

Defining Dependency

A useful thing about a word like "dependency" is that it is familiar; most people have some understanding of the word and what it means. However, we are going to use the term in a very specific way, based on research and theory that have defined the concept of dependency within the context of depression. In various decades, this concept of dependency has been called by different names. Some depression researchers call it *sociotropy* (Beck 1983), and some call it *interpersonal relatedness* (Blatt and Zuroff 1992). In general, however, there is reason to believe that people are talking about the same concept from different perspectives (Alden and Bieling 1996), so we will stick to the simple term *dependency*.

First off, dependency does have to do with relationships; that is, dependency means that one is in need of, or is relying too much on, other people. Even though dependency occurs in the context of a relationship with another person, we see dependency as something that is internal. We believe that dependency is a core, personal motivation. We should also point out that many people think of dependency as something that develops in certain relationships, and this may be true to some extent. It certainly is true that, as a result of depression, interpersonal relationships can be altered, even damaged, and depression does seem to lead to greater neediness. We talk about all of this in chapter 13, where we address the issue of relationships in relapse prevention. But levels of dependency seem to be fairly constant over time; that is, level of dependency does not change with every relationship, but tends to exist at a similar level within a specific person over long periods of time (Blatt and Zuroff 1992). Chances are if someone is dependent in one intimate relationship, they are likely to be dependent in another intimate relationship. Dependency appears to be a fairly basic part of our internal makeup or personality, and thus it is reasonable to call it a core motivation.

What does it mean to be too dependent? It certainly is true that some amount of interdependence with people is normal. This is what allows us to form attachments and long-term relationships; we all need others in our lives and we all benefit from good relationships. How then do we draw a line and say that some amount of dependency is problematic, or say that one person is too dependent on others? There are several ways to answer this question, but all of them come down to the idea that too much dependency is actually counterproductive, that essentially dependency can interfere with one's sense of well-being, and can actually disrupt rather than enhance relationships.

Let's start with the question, "Why does too much dependency develop?" It seems that excess dependency emerges in response to a very basic sense of unlovability; that is, a sense that a person is flawed in some way, and perhaps not deserving of love, affection, or attention. Most people who are simply interdependent do not have this sense of unlovability; it is something that is unique to being overly dependent and appears to be a very critical and negative belief about the self. According to therapists who work with such beliefs, it is a common theme in depression (Beck 1983). This fundamental sense of unlovability is such a strong motivator that a person is likely to do many things to try to ward off the belief or prevent it from coming true. In other words, someone who deep down sees themselves as unlovable may be motivated to do a number of things to try to prove just the opposite, that they are lovable. Dependency behaviors are the result of these attempts to prove that one is lovable. But as you will see, behaviors that are designed to prove our lovability have a tendency to do just the opposite. Dependency behaviors have the counterintuitive effect of making relationships more and more problematic.

Dependency shows itself in many interpersonal behaviors, all of which go back to the idea that fundamentally the dependent person feels unworthy of love. For one, dependent people are often preoccupied with what others, especially intimate partners, family, and friends, think of them. Any sign that things are not perfect in the relationship has the potential to be seen as a sign of impending rejection, the worst fear of the dependent person. As a result, dependent people are usually hypervigilant or on guard for real or imagined signs of rejection. Therefore, they may exaggerate the importance of keeping communication lines open and of ensuring that someone loves them and cares for them as much as they love and care for the other.

Dependent people tend to use various strategies that they think will help them get along with others and keep others around (Beck 1983; Bieling and Alden 2001). Unfortunately, many of these strategies have the potential to backfire. Dependent people often try their best to please other people, perhaps by being overly kind, by giving in to others' wishes, by not standing up for themselves, or by making themselves constantly available. Dependent people are likely to see these kinds of behaviors as positive and important. They view their own behavior as correct and seem to believe that pleasing others, being passive, and going along with others is the best way to make people like them. But sadly, their approach is often too extreme. Indeed, research has shown that seeking reassurance and using other dependency strategies are not terribly attractive to other people (Joiner and Coyne 1999). Dependent people actually increase the odds of rejection by others when they engage in behavior that, on its face, is designed for just the opposite purpose. Exactly why this should be is unclear, but social psychologists believe that most people show an affinity towards others who display many capabilities, have a strong sense of themselves, and who pull their weight in social interactions. Passivity, eagerness to please, and going along to get along communicate neediness that seems to be unappealing to others. Also, perhaps the biggest problem with dependent behavior is that it never can really achieve its goal. Remember that dependent behavior has the supposed goal of maintaining love and care from other people. However, the underlying problem is that, inside, the dependent person does not feel lovable. No relationship, no matter how wonderful, can really repair that internal sense of unlovability. To reduce dependency, the person needs to work on him- or herself to develop a sense of being lovable. We describe some methods for starting this process later in the chapter.

What happens when dependent people experience problems in their relationships? As you'll see below, there are good reasons to believe that relationship problems in dependent people trigger episodes of depression. In any case, the dependent person who is cut off from a relationship is likely to be highly motivated to either reestablish a dependent relationship or to become hopeless about the situation and to withdraw into a state in which they feel abandoned and alone. When dependent people are motivated to look for an alternative source of love, comfort, and affection, they may not be making the best choices for themselves and may find themselves in relationships out of need rather than mutual respect, attraction, and affection. Similarly, some dependent people withdraw entirely and imagine that they will never be able to find a satisfying relationship. In either case, risk of emotional upset and depression is increased.

To sum up, we have defined dependency as related to a deep sense of unlovability and have tried to describe the sorts of behaviors a dependent person engages in. The central point is that dependency is, in the end, self-defeating and likely to put a person at risk for depression. Next we describe the evidence that links dependency and depression.

Dependency and Depression

As we said earlier, the idea that dependency is associated with depression has been around for decades, and a considerable amount of research has been done on this topic. We will highlight two areas that are important for the prevention of relapse and recurrence in depression. First, it seems that, overall, dependent people respond best to group (rather than individual) cognitive therapy, and that dependent people have some unique types of depression symptoms (Clark, Beck, and Alford 1999). This may suggest that dependent depression is caused by a different kind of mechanism, and that it may be important to match the treatment approach to the person rather than applying the same treatment for everyone. Second, it also seems that people with a dependent core motivation are much more vulnerable to depression when they have had an interpersonal setback (such as a relationship breakup) as opposed to any other kind of stressor (Clark, Beck, and Alford 1999). Researchers have done many studies in which they follow both dependent and nondependent people, and then determine what kinds of stresses were associated with a new episode of depression or symptom worsening. Most of these studies find that dependency and relationship troubles interact in a way that increases a person's risk for experiencing depression. This finding is important in regard to relapse because it points to a very specific relationship between the kind of person you are and the kind of life event that might result in a new episode of depression. Reducing these negative relationship events or levels of dependency can perhaps reduce the risk of relapse.

The findings about depression and dependency are really not surprising when we look back at the definition of, and the behaviors associated with, dependency. Breakups and disruptions in relationships are part of everyone's life, and certainly there are few among us who haven't suffered from a broken heart. But for a dependent person, not only is his or her behavior likely to undermine relationships, but the ending of a relationship can seem catastrophic. When a relationship ends, the dependent person is confronted with their unlovability belief and this can turn a time of difficult emotions into a full-blown episode of depression. Finally, because dependency focuses people on relationships, dependent people will benefit more from a form of therapy that emphasizes interpersonal relationships, or in which their relationship is part of the process of treatment. In fact, there is some evidence that treatment with certain types of psychotherapy reduces levels of dependency (Bieling, Beck, and Brown 2002).

The Implications for Relapse Prevention

What are the implications for you and your desire to prevent a relapse of depression? First, it is important to determine whether you have a problematic level of dependency. To reiterate, not all people who are depressed are dependent, just as not all people who are depressed are perfectionists, something you learned in chapter 11. In fact, it is not easy to know exactly what proportion of people who suffer from depression have a problematic level of dependency, but we provide some guidelines to help you identify whether dependency is an important issue for you.

Second, the link between dependency and onset of depression is important enough that you may want to address your level of dependency. We suggest that there are two ways to really work on dependency. The first way is to pay attention to your dependency behaviors. You'll need to ask yourself whether your dependency behaviors set you up for depression. Do your dependency behaviors undermine your relationships? The second approach is to reduce your level of dependency by looking at its underlying cause, that sense of unlovability. By acknowledging a sense of unlovability and identifying ways in which you are lovable, you will eliminate this motivator for dependency.

Examining Your Level of Dependency

There is no simple or comprehensive test for dependency, though there are several research scales that are used in studies to assess levels of dependency across groups of individuals. Unfortunately, these scales cannot be used to accurately say whether a particular person is dependent or another person is not. So, although they are very useful in sizable studies, these scales are not much help for measuring dependency in any one individual. Nonetheless, by looking at these measures of dependency and the research on dependency and depression, we can provide some guidelines to help you start to answer the question of whether dependency is a problem for you. Here are several questions that you can ask yourself.

Question 1: Can you recall an episode of depression that may have been triggered by the ending of a relationship or a disruption in a relationship? It is not always easy for people to recall or completely establish the trigger for an episode of depression. However, sometimes a trigger can be very clear and hard to ignore. For an individual who is overly dependent, triggers for depression may include disruptions in intimate relationships, as well as problems in an important friendship or in family relationships. It may also be that a relationship didn't break up per se, but rather that the person moved away, or the relationship was cut off in some other way.

Question 2: Are phases of depression, or the times immediately before you become depressed, marked by thoughts and feelings about rejection, loneliness, or loss? This question is related to question 1, but it is more focused on the kinds of thoughts and feelings you may have had. As you may recall from chapter 6 on thinking and depression, the kinds of thoughts one has when depressed tell something about the individual's beliefs and core motivations. If you have thoughts such as "No one will ever care about me" or "I'll be alone forever," it is possible that dependency is an issue for you.

Question 3: Are you the kind of person who, above all else, tries to please other people? Do you have rules about how you must behave to get along with others? People with a dependency problem often have beliefs about what they must do in relationships. They often feel that the most important thing they need to do is to please other people. Other beliefs may be along the lines of "If I do everything right, people will like me" or "My needs come last, other people are the priority." These beliefs tend to be rigid and hard to live up to, and they are very similar to the problematic rules we discussed in chapter 6. Sometimes these beliefs are summarized in the phrase "the disease to please," which is a fairly good description of what these beliefs do. Of course, we have already addressed how these beliefs are actually quite problematic; they do not allow people to get what they want for themselves, and trying to please others has very little to do with whether others actually do like us or are pleased with us.

Question 4: Do you feel that you need to be connected to people constantly? To answer this question, you may want to think about your behavior—what you actually do in relationships every day. Important questions to ask yourself include

- Do you try to spend as much time as possible with others?

- Are you uncomfortable being alone?

- Do you find yourself often reaching out to others by talking to them in person or on the phone?

- Does it seem like you just have to talk to someone most of the time?

- Do you take great comfort from getting reassurance from others, but find that this wears off and you need to seek reassurance again from that same person or someone else?

Of course, it is helpful to keep in mind that we all rely on relationships for support, nurturance, and a sense of connection. The more critical question is whether you believe that you are *overly* reliant on other people. One way to look at this is to ask yourself whether you wish you could be more independent. Do you wish you could do things alone, like go to a movie, eat in a restaurant, or travel? If doing things alone makes you very uncomfortable, you may have a problem with dependency.

Question 5: Can you only make decisions with input from other people? Here too, you may want to think about your usual patterns of behavior. Do you struggle to make decisions, even in relatively minor everyday matters like what errands you need to do first, how you want to spend your day, what groceries to buy, or what route to drive on a routine trip? Dependent people seem to like others to make decisions for them, often because they feel incapable themselves or because they believe that other people will get mad if they choose something wrong. Some dependent people end up reporting that they have no preferences; that is, they don't care what movie they go to see, what restaurant they eat in, or how they spend their time. Dependent people subjugate or put down their own needs relative to the needs of others. It is not necessarily the case that they don't have a preference, but rather that they would feel very uncomfortable saying what their preference is in case someone disagrees.

Question 6: Are you willing to give up a lot to get along with others? People with dependency needs will try very hard to keep lines of communication open and to have others think well of them. This sometimes means that a dependent person is willing to do or say things that deep down he or she would prefer not to do or say. The only reason he or she does or says these things is to keep the other person happy. Dependent people may even volunteer for unpleasant tasks just so that others will think well of them. Above all, dependent people do not like to rock the boat and may be willing to endure a lot of personal hardship to keep things calm in relationships. Getting into a disagreement is often the worst-case scenario for a dependent person. Rather than seeing a disagreement as a legitimate difference of opinion, as a chance to get more of what he or she wants, or as an opportunity to have a meaningful dialogue, the dependent person sees a disagreement as a very threatening sign that the relationship is going to end. The dependent person may be willing to give up a lot to avoid arguing, but often his or her resentment can build to the point where there is a very emotional conflict. This is unfortunate since small disagreements are part of relationships and probably best handled quickly so that both parties get more of what they want and end up happier in the long run.

Summing Up Your Level of Dependency

Looking at your answers to these six questions should be useful in determining whether dependency is a problem for you, especially if you found yourself answering yes to all six questions. We suggest that even if you answered three of these questions yes, especially the first two about triggers for depression, dependency is something you should consider working on. If you answered all of the questions no or only answered yes on one question, you may not have any problems with dependency. However, there may still be some things in this chapter that you will find useful. Remember that dependency is probably unrelated to age, gender, or the stage of life you are in. People who are in a committed relationship may struggle with dependency, but so might an unattached person. We should also point out that just because you are dependent does not mean that you will constantly be depressed or struggle in relationships. It is true that dependency often interferes with relationships. Dependent people are often disappointed by others because they place such a high value on their relationships and other people may not live up to their wishes. And yet, when dependent people are in a strong relationship and have many friends and good ties with family, they may feel quite well and not be depressed. However, they will be vulnerable should something go wrong in a relationship, whether by their own doing or through other circumstances. Because life offers no guarantees that relationships will always run smoothly, it makes sense to be ready to cope with disruptions in a relationship and to try to ensure that such situations do not trigger an episode of clinical depression.

If you identified dependency as an issue for you, you are already far ahead of the game. After all, you need to be able to put your finger on the source of the problem before it can be fixed. Many people never discover what core motivation makes them vulnerable to depression, which in turn leaves them unable to make themselves less vulnerable. Once dependency is identified and you have been able to see how the descriptions we have provided might fit you, it will become possible to improve the situation.

Reducing Dependency

Earlier in this chapter we wrote that there were two general ways to reduce dependency—working on reducing dependent behavior and changing the core motivation by working on the sense of unlovability that motivates dependency. The reality is that to get true change, you probably will need to work on both of these things. It is also important to work on this in stages, beginning with taking a look at why you became dependent in the first place. Understanding this may not in itself change the behaviors that are associated with dependency. However, by seeking to understand the question of why, without losing sight of the fact that behavior also needs to be changed, you will have the best possible chance of protecting yourself from patterns of dependency.

How Did I Get This Way?

Where does dependency and a sense of unlovability come from? Most theories of dependency and depression suggest that this process begins when we are very young. Most authorities on child development and most depression researchers assume not only that children are born with different kinds of temperaments, but also that children generally share very similar needs—to be cared for, both emotionally and physically, and to have at least one reliable, responsive caregiver. However, if these basic needs are frustrated or disappointed in some way, dependency can be fostered. For example, a child may experience the loss of a caregiver through illness, death, or divorce. Parents may be inconsistent in the level of attention they give, and the child's need to be loved may or may not be met. In fact, there is fairly strong literature suggesting that people who are prone to depression tend to have grown up in homes where there was a lack of affection and perhaps too much heavy-handed parental control of children (Bieling and Kuyken 2003). In these kinds of circumstances it makes sense that some children would question whether they are lovable. This may even happen before a child can really express that sentiment in words. A child may develop strategies to ensure getting the attention he or she needs. Those strategies are very similar to dependency behaviors that sometimes carry through to adulthood. If a child cannot be sure he or she will get the love and attention of a caregiver, the child may doubt his or her lovability and develop dependency behaviors, such as trying to please their parents, not stating their wishes for fear that this will lead to rejection, or asking for reassurance from parents.

What is most important here is that the core motivations we have make sense when we consider the context in which they were formed. Dennis Greenberger and Christine Padesky make a similar point in their excellent book *Mind over Mood,* when they write, "Because . . . beliefs help us to make sense of our world at such an early age, it may never occur to us to evaluate whether they are the most useful ways of understanding our adult experiences" (Greenberger and Padesky 1995, 130–131). Part of growing up is figuring out the way the world works—the rules that we need to live by—even when we are young children. And while we are young, our parents and environment are really all we know. We have little choice but to adopt these rules in order to get along because children have only a limited ability to critically appraise what they are learning. But those rules we learn as kids may not make sense in an adult world; they may not even be true. Fear rules are a good example. A child may be told by a parent that snakes are poisonous and come to fear, avoid, and even hate snakes because of this belief. The parents of the child might reward the child for staying away from snakes or expressing their fear of snakes. But of course most snakes are not poisonous and have little interest in humans. The belief that snakes are poisonous has a lot of logical holes and is not a very adaptive rule for being in a natural setting that you may be sharing with a harmless garter snake. The bottom line is that some of our beliefs may be useful tools for having our needs met as a child, but they turn out to be a poor fit with adult realities or they do not help us live a happy and productive life.

When it comes to understanding dependency, it is important for you to determine where your sense of unlovability comes from. This will require giving some thought to your experiences growing up, and determining if and when some of your needs were frustrated or unmet. Often when people look at these issues in therapy, they search for something very traumatic and memorable, such as abuse of some kind or long separations from caregivers. Such things may indeed be very important, but for many people their experiences are somewhat more subtle and not as clearly defined. If a parent or both parents are consistently not meeting a child's needs in some way, the impact may be just as relevant, or perhaps even more relevant, than a single episode of abuse or separation from a caregiver. In any case, what is most important is to try to understand the situation that led up to feeling unlovable as a child or adolescent. This can be started by simply writing down some of your recollections, especially very emotional memories from childhood. You can also try to write down some impressions of your parents' personalities, not so much as they were later in life, but how you remember them from your childhood. The bottom line is that looking at why you first felt unlovable as a child is a key step toward changing.

As people engage in this process of looking at where core motivations come from, something very important happens; the person begins to view his or her own experiences in a way that is more objective than usual. In a way, the person begins to develop empathy and understanding toward him- or herself. By looking at how you acquired a sense of unlovability, you are also saying that what happened to you was not inevitable, that there is nothing inherently flawed about you, and that what happened is quite understandable given the environment you grew up in. Remember that when we are children, we are not able to critically examine our experiences, or to compare our experiences with others in a meaningful way. Prior to the age of twelve or thirteen, we unquestioningly accept our home, our parents, our friends, and the school we attend because we have no capacity yet to look beyond our immediate experiences. It is not until we reach our teenage years that we start to critically examine our own experiences and start to make up our own minds on things. That is why teenagers often go through a stage in which they are oppositional and rebellious; they are beginning to understand that there are lots of different ways of being and behaving.

While looking back on your early childhood, you may conclude that some of the things that happened to you were unfair, harsh, or very sad; this is a sign that you are experiencing empathy and understanding for yourself. As an adult, you are able to acknowledge that what happened to you when you were young was not justified by your actions, and that it was unfair or even wrong. Once you get to this point, it becomes easier to see that you deserve something different than what you received. Of course, it is also true that we cannot relive the past, and there is probably no way to completely make up for what happened. That is the bad news. The good news is that, with some careful thought and planning, you can take steps to make up for what happened in a way that is healthy and that will make your dependency less of a problem.

Before we go on, we should say a word about anger and blame, especially blaming of caregivers. This is a fairly common response when people discover how their needs as a child were not met by their parents. However, anger and blame are not very productive emotions. Getting angry might be useful if there was something your parents could do now to help, but chances are that your parents can do very little. At most they might acknowledge their imperfections and mistakes, and apologize. Parents who make mistakes with their children often had no ill will at the time, and probably did not have a sense that what they were doing was problematic or wrong. In fact, parental behaviors that are wrong for one child may be completely appropriate for another child because different children have different needs.

Most parents do what they do with children because they think it is good for the children. For example, overly strict parents might say that they are doing their child a favor by teaching him or her how hard the world can be. Similarly, parents who are overly protecting (such as telling a child that snakes are poisonous) and do not allow their child much freedom to explore and test their limits might say their goal is to protect the child from an unsafe world. Few parents set out with the agenda of making their child miserable, and problematic beliefs are usually unintended consequences. This is not to say that parents bear no responsibility for your core motivations, but rather that they likely did not see there was harm in what they were trying to do.

To sum all this up, it is important to try to understand where your dependency and sense of unlovability come from. The purpose of this exploration is not to find some critical event and try to undo the past; rather, the aim is self-understanding, empathy for yourself as a child, and even sympathy for what you went through. Sometimes people see this as feeling sorry for yourself, a notion that holds a fairly bad reputation in our culture. It is true that if all you do is feel sorry for yourself, you may not get very far in changing your thoughts and behaviors, or in preventing depression. But acknowledging that what happened to you was sad, wrong, unfortunate, or unnecessary is important. Many people who struggle with depression do not allow themselves to have any sympathy for themselves; however, when it comes time to explore their core motivations in therapy, they often get quite emotional and sad. This is probably a necessary step. Exploring the origins of your dependency and perceived unlovability will set the stage for answering the question, "Now what?"

At the end of this process of self-understanding, you should try to write out, in as simple a form as possible, what conclusions you have drawn about yourself and your level of lovability, based upon your early childhood experiences. This will represent your core motivation in the area of dependency, and it could be something as simple as "I am unlovable" or "No one loves me." Writing this out may make you feel very sad, and confronting these deeply held beliefs is difficult for most people. However, in order to change or fix something, you must first understand the problem. Once you know what your core motivation is, you will be able to track how it affects other beliefs about yourself and your relationships, as well as your behavior. The next section deals with what you can do about dependency and your maladaptive personal core motivations, with the ultimate goal of preventing relapse and recurrence of depression.

Understanding is a prerequisite for change, especially the kinds of changes we want to make to core motivations. We mention this again only to make sure that you are not tempted to take a shortcut straight to the next section on change and skip the above section on self-understanding. If you read this section and try to follow the steps without reading and working through the earlier section on understanding where your dependency comes from, your experience may be like traveling without a road map.

Use Your New Understanding to Work on an Alternative Core Motivation

The first step to reverse dependency is to gather together what you know about your sense of unlovability and to answer this question: Considering all of the information from your past, and the problematic core motivation you have identified, what belief about yourself is going to be more functional, positive, and realistic? For example, if you believe that you cannot make decisions for yourself and you recognize that this passivity is a result of early learning, you may decide that it makes more sense to try to believe something like "I can make decisions for myself." This belief is more functional in the long run and is probably quite realistic for most people. Having said that, trying to have a new belief or core motivation is not something that happens quickly or suddenly. Let us take another example: A person who feels unlovable because of a history of childhood neglect may choose to try out a new belief such as "I am as lovable as anyone else." Again, the person will not immediately believe this new core motivation or wish to act accordingly. At first, keeping the new belief in mind may take quite a bit of effort. That old belief concerning unlovability may want to rear its head, especially when something happens that is not completely positive (such as a quarrel with a loved one). At the same time, if you do not provide yourself, on paper, with an alternative core motivation, it will be hard for you to know what to think or what to aim for as a goal. To sum up, try to write down a set of new core motivations that you think are more in keeping with reality and less biased by past events, and that you think will be more functional for you.

When people try this for the first time, they often have a very strong reaction that goes something like "My head says one thing, my heart says another" or "I see it but I don't believe it." This is completely normal. Remember, for years you have seen things a certain way, and now you are proposing to see them in another way. This new way of thinking will feel quite alien. It is a bit like people must have felt hundreds of years ago when they were told the Earth was round and not flat as they had been taught all their lives. At first, people would have had a reaction pretty close to shock. Remember, the idea that the Earth was round was considered scandalous in the Middle Ages. How could everyone have been so wrong about something as basic as the shape of the world? How come the world looks so flat to us? If it is round, why do we not fall or roll off? There are answers to these questions of course. The very fact that we can see a horizon that moves forward as we move forward tells us that the Earth is curving down and away from our view. This is simple proof that the Earth is round, and you don't really need to sail around the globe to prove it.

Saying that you are lovable, that you can make decisions for yourself, or that spending time with other people is a choice rather than a need may feel just like saying the world is round when you thought it was flat. It will seem strange at first, but the value of these new motivations will be proven in time. Remember too that these new core motivations are a more functional alternative, and that they will have many advantages over your previous, negative beliefs.

To help with the process of creating and nurturing new core motivations we have created a worksheet. Worksheet 12.1 is a sample Dependency Core Motivation Worksheet completed by Allison, a thirty-four-year-old woman who identified dependency as a major factor in her depressions, especially in the context of intimate relationships. Worksheet 12.2 is a blank Dependency Core Motivation Worksheet. In step 1 the idea is to record what you have discovered in the section "How Did I Get This Way?" and to express what your problematic core motivation is in a simple phrase. In the example, Allison has recorded the core motivation as the belief that "No one will ever love me as I much as I need to be loved." In her case, this was based on her relationships with her parents. Her father had developed a rare medical illness when she was eight years old and had required constant care from Allison's mother. Her father's illness changed everything for Allison, not only because her father was often incapacitated and too sick to interact with the children, but also because Allison's mother had to take care of her ill husband and there-fore was also often unavailable to the children.

Step 2 simply asks you to make sure that what you have written makes sense to you, just as Allison's sense of unlovability made sense to her in light of what happened. This is not, of course, to say that the old core motivation is correct in an absolute sense, but rather that you can understand where this negative set of motivations originated.

Step 3 asks you to list the negative consequences of this motivation. Remember, the ultimate goal here is to protect you from relapse, so it is particularly important to focus on how a core motivation makes you vulnerable to negative feelings or sets the stage to create problems for you. In step 3 you might consider how your own behavior could result from that negative core motivation. Consider especially whether that behavior, in the long run, is helpful or hurtful for you. For example, do you always act in your own best interests when you see yourself as unlovable?

On the sample worksheet, Allison identified that her core motivation not only makes her reluctant to get involved with people sometimes, but also can lead her to be overly involved and needy. In either scenario, those behaviors are likely to lead to problems for Allison because they will negatively impact any relationship she has. In the first case, being standoffish may result in the insufficient building of necessary intimacy for Allison; alternatively, being overly involved might cause the other person to want to put some necessary distance back into the relationship. In either case, the behavior is self-defeating; not only does it undermine good relationships, it may also confirm her fears of being unlovable. As we mentioned earlier, dependency does undermine relationships, not because the dependent person is flawed, but because their relationship strategies are not as helpful as they could be.

In step 4, you are asked to create an alternative core motivation that should be based on reading this chapter. Remember, the critical elements in doing this are self-understanding and using a more rational approach to come up with a more helpful belief that is a closer fit to reality. Sometimes, the adaptive core motivation can simply be the opposite of the negative core motivation. For example, if the negative core motivation is "I am unlovable," the adaptive core motivation might be "I am lovable." This strategy of using the opposite belief might not always seem right to you, so feel free to use your own words. In the example, for step 4 Allison has written, "Everyone is lovable, so that includes me! When relationships don't work out, there are many reasons. It's not because I have a fatal flaw. Finding a match is what's important." Notice how this is a much more elaborated idea than "I am unlovable," which is quite harsh and not very subtle. The alternative has nuances, including the idea that all people are lovable, and that relationships involve two people who need to get along, not one person who is lovable and one who isn't!

In step 5, you are asked to do a quick check on your alternative thought to make sure that it is going to have positive consequences for you. You are also asked whether you would recommend that other people have this belief about themselves. If you cannot come up with advantages for the new core motivation over the old one, or you would be reluctant to recommend this motivation to people you love, you probably have not identified a healthy or adaptive alternative. Step 6 will tell you, in the absence of identifying advantages to the adaptive belief, to return to step 4 and come up with another alternative.

Finally, step 7 asks you for a kind of bottom line—a single sentence or catchy phrase to remind you what the new adaptive motivation is. This final phrase is what you are aiming to cultivate. In the example, Allison's final alternative belief is "I am lovable, no matter what happens." This phrase incorporates the idea of lovability, and the idea that this lovability exists even when things are not going well.

As a final note, it is important to remember that having an alternative belief is not a "cure" for dependency. Like self-understanding, having an alternative is a necessary component of healthy change. The alternative core motivation is the goal but the goal is not an end in and of itself.

Try to think of this alternative core motivation like it is another kind of goal. For example, a fitness goal might be that you would like to be able to jog six miles without stopping. This is not something you can just do right away, even though it's a wonderful goal to have. This goal must be combined with some kind of regimen for getting there, like starting off jogging for ten minutes and jogging an additional five minutes every few days. If you followed this plan, you would soon be a jogger, you would be fit, and you would probably reach your goal of jogging six miles. This would occur because you had a well-thought-out goal that was combined with behavior; neither of these things alone would work as well as the combination. By completing the worksheet, you now have a goal, or an alternative core motivation. Next, we need to make a plan of behaviors to take the final step in ridding yourself of excessive dependency.

Worksheet 12.1
Sample Dependency Core Motivation Worksheet

Step 1: Considering my past, both while growing up and during recent times when I have felt vulnerable, one of my core motivations related to unlovability or dependency that puts me at risk for depression is:

No one will ever love me as I much as I need to be loved.

Step 2: Do I have a good understanding of where this negative core motivation originated and can I acknowledge its unfairness or bias?

   (YES) or NO

   If YES, proceed to step 3. If NO, spend more time on trying to understand the belief, or reread the section "How Did I Get This Way?"

Step 3: What are the consequences of this negative core motivation? How does it lead me to be vulnerable? What disadvantages does the core motivation have?

It makes me too cautious, and sometimes leads me to be overly needy in relation-

ships. I'm not content, and I'm always on the lookout for something to go wrong.

Step 4: An alternative core motivation that is more realistic, that could be more functional, and that takes into account what I have control over in my life now is:

Everyone is lovable, so that includes me! When relationships don't work out, there are

many reasons. It's not because I have a fatal flaw. Finding a match is what's important.

Step 5: Does this alternative core motivation have any advantages, especially if I believed it completely? Would I encourage other people I know or love to have this perspective, and why?

This motivation does have advantages. I would be more hopeful when

relationships don't work out. I could see my relationships in a more realistic way,

perhaps be more independent.

Step 6: Do I have sufficient information about the advantages of this alternative core motivation to say that it would be more functional or advantageous?

(YES) or NO

If YES, proceed to step 7. If NO, create another alternative core motivation.

Step 7: Based on all of these steps, the new core motivation that I will try to work with is:

I am lovable, no matter what happens.

Worksheet 12.2
Dependency Core Motivation Worksheet

Step 1: Considering my past, both while growing up and during recent times when I have felt vulnerable, one of my core motivations related to unlovability or dependency that puts me at risk for depression is:

_____

_____

Step 2: Do I have a good understanding of where this negative core motivation originated and can I acknowledge its unfairness or bias?

YES or NO

If YES, proceed to step 3. If NO, spend more time on trying to understand the belief, or reread the section "How Did I Get This Way?"

Step 3: What are the consequences of this negative core motivation? How does it lead me to be vulnerable? What disadvantages does the core motivation have?

_____

_____

Step 4: An alternative core motivation that is more realistic, that could be more functional, and that takes into account what I have control over in my life now is:

_____

_____

Step 5: Does this alternative core motivation have any advantages, especially if I believed it completely? Would I encourage other people I know or love to have this perspective, and why?

_____

_____

Step 6: Do I have sufficient information about the advantages of this alternative core motivation to say that it would be more functional or advantageous?

YES or NO

If YES, proceed to step 7. If NO, create another alternative core motivation.

Step 7: Based on all of these steps, the new core motivation that I will try to work with is:

_____

Alternatives to Dependency Behaviors

There is a saying that old habits die hard, and this idea is something we have to keep in mind during this section. It is all well and good to have a new, alternative core motivation that is balanced and healthy. The trouble is, unless you are paying close attention, it will be easy to slip back into old, self-defeating behaviors. This is because, to some extent, the old and problematic core motivation is still around somewhere. It will not go away quickly or quietly. Especially when something goes wrong, you need to be on alert for that old core motivation to rear its head in the way you feel and the way you think about yourself. Part of helping yourself with this will be using the thinking strategies we described in chapter 6 and the mindfulness strategies we described in chapter 8. These techniques can help you to detect a change in your thinking and emotions when things are not going well. Another reason dependency behaviors are hard to change is because they are just like any other habit. They are a bit like tire tracks or well-worn grooves that are easy to follow almost automatically. Dependency behaviors may also simply feel comfortable because they are so familiar, and they may be the way you have always done things in relationships.

As a result of these factors, the most important thing you can do as you try to reduce dependency behaviors is this: pay attention to your own behavior in relationships and stop to ask yourself questions about your real motivations, especially when things are not going as well as they could or your mood is lower than normal. Common dependency behaviors include

- seeking reassurance from another person that they still care for you

- needing to check to make sure someone is available at all times

- going out of your way to make everyone around you pleased with you

- being passive so as to not rock the boat in a relationship

- not making decisions for yourself or never doing things alone

- not standing up for yourself in order to avoid conflict

- being overly sensitive to how others might be perceiving you

These behaviors are all designed to meet your own need to feel loved, protected, and cared for. By paying attention to and carefully evaluating the reasons why you are engaged in some of these behaviors you will catch yourself in many more dependency behaviors. You also need to be sensitive to the sorts of situations in which dependency behaviors are most common for you. These sorts of situations are difficult to predict with complete confidence, considering how complex relationships are and how different people can be from one another. At the level of the individual, however, there may be repeated scenarios that bring out dependency behaviors in you. Keep in mind that such behaviors are likely to happen when

- there is some doubt in your mind about the stability of an intimate or close relationship

- there has been some conflict between you and another person

- your mood is lower than normal, and perhaps there have been other stressors that are triggering negative thoughts

- another person is behaving in an ambiguous or confusing way

- a relationship is ending or is going through a difficult time

- another person has been critical or difficult to get along with

In fact, dependency behaviors may occur at any time when you are experiencing a dependency need. Assuming that you have identified a time or place when you find yourself wanting to use a dependency behavior, we next describe some strategies to help you track and stop dependent behaviors. If you catch yourself in the early stages of such behavior you should do the following:

1. Stop or suspend the behavior. Take a moment to give yourself space and time to think things through.

2. Bring to mind your old core motivation. Could this core motivation be driving your behavior in this instance?

3. Think carefully through all the consequences of the behavior. Will it really improve things in the long run or will it only help in the short run? Will this behavior really make the relationship better or will it really make you feel better about yourself later on? Will this behavior actually do what it is intended to do, or does it have the potential to undermine you or your relationship?

4. Bring to mind your new, alternative core motivation from worksheet 12.2. If that alternative core motivation were driving you now, would your behavior be any different?

5. If your behavior would be different when operating under the alternative core motivation, what would that different behavior be?

6. Do that new behavior instead.

As you move through these steps, they should make clear whether the behavior you are about to use is based on dependency motivations, and whether it is healthy. The questions also ask you to use what you have learned about yourself and the new, alternative core motivation you developed. If the old behavior you are considering is at odds with the new core motivation, you can be pretty sure that the behavior you were engaged in or are considering is going to be problematic. The questions then ask you to come up with a new behavior that is consistent with the alternative core motivation and to use that behavior instead. This new behavior is going to seem a little strange, perhaps even uncomfortable. Over time and with practice, the alternative core motivation will become second nature.

As you become used to tracking and stopping these dependent behaviors, you will probably notice that there are several that occur repeatedly. For those behaviors that occur more frequently, we have developed a worksheet to help track behaviors and develop healthier alternatives. The worksheet is fairly straightforward and relies on information from worksheet 12.2 to get you started. First, from worksheet 12.2 write down the old core motivation from step 1 in the left column of worksheet 12.4 and the new, alternative core motivation from step 7 in the right column of worksheet 12.4. We have done just this in worksheet 12.3 using Allison as the example.

Next, keep track of the common dependency behaviors associated with that problematic core motivation in the left column. We have left space for five, but there may be more or fewer. If there are more, you could use another sheet or a notepad to keep track. Allison has recorded three problematic behaviors that she noticed not only in her current relationship, but in recollections of past relationships as well. First, she found herself trying too hard to please her boyfriend, including trying to anticipate all his needs, constantly doing unasked favors, and always trying her best to keep him happy. In fact, he didn't always appreciate this seemingly nice behavior. Instead, it made him uncomfortable sometimes and made the relationship seem unbalanced to him. Second, Allison frequently asked her boyfriend questions like "Do you love me?" rather than letting him tell her how he felt more spontaneously. She would also call him and then measure how long it took him to return her call. If it exceeded a few hours she became extremely upset, reckoning that it was a sure sign he had lost interest. Third, she never made any decisions in her relationship. She would never make suggestions about restaurants they would eat at, movies they might go to, or other plans. This frustrated her boyfriend, who always wondered what Allison *really* wanted, and made him feel overburdened with having to make all the decisions for the two of them. For your own worksheet it will be important to identify your common dependency behaviors and what the consequences of these behaviors are for you and for the relationships you are in.

Next, in the right column of worksheet 12.4, keep in mind the new, alternative core motivation and record next to the old dependent behavior what the new, alternative, adaptive behavior would be. As you do this, keep the following questions in mind:

- Do the adaptive behaviors support the new, alternative core motivation and strengthen it?

- Are the adaptive behaviors healthy for you?

- Are the adaptive behaviors healthy for the relationship?

- Are the adaptive behaviors reasonable for you to carry out?

The answers to most of these questions should be yes, but the real test will come when you try out these new behaviors. In Allison's example, most new behaviors involved backing off in some way. However, she also made it more of a priority to make decisions and express her preferences and feelings. Once you have alternatives to your dependent behaviors, you will really have gone a long way toward developing a list of new strategies that you can consult as needed. Eventually this worksheet can help you to identify alternative behaviors quickly, when you most need them. Finally, the real test of this worksheet is whether, in the long run, the alternative, core motivation is strengthened and begins to be easier to work with.

Worksheet 12.3
Sample Dependent Behavior Alternatives

My old core motivation is:

No one will ever love me as I much as I need to be loved.

This leads to the following dependent behaviors:

1. *I try so hard to please a boyfriend that I get exhausted by it and he wants me to back off.*

My new, alternative core motivation is:

I am lovable, no matter what happens.

This would lead to the following adaptive behaviors:

1. *I should be polite and ask about his needs sometimes, but also make sure I am happy.*

2. *I ask for reassurance all the time and find ways to test my boyfriend's love for me.*

2. *Assume that he loves me unless there is evidence to the contrary. Testing him could only create many more problems.*

3. *I let him make all the decisions so he will not resent me for trying to get my way.*

3. *Make more decisions. He may not even like making all the decisions anyway, and I may get more of what I want by looking at what I prefer.*

Worksheet 12.4
Dependent Behavior Alternatives

My old core motivation is:

_____

_____

My new, alternative core motivation is:

_____

_____

This leads to the following dependent behaviors:

1. _____

   _____

2. _____

   _____

3. _____

   _____

4. _____

   _____

5. _____

   _____

This would lead to the following adaptive behaviors:

1. _____

   _____

2. _____

   _____

3. _____

   _____

4. _____

   _____

5. _____

   _____

A Healthy Feedback Loop

Once you have provided yourself with a new core motivation and have put into place new behaviors to support that motivation, you will have established what we call a *healthy feedback loop*. The new core motivation, which amounts to a new way of seeing yourself and relationships, should help you to realize new adaptive behaviors. Carrying out these new adaptive behaviors in turn should strengthen the new core motivation. Eventually, the old core motivation may become more of a distant memory and less of a problem for you, and the new motivation will begin to dominate and drive your behavior. Remember, this is a process that can take months or years and it requires careful attention and hard work. You may have setbacks at times, if only because relationships are complicated and often unpredictable. But, as for any change you try to make, the important thing is your overall trajectory and moving in a generally positive direction.

Summary

In this chapter, we have discussed how dependency, stemming from a deep sense of unlovability, puts people at risk for depression. We described some of the background that links dependency to both episodes of depression and problems in relationships. We also suggested that the vicious cycle of dependency, relationship problems, and increasing depression is one that should be avoided, and we proposed that the best way to reduce these risks is to tackle dependency directly. Remember, the steps to reducing dependency at its roots are self-understanding and empathy for how the dependency developed, creating a new, alternative core motivation, and, finally, developing new behaviors to support that motivation. Of all the issues we raise in this book, altering core motivations is probably the most time-consuming and difficult. Because these are factors that have been present for most of one's life, core motivations are difficult to change. A lot of diligence and patience is required; however, the payoff can be great. By changing core motivations, your risk of relapse will be reduced. But even more than that, your relationships, sense of self, and quality of life will be much improved.

Summary Exercise

Record what you believe is the bottom line from this chapter, then record what practices or exercises you would adopt as part of your wellness plan.

Chapter 12, Dealing with Dependency, examines the issue of interpersonal dependency and the risks dependency poses for relapse. My bottom line in this chapter is:

_____

_____

The practices, exercises, or worksheets I will use from this chapter are:

_____

_____

Chapter 13

Developing Healthy
Intimate Relationships

One of the most complex and important areas of life that contributes to the experience of depression is the area of relationships. At its core, the experience of depression is of course something that happens to the individual. Many experts would call depression a mostly *intrapsychic* problem; that is, it is an experience that the person feels inside of themselves, including the many internal signs and symptoms related to the emotion, as well as the physical symptoms. A casual observer may not notice that someone is clinically depressed unless the depression is very severe. Having said that, it is also true that depression has important consequences for our relationships and interactions with others, including friends, family, and intimate partners. Depression is clearly interpersonal as well as intrapsychic.

There have been dozens, perhaps hundreds, of studies looking at the interpersonal relationships of people with depression. As best as researchers can tell, it seems that relationships and depression are related in two fundamental ways. First, it is clear that the experience of depression impacts relationships that the depressed person has with other people (Joiner and Coyne 1999; Segrin 2001). Second, it is also the case that interpersonal relationships affect, and perhaps even trigger, the experience of depression (Weissman, Markowitz, and Klerman 2000). In fact, one of the most effective treatments for depression is Interpersonal Psychotherapy (IPT), which has been shown to be as effective as antidepressant medications (DeRubeis and Crits-Christoph 1998) and seems to lead to decreases in depression symptoms by directly affecting issues related to an individual's relationships (Weissman, Markowitz, and Klerman 2000).

Given these facts, we think it is important to discuss the issue of relationships as they relate to relapse prevention. In the first section of this chapter, we describe some of what is known about the way in which depression affects interpersonal relationships. Then we will consider how damage to relationships might be repaired by using various strategies that are derived from interpersonal psychotherapy and other approaches. Ultimately, the goal of the chapter is to give you a plan that will help to heal any difficulties that past depressions have caused in your interpersonal relationships, and then to help you construct healthy relationships that may further protect you from relapse. What you get from this chapter will complement what you learned in chapter 12 about dependency. However, developing healthy relationships is not written only for people with dependency issues but also takes a different perspective on the issue of relationships that should be useful for anyone who has been depressed and is looking to stay well.

The Impact of Depression on Relationships

The idea that depression creates problems in interpersonal relationships is not as old as one might think. In fact, the roots of this idea can be traced back less than thirty years, to when the interpersonal nature of depression was first described by well-known psychologist and researcher Jim Coyne, in 1976. Coyne described a kind of vicious cycle that begins when a person first starts to become depressed (Coyne 1976). Interestingly, in Coyne's theory the trigger for the depression can be any number of factors. However, once a person is depressed, the various symptoms of depression—sad mood, loss of interest, fatigue, and feelings of worthlessness—are quickly apparent to others, especially people who are close to the depressed person. Also, the depressed person may be motivated to seek help and support from others and to share what is happening to him- or herself. The spouse, friends, and family of the depressed person are initially very supportive, and will likely offer all kinds of advice and emotional support. Along with that, other people may try to boost the depressed person's mood, as if what he or she is experiencing is a temporary sadness. After all, everyone can feel sad sometimes, and the sorts of advice people offer to a depressed person are often things that may have helped the advice-giver to feel better in the past. Other people might offer strategies such as taking some time off, relaxing, having some fun, going to see a movie, going shopping, going for a jog, taking a nice bath, or having some ice cream. All of these bits of advice are, of course, well-intentioned, but they are really the equivalent of throwing a snowball into a roaring fire when it comes to clinical depression.

According to Coyne, what happens next is critical. The depressed person, having sought the advice and maybe even taken up some of the advice, is not likely to feel better. This lack of response will be noticeable and the depressed person will probably continue both feeling sad and talking to others about his or her sadness. This sets the stage for a certain kind of interpersonal ambivalence. The depressed person's friend or spouse is likely to start feeling increasingly helpless; after all, he or she has provided advice and yet nothing is different for the depressed person. People around the depressed person may start to wonder what else they can do or say, and they may feel like they have little left to give. This is especially likely to happen when other people interact with a depressed person for a long time.

As time moves on and the depression continues, people are likely to have an ever-increasing sense of frustration and of powerlessness to help the depressed person. Meanwhile, the depressed person may also be worn down by the sad mood and, understandably, may make the depression the focus of his or her conversations with other people. Eventually, the relationship with the depressed person may become increasingly two-faced, with the spouse or friend of the depressed person saying one thing, and yet feeling another. For example, others may reassure the depressed person that the relationship is as strong as ever, when in fact they are frustrated and find it harder and harder to enjoy the company of the depressed person. Coyne suggested that ultimately this cycle can result in rejection of the depressed person, and that rejection will only add further fuel to the depression (Coyne 1976).

Since Coyne's description of this process, dozens of studies have confirmed, sadly, that depressed people are likely to be rejected by others in interpersonal interactions. This rejection effect is especially likely to occur in long-term relationships that involve a lot of closeness and time spent interacting (Marcus and Nardone 1992; Segrin 2001).

Since Coyne's original work on the topic, other people have continued to refine these ideas and to support them through careful research. More recently, psychologists working in this area have begun to look at the way in which these relationship factors might contribute to depressions that reoccur or become chronic (Joiner 2000). This kind of work is especially relevant for relapse prevention because it describes interpersonal problems that may have an erosive quality. Here the term *erosive* refers to a gradual wearing away of positive relationships that leaves the individual at an ever-increasing risk of depression.

Joiner (2000) has written about a number of these interpersonal processes or dynamics that can develop as a result of depression. Once started, these difficulties may be perpetuated even after a depression ends. Joiner has described four of these kinds of processes. The first is *negative feedback seeking*. There is a large body of psychological literature that suggests that people respond most to feedback about themselves that is consistent with their own personal view of themselves. This makes perfect sense when you consider a person who has a positive view of him- or herself; such a person would prefer, or choose, to receive positive feedback from others. What may be more surprising is that people with a negative view of themselves also prefer, and even choose, negative feedback from other people. This process is often called *self-verification* (Swann et al. 1992). No one completely understands why there is this preference to get external feedback that is consistent with our own views of ourselves. It may be that consistent feedback simply feels more comfortable than inconsistent feedback. However, the implications for interpersonal relationships and depression are clear. A person who has been depressed may go out of his or her way to seek negative feedback, and therefore maintain a negative self-image even if that view is unrealistic or unfair.

The second erosive process described by Joiner is *excessive reassurance seeking.* In many careful studies, Joiner has found that depressed people who repeatedly ask for reassurance about their lovability and worth are most likely to be rejected by others. Put plainly, requests for reassurance may be one of the most aversive things that depressed people do in their relationships with others. In terms of relapse prevention, it is important to focus on reduction of reassurance seeking, especially when symptoms first start. Reassurance seeking should not be confused with talking about or seeking help with your mood.

The third erosive process is *interpersonal conflict avoidance.* According to Joiner, general shyness and nonassertiveness are common in depression. These factors combine to make the depressed person reluctant to assert their needs. Assertiveness generally means asking for things we want and being able to say no to unreasonable requests. A lack of assertiveness is one warning sign of dependency that was discussed in chapter 12. More generally, people with depression may be afraid to assert themselves for fear of other people's reaction. However, in the long run, nonassertive behavior results in more and more needs not being satisfied and, of course, unsatisfied needs lead to increased feelings of frustration and sadness. For someone who is interested in preventing depression relapse, it is important to make sure that in your interpersonal relationships you are getting your needs met and that you are able to ask for things that you want or need.

The final factor described by Joiner is *blame maintenance.* Blame maintenance has to do with how other people see the depressed person. Other people may perceive that a depressed person is always sad or unable to cope, or they may attribute other negative qualities to the person. Even when the depression has remitted, other people's impressions may already be fixed, and, worse, they may actively look for signs that are consistent with their previously formed opinion. The implication is that a person who has been depressed is in a difficult position; even though the person may have recovered completely, other people will have an impression that is relatively fixed and hard to change. For someone who has been depressed and has recovered, it will be important to correct other people's perceptions. Of course, we cannot hold ourselves 100 percent responsible for others' opinions of us. Nonetheless, with the goal of relapse prevention in mind, constructing the best possible and most supportive interpersonal environment is in your best interests. In the next section, we move beyond describing these difficulties and discuss some methods to improve relationships affected by depression.

Developing Healthy Interpersonal Relationships

As we described earlier, interpersonal therapy, or IPT, is one of the best-known and most useful treatments for people who are acutely depressed (Weissman, Markowitz, and Klerman 2000). Again, taking an interpersonal perspective on depression is not to say that relationship problems necessarily cause depression, but rather that focusing on making relationships better and stronger does seem to help reduce depression symptoms. In this section, we focus on some of the basic ideas in IPT, with particular attention to how these ideas can be used in relapse prevention. In the same way that we adapted some of the strategies of cognitive behavioral therapy for relapse prevention in chapter 6, we look here at how IPT can help you to protect yourself from relapse. You may also discover from your reading and working with the materials we present that IPT is something you would like to pursue with a professional therapist. If that is the case, you may want to consult the Additional Resources at the end of this book to help you locate a therapist. If you are going to pursue IPT with a professional, make sure that you find out something about the person's training and experience in IPT so you can be sure that the therapist has been trained in the approach and has experience using it. Remember, our intent is only to provide an overview, and you may want to explore these areas in more detail on your own. If you are approaching this topic from a self-help perspective, Myrna Weissman, one of the founders of IPT, has published an excellent book called *Mastering Depression through Interpersonal Psychotherapy: Patient Workbook* (Weissman 2000). This book provides a wealth of detail about how to use IPT to overcome problems with depression.

Finding Your Interpersonal Focus

The descriptions we provided of the interpersonal processes that contribute to depression were very general. For many people, the kinds of interpersonal issues that arise from depression are confined to one or two specific areas, perhaps a particular relationship or a particular aspect of several relationships. In order to make changes to your relationships, it will be important to find a specific relationship issue that has affected you during your depression or that has developed as a result of your depression. When someone attends IPT sessions with a therapist, that person will usually be asked to choose one of the following four areas to work on: (1) grief, (2) interpersonal role disputes, (3) role transitions, and (4) interpersonal skills. From the perspective of relapse prevention, it may be most useful for you to take a look at the description of the four areas and choose the area that you believe has been most affected by your depression. This should also point the way to the aspect of your interpersonal relationships that is most in need of repair or strengthening. Later in this chapter, we provide an overview of what you might do to help yourself in all four of these areas. But first, we describe the four areas in more detail.

1. **Grief.** This is probably the most straightforward area to recognize. In the IPT context grief concerns the death of a loved one. If a death occurred before or during your depression, you will want to be sure that those feelings are being recognized and handled as best as possible. If the predominant emotion is grief over some other kind of loss, for example, the end of an intimate relationship, this is considered a role transition.

2. **Interpersonal role disputes.** This is the area to focus on if now, or during your depression, there is some disagreement about what you want in a relationship and what other people expect from you. For example, a young mother may have expected that her husband would provide much more child care than he thought he would provide, or a newly married man may have expected that his wife would spend all of her leisure time with him, whereas she prefers to spend some time with her friends. In both cases, one person has one set of expectations about what should be happening in the relationship, and the other person has another set of expectations. Clearly, when this occurs in the long run, there is potential for some conflict. One sign that role disputes are the area you should focus on is if, during your depression or even right now, you have a sense of resentment over an important relationship or there has been a lot of conflict in a relationship. This probably means that your needs and expectations are not being met, and that some amount of adjustment or compromise to either your expectations or the other person's behavior is going to be useful.

3. **Role transitions.** This is the area to work on if you have had difficulties with adjusting to life changes, particularly when these changes involve taking on new demands or a different kind of identity. For example, one very powerful role transition occurs when people get married. A person may go from just being him- or herself to having the additional role of husband or wife. Another set of transitions comes with having children; the person is still a husband or wife but now is also a father or mother. When we take on new roles, we often do not completely anticipate what the change will involve—just ask any new mother or father. However, many role transitions require us to make very fast changes that we may be underprepared for or that we do not wish to make.

   Keep in mind that many role changes are associated with life changes or stages of adult development, like becoming a parent, becoming a grandparent, or becoming a retiree. When role transitions are a problem, you may have felt out of step with or falling short of what was expected of you. If this is what your depression was like, role transitions may be what you want to focus on.

4. **Interpersonal skills.** This is the area to focus on if, now or during your depression, you find that most of your relationships seem to be inadequate or if you feel dissatisfied more generally with the number and quality of relationships in your life. This may indicate that you are having problems with a particular area of relationship building or your ability to maintain relationships. There are many skills and specific behaviors that are important for establishing relationships and keeping relationships going. Like any skills, these can be learned with sufficient practice and a clear understanding of the problem. However, because the range of issues related to relationship skills can be very broad, it is beyond the scope of this chapter to describe all the possible interventions. For example, skills in assertion are very different from skills related to intimacy. Each different interpersonal skill area

(such as forming intimate attachments, assertiveness, and so forth) that helps us to build satisfying relationships is large enough that it deserves more space than we can provide here. We recommend the following in-depth resources on the topics of communication and interpersonal skills (see the bibliography for details on each). For communication skills, one the best books is *Messages: The Communication Skills Book* by McKay, Davis, and Fanning (1995). Also, Deborah Tannen has written several books on communication patterns, both in general relationships (Tannen 1991) and in relationships between men and women (Tannen 2001). Finally, there are several good books on assertiveness that are useful if you have long-standing difficulties asking for things you need or have difficulty saying no to unreasonable requests (Fleming 1997; Paterson 2000).

Although self-help books may be useful for improving interpersonal skills, these issues are complex. Therefore, we suggest that a person may be better off consulting with an IPT therapist to develop and improve interpersonal skills. Sometimes, it may not even be clear to the individual exactly which interpersonal behaviors are causing problems in his or her relationships. That is where a professional opinion can be very useful.

Techniques for the Different Interpersonal Areas

As you may have recognized in reading the above section, each of the four areas emphasized in IPT is quite distinct and will require different approaches when it comes to treatment. For some areas, the best way to bring about positive change is through some new behavior, for example, to do some skill building. In other areas, the focus is much more on changing psychological factors like emotions and expectations about relationships. It is generally recommended that individuals start by focusing on one area and working on that area consistently to maximize their chances of making progress. If you find that there is more than one area that you need to work on, pick the most important or most problematic area and work on that first, followed by the area that is next in importance. Also, if you believe that more than one of these areas needs to be worked on, it may be a sign that you ought to seek help with a professional therapist, because treatment will likely be more complex and therefore difficult to do on your own. On the other hand, if you immediately identified one of the areas as the focus for you, you may find the interventions to be more straightforward and you may be able to do much of the work yourself.

Grief

Grief is a natural reaction to loss that is necessary and normal when someone dies. Certainly, the experience of grief has a lot in common with the experience of clinical depression, but normal grief starts to resolve over a period of several months to a year. As grief dissipates, the affected person gradually focuses less and less on the death and his or her emotions become less overwhelming. Keep in mind that grief itself is not a disorder and it is not something you should necessarily want to stop through some sort of intervention. However, there is a form of grief, known sometimes as *complicated grief,* that may not resolve on its own. This kind of grief can last a long time (sometimes years), can be associated with more severe symptoms of depression, and can lead to greater impairment in a person's ability to function. This is the sort of grief reaction for which the techniques described here are intended. When this kind of complicated grief is the focus, the aim is to facilitate the emotional mourning process. Next, the person is helped to reestablish previous interests and activities, and to create relationships that can, in some ways, begin to make up for what has been lost (Weissman, Markowitz, and Klerman 2000).

One of the assumptions about complicated grief is that the normal process of grieving may not be operating as it should be. In some cases, people who are grieving may not have been allowed to properly express their feelings, or when they have tried to express their feelings, the reactions from people around them may have been negative. If this is what happened to you, a real priority is to find someone with whom you can discuss your grief. That person ought to be available, willing to listen, nonjudgmental, and able to offer you some kind of reasonable feedback. When people are involved in IPT, it is usually the therapist who fulfills this role. But if you are doing this without a therapist, you will want to find someone, perhaps even a group of people, with whom you feel comfortable sharing your feelings. In most communities there are grief support groups that might offer a good forum to talk. Perhaps you have a friend or family member whom you respect, trust, or admire, with whom you want to share your feelings, if you have not done so already. IPT emphasizes the importance of talking through the story of what happened, such as who the person was and what he or she meant to you, the timing and order of events that led up to the death, and what happened after the death (Weissman 2000). In IPT, there is a real emphasis in getting it all out. Often, until we say things aloud or write them down, we do not know exactly what we may be feeling or thinking. When we disclose, we aren't just recounting things that we already know, we may also discover lots of things that we didn't know about ourselves.

If you are suffering from complicated grief, one of the things that may be inhibiting the normal grieving process is a fear of talking about the event. People sometimes think they will not stop being sad once they start talking. Or they may be experiencing guilt about something they did or didn't do around the death. They may have all kinds of emotions that they think are wrong, for example, anger at the person who has passed away. But in grief, there is no such thing as a right or wrong emotion; in fact, experiencing a range of emotions is probably very necessary to the grieving process. You may also want to consider (perhaps using strategies from chapter 6) whether you have some overly rigid rules regarding the discussion or experiencing of emotions.

A next step in resolving grief is to focus less on the death itself and more on the person who was lost and your relationship with that person. When someone close dies, there can be a tendency to view that relationship in an extreme way, as either all good or all bad. It is important over time to come to a balanced view of the relationship. You may want to write down all the things that were good about the relationship, and also all the things that were not so good or that were bad. By helping to understand what the relationship meant, you will be better placed to understand what to do next.

Interpersonal Role Disputes

Technically speaking, the term *interpersonal role disputes* refers to a situation in which one person has *nonreciprocal expectations* about a relationship. Put simply, this is when one person's expectations in a relationship are different from the other person's expectations. This is most problematic in very close relationships. For example, Alex, who has been married for three years to Ginny, expected his wife to find outside employment after they had a child one year ago. Ginny wasn't quite sure what she wanted when she was pregnant, but soon after their son was born it became clear to her that she wanted to spend her time raising her children. Chances are that Alex and Ginny's contradictory expectations may cause a lot of friction between them. Both of their positions on this matter are not at all unreasonable, but they are very different and their opinions will affect their lives together in important ways. For depression and relapse, the central issue in conflict is often whether the individuals in the relationship have expectations that are inflexible. A repetitive pattern of expectations that are in conflict but never resolved fully can wear down people's sense of control over their lives, and ultimately leave them hopeless. For example, in Alex and Ginny's case the situation could drag on for months or years. Alex may continue to put pressure on Ginny to find outside work. Ginny may resist or at least delay searching for a job. There will be no winners in such a conflict—both Alex and Ginny will eventually feel frustrated and resentful. It may be that Alex and Ginny argue over this topic frequently. It may also be that the conflict remains unspoken and simmering, but just as damaging. If either person in such a conflict is vulnerable to depression, this kind of conflict may well trigger an episode.

To move forward, it is also important to determine what stage a conflict is at (Weissman, Markowitz, and Klerman 2000). In IPT, conflicts are thought to have three stages: (1) *impasse*—this is when there are clearly different expectations, but there is no discussion or open acknowledgment of this; (2) *renegotiation*—this is when both people are aware of the conflict and are talking about the differences between them; and (3) *dissolution*—this is when differences are so obvious and great that the relationship is too broken to be mended. For this last stage, many of the techniques for grief are going to be useful because, ultimately, the relationship is going to be lost.

For the impasse stage, the place to begin is discussing the differences. This may initially lead to more conflicted feelings between the two people. On the other hand, nothing will be gained if the differences are not acknowledged and discussed. If you are in the impasse stage, the first step will be to have a frank discussion about the nature of the different expectations, and to encourage more open communication about this conflict. The goal here is not to create more negative emotions or hostile communication, but to put the problem on the table and to discuss possible solutions. Going back to the example of Ginny and Alex, who have stopped talking to each other about anything but the most basic matters related to their children, Ginny might ask whether Alex would like to sit down and talk about the topic of working and children. Both Ginny and Alex should take some time to gather their thoughts in preparation for sharing them with one another. They should then find a mutually agreed upon time and a quiet space to put their different opinions on the table. There is, after all, no way to negotiate in relationships unless the players have shown all of their cards in good faith.

The next step is to look at all of the differences between the two sets of expectations. The following questions will be helpful:

- What are the differences in expectations?

- What are the different values that each person has that might be driving their different expectations?

- What are the options? Which are possible? Which are realistic?

- What are the strengths of the relationship? What is the common ground?

- Has this happened before? If so, how was it solved then and what can be learned from that?

Negotiating disputes is like any other type of negotiation. Participants must make clear their own positions, try their best to appreciate the other's position and values, and then come to an agreement that incorporates the needs of both people. When Alex and Ginny agreed to negotiate, they kept these steps in mind. They discovered that the core value they had in common was that they wanted to do the best possible job raising their children. For Alex, this meant trying to earn enough money to perhaps afford a more spacious home, or to start planning for the children's college funds. For Ginny, this value came down to providing the best possible child care, which meant staying at home. Both Alex and Ginny were able to see merit in each other's views. Ultimately, they were able to reach a compromise. Ginny would work part-time so as to have at least the majority of her time with the children. The money she earned would go toward a college fund, which is something Alex had wanted.

Like all negotiations around role disputes, not everyone gets exactly what they want. However, both people get some of their expectations met, and the conflict is reduced. Over time, negotiating successfully in role disputes will help a person to minimize conflicted feelings and frustration.

Role Transitions

Everyone has multiple roles in life, though we often do not think of ourselves in this way. It is important to understand the idea of roles before moving on in this section. For example, many people have a work role and a home role. The home role may be further subdivided into mother and wife, or even mother, wife, and grandmother. Each role brings with it different expectations and skills, and a person may behave quite differently in each role. Think for a moment about how you behave and what you do at work. Would this same behavior make sense at home? Chances are it would not; that is, you adopt a different version of yourself when you are at home versus work.

Roles are important because they have numerous benefits. For example, they make us feel worthwhile and they allow us to accomplish things that matter to us. However, there are times in life when something does not go as well as it should in the different roles. This may happen because of a recent change in roles to which we have not been able to adapt as smoothly as we might like. For example, a woman who has just had her first child will now have a new "mother" role that she may not be completely comfortable with. As we said earlier, many role transitions coincide with life stages, such as leaving home, getting married, having children, and retiring. But transitions at other points are possible. For example, a promotion at work or a change in job status is a common transition, and these too can sometimes trigger depression. For relapse prevention, the main intent here is to sensitize you to what a role transition is, and how these can be managed with the least possible distress.

To identify whether a role transition is a problem, you might want to ask yourself what recent changes have occurred in different areas of your life, including work, home, school, and child rearing. The bottom line is, has your life recently changed in some important way, and is there some discomfort around those changes? Once you have identified the role transition that seems to be the source of the trouble, the next step is to get more details on the matter. It will be important to identify what old role you have given up. In the case of a new mother, the old role maybe "newlywed." Also, you will want to specify the requirements of the new role (such as what is expected in the new role).

Four stages in successful role transitions are (1) grieving the old role, (2) developing new skills needed for the new role, (3) establishing supports to help in the new role, and (4) identifying positive aspects of the new role. To help describe these steps, we will use the example of John, who went from being a factory worker to being an area manager where he worked. After only a couple of weeks in the new job, John began to develop some periodic sad moods, irritability, and, for the first time in his life, a lack of confidence. With a fairly clear relationship between his change in job status and his negative moods, he elected to focus on role transition during IPT.

The first step in the process of dealing with role transitions is to talk about the old role and to grieve whatever positives have been lost along with that old role. It is interesting that role transitions often appear, to the outside world, as positive steps. Getting promoted, getting married, or having a baby often seem like things that should make us happy, but in each case there is something we give up, such as freedom or self-sufficiency. It is often helpful and sometimes necessary to mourn those things we have lost and to express our emotions around those losses. In John's case, his promotion was associated with some real losses. As a worker in the factory, he had more freedom and was less accountable for his individual performance. He also had excellent camaraderie with his coworkers and noticed that when he moved on to management, his coworkers became less friendly and acted more aloof around him. He didn't fully expect these changes when he accepted the promotion. He also didn't fully appreciate how the social part of his old job (like lunches with coworkers) led to a sense of satisfaction with his work. For John, it was important to come to terms with these expected and unexpected losses.

The next phase is to focus on new skills that may be needed. Often, new roles are thrust upon us with the expectation that we are supposed to know just what to do or that we will learn what to do by simply being in the new role. But this expectation may be both artificial and untrue. A person in a new role may be able to avoid a lot of difficulty by seeking out skills training or resources (like self-help books) in order to learn the information they will need. For John, although he clearly knew the work that the factory did, he had not been trained as a manager. As a result, he was often uncomfortable making decisions. John decided to take some weekend management seminars at a local college. This allowed him to gain new information and also to use the seminars as a kind of sounding board for the way he was going about his work.

The third step in transition to a new role is to establish a new social support system. This would involve finding social contacts that are associated with the new role. For example, a new mother may seek out a group of other new mothers who meet regularly. John decided that he would try to befriend other managers because they might be able to provide some support and knowledge. Whatever the new role a person is moving into, the general idea is to find social contacts within that new role.

The final step in transitioning is to focus on the benefits of the new role. Positive aspects of a new role may not be noticed by someone in transition. For example, with the difficulties John was having, he was unable to appreciate the substantial raise he received with his new job and the greater flexibility in his work hours as a manager. Also, negative views of a new role may be based on certain stereotypes or assumptions that the person has. These kinds of assumptions or thoughts can be challenged by some of the strategies we described in chapter 6. Paying attention to difficulties that result from role transitions and putting into place strategies to minimize the disruption and maximize a smooth transition will help to reduce times of negative emotion substantially.

Summary

The impact of depression on interpersonal relationships is one of the most important, though subtle, areas in which depression takes an enormous toll. Depression undermines relationships with other people in a way that is sometimes difficult to notice at first, but is nevertheless very real. It is as if the depression erodes the foundation of the relationship so that everything might look just fine, when in reality the relationship is very fragile. This makes relationship rebuilding after depression a real priority. The other challenge with trying to improve relationships is that it is not up to just you. Unlike exercising, taking medication, or using worksheets from this book to examine your thoughts, relationships involve another person who will have his or her own behaviors and motivations. This only highlights how important it is to communicate what has happened during the depression and to start talking about how things might be repaired. When a person has recovered from depression, relationships are not an area that he or she should leave to chance. We derive such important satisfaction and support from others, that it makes sense to actively heal our relationships and to put in the effort to make them thrive. Once you let the people you love know that your aim is to build the best possible mutually satisfying relationship, whether they are family, friend, or partner, you will likely find that others will make the very same pledge to you. After that, you will be building new, healthy relationships and adding supports for wellness every day.

Summary Exercise

Record what you believe is the bottom line from this chapter, then record what practices or exercises you would adopt as part of your wellness plan.

Chapter 13, Developing Healthy Intimate Relationships, reviews the links between interpersonal problems and depression. My bottom line in this chapter is:

_____

_____

The practices, exercises, or actions I will take from this chapter are:

_____

_____

Chapter 14

Vital Involvement in Life

In this final chapter we offer a somewhat different perspective on the idea of wellness and relapse prevention. In fact, in this chapter we go out of our way to not even think about depression very much at all. Why would we do this in a book about relapse prevention for depression? The answer is that what we are going to focus on here are developments that come from a different area altogether, sometimes called *positive psychology*. Most of what we know about depression and what has been described in this book comes from the fields of *psychiatry, abnormal psychology,* and *clinical psychology.* All three approaches focus on the idea of *dysfunction;* that is, they focus on understanding whatever is going askew that makes a person unhappy or interferes with a person's ability to function. Huge amounts of resources in the form of research and writing have been invested in this notion of psychological dysfunction, and certainly we know a lot more about mental illness than we once did. In contrast, only a tiny fraction of our intellectual resources have been devoted to understanding what it is that makes people happy or satisfied with their lives, and many people argue that we ought to know more than we do (Seligman and Csikszentmihalyi 2000). Indeed, the idea that psychology should do more to understand happiness and well-being is not new. Some thirty years ago, one of the earliest positive psychologists wrote that in the first half of the century Sigmund Freud and others "had supplied to us the sick half of psychology and we must now fill it out with the healthy half.... Perhaps this will be more fruitful than asking 'how to get unsick'". (Maslow 1968, 5). One difficulty with positive psychology is that it is not an easy area in which to conduct rigorous research. Positive psychology fairly quickly runs into questions related to the meaning of living, spirituality, faith, and exactly what the word "happiness" means. These kinds of things are difficult to quantify and measure in an exact way—try it out yourself by defining what happiness means precisely. It is not so easy. Nonetheless, there are several areas that we will highlight that have been looked at in some detail. The first of these areas, self-actualization, will serve as a kind of overview of the field. We will then go on to talk about some other ideas: flow, hardiness, values, and meaning. In the end, all of these concepts from positive psychology lead to the idea that happiness and satisfaction come from active engagement in living, or *vital involvement*.

One final word about relapse before we leave that concept behind for the rest of the chapter. Our idea here is that if, in addition to the relapse prevention strategies presented throughout the book, you cultivate aspects of positive psychology in yourself, you will indeed be killing two birds with one stone. That is, your life will become more positive, fulfilling, and meaningful, and this should offer some additional protection from the return of depression.

Self-Actualization: An Ideal State of Living

One of the most frequently described, but hard-to-pin-down and controversial, ideas from positive psychology comes from Abraham Maslow (1968). That idea is called *self-actualization*. Maslow described humans as having a hierarchy of needs, ranging from basics like air to breathe, water, food, and shelter, to the comfort of loved ones, to wanting to become self-actualized (Maslow 1968). For Maslow, being self-actualized is living to your fullest potential. He described many famous people who seemed to have reached a state of human potential that few others do. Maslow was able to study these people from biographical information and even interviewed some himself, and then described their characteristics. But a truly precise definition of self-actualization never really emerged. Neither Maslow nor anyone else since has ever gotten past the fact that there is something circular about the concept of self-actualization. It is defined by the characteristics of people who are self-actualized, and they are seen to be self-actualized because of their characteristics. Nonetheless, the idea of self-actualization has been so compelling that it still dominates many fields including business and management, industrial/organizational psychology, counseling, and even school curricula. In these fields, self-actualization is often described as the ideal state that people are motivated to strive for in their life.

There are many people who have been described as self-actualized, including Thomas Jefferson, Benjamin Franklin, George Washington, Albert Einstein, Aldous Huxley, William James, Simone de Beauvior, Maya Angelou, Jane Goodall, Marie Curie, Emma Goldman, Walt Whitman, Eleanor Roosevelt, Albert Schweitzer, and Ralph Waldo Emerson. What do these diverse people have in common? Certainly, they are famous and well-known, but Maslow would say that many people including ourselves and people we know and love, may also be self-actualized. These people share common features, such as

- They accept themselves for what they are, both good and bad.

- They are less interested in cultural norms than most people, they feel free to express desires that may be counter to the mainstream, and they don't allow themselves to be hemmed in by "shoulds."

- They are creative, not necessarily in the artistic sense, but in their approach to living and the problems of living.

- They have a particular sense of humor, taking themselves and life with a grain of salt and being able to laugh at themselves, not at others.

- They have a strong need for privacy and have a relatively small number of acquaintances. However, the friendships they do have are deep and lasting.

Another aspect of the self-actualized person that we will describe later in detail is that they have *peak experiences,* moments when their experience goes beyond place and time, when thoughts about past and future disappear, and they are in the moment completely. When you look at the list of self-actualizers above, these peak experiences seemed to come in their vocations, for example, in writing, performing, leading, caring, or philosophizing. Trying to think of people who might be self-actualized is an interesting exercise, not least because it takes more to be self-actualized than fame, money, or talent. In fact, none of those things are any guarantee. Just think of all the famous, moneyed, talented people who we hear about in the media having troubles in their lives like substance abuse, multiple marriages and divorces, dysfunctional families, or run-ins with the law. And yet Western culture focuses us on these qualities of fame, money, and talent as the important things to strive for, and tells us that the ideal is to have a life of opulent leisure. Maslow would have disagreed with this strongly and it may surprise you to learn that factors like personal income and wealth really have very little relationship to happiness and satisfaction either for individuals or when one compares rich and poor countries (Diener 2000). So if celebrity, fame, and money are really a false portrait of happiness, what kind of goal is ideal? Certainly, one should always be wary of being told to work toward a very specific ideal or perfection; remember chapter 11. But if you did set one personal goal, becoming self-actualized would be a very good one. Also, the idea of self-actualization in many ways incorporates some of the other concepts we will introduce here, like optimal experiences or flow; living in a way that is consistent with your values; cultivating hardiness; and finding a meaning in life.

Flow

The origin of the idea of *flow* is a very interesting one, and the term itself is interesting because it actually defines and also describes the experience it refers to. Mihaly Csikszent-mihalyi (1988) (pronounced chick-sent-me-high), who created the concept of flow, was very interested in understanding the experiences that made people happy. He was studying a group of artists as part of his doctoral research and noted how enormously devoted and passionate they were in their painting (Csikszentmihalyi and Csikszentmihalyi 1988). He noted that these artists seemed to be enjoying themselves in a very profound, lasting way, and that they believed what they were doing was very important. Yet these unknown artists had not been commissioned to do the work and probably had no idea whether they would ever be able to sell their work or achieve any kind of critical success. He also noticed that, once they finished a work that had been their sole focus for days, they would often put it away and not ever look at it or think of it again. Csikszentmihalyi began to believe that what he was seeing here was a form of optimal experience, an experience beyond a mere moment of laughter, pleasure, fun, or leisure, a very deep experience of satisfaction and contentment (Csikszentmihalyi 1990). He came to call such experiences flow because, whether it was artists, musicians, surgeons, writers, or gardeners, they described their peak experiences in similar ways. When reading about the work of Csikszentmihalyi, one is often surprised that people report being ultimately happy in moments we would not necessarily suspect. Judging by cultural stereotypes, we should be most happy on a ride at Disneyland, standing at the railing of a cruise ship, as we drive our brand new car off the lot, enjoying lavish meals with family or spouses, or lounging on the beach at a tropical resort. Csikszentmihalyi's work shows us that true happiness and contentment does not require extravagant expense or exotic locales. Also surprisingly, flow seems to happen more often when we are alone and when we are challenged by a task; flow is far more likely to happen in our work than it is in our leisure time. Again, this is at odds with cultural stereotypes that say happiness only occurs with others (often in the context of romantic love) or when we are in a leisure mode, and that work is a negative aspect of our lives that we should seek to minimize.

But to really illustrate flow, we need to describe what it is like. Once you are aware of the characteristics of flow, it then makes sense to look at flow in your own life. In one of his many writings on flow, Csikszentmihalyi (1990) described eight components of flow, aspects of either the activity or the state of the person doing the activity:

1. The activity is challenging and a certain skill is needed. The tasks that result in flow are challenging, but not overwhelmingly so, for that individual.

2. Your full attention is absorbed by the task. In a sense, for that time period, you become that task.

3. The activity has clear goals, endpoints, or a way of seeing that you are making progress.

4. There is clear feedback about whether you are moving in the right or wrong direction.

5. Nothing else intrudes into consciousness; that is, you do not think about your physical state, what time it is, what your mood is or whether you might be hungry.

6. There is a deep sense of personal control over your body and the activity.

7. One loses a sense of self or "I"; self-consciousness is absent.

8. One loses a sense of time; hours pass like minutes, or sometimes the other way around—time seems to slow down so that seconds seem like a very long time.

When people write about flow, it is often in the context of something creative, like the painting of artists that originally fascinated Csikszentmihalyi. Musicians describe flow when playing, surgeons describe flow when operating, but what about flow in everyday experiences? When we talk to people about flow, such as in a large college course, we get some interesting descriptions of their flow experiences. Some talk about sports, from playing soccer to rock climbing. Others talk about hobbies, especially those that require building or making something, like sewing, knitting, making model sailboats, or woodworking. Flow does not have to be about brain surgery or violin concertos; it can occur in any activity that you are invested in and that involves skills.

So flow is experienced uniquely by everyone, but it is the kind of thing that can only be achieved if you seek it out, that is, if you put yourself in a position to feel challenged and to become engrossed in something that you want to master. We will never stumble across a flow experience, we have to create them (Csikszentmihalyi 1990). And true flow experiences are likely to be somewhat irregular and not necessarily something that will happen every day. But the more flow you have, the more satisfied and passionate you will be about life.

Hardiness

The concept of hardiness was first introduced into psychology literature almost twenty-five years ago by Suzanne Kobasa (1979). *Hardiness,* in this context, refers to certain strengths within a person that make them resilient to stress. The term was coined when Dr. Kobasa and some of her colleagues were looking into the relationship between stressful life events and emotional and physical health. However, rather than looking at the relationship between stress and various problems to see what might be going wrong, Dr. Kobasa was looking at it from another perspective: what was it about a person that could help them get through difficulties relatively unscathed emotionally and physically? Dr. Kobasa and her colleagues were particularly interested in people who were under a lot of pressure and who would be in high-stress environments almost daily. Much of the research was conducted with executives, lawyers, and army officers who were involved in high-stress roles and living through large-scale shifts in the organizations or companies they worked for (Kobasa 1982). Her numerous studies found that there were certain aspects of a person, in a way related to coping style and beliefs, that did seem to reliably allow some people to better deal with stress. Even though these factors are sometimes thought of as personality styles (and perhaps difficult to change) recent evidence suggests that hardiness can, in fact, be instilled in people through training (Maddi, Kahn, and Maddi 1998). Next, we present the three different aspects of hardiness.

Hardiness appears to consist of three different components, all interrelated but unique in some way. The first of these building blocks is *commitment,* "the ability to believe in the truth, importance, and interest value of who one is and what one is doing" (Kobasa 1982, 6). Commitment is about a tendency to be completely engaged in all aspects of life, work, family, and other relationships. Like all components of hardiness, no one is quite sure exactly why commitment offers such good protection from stress, but one idea is that a person who is committed to all aspects of life deal might better with a loss in a particular area. For example, someone committed to job, family, and friends will likely cope better with losing a job than someone who is committed only to that job. Commitment also fits well into some of the other sections of this chapter, particularly meaning and values, since these form the cornerstone of what one commits to.

The second component of hardiness is a sense of *control* (not actual control though). Here control refers to "the tendency to believe and act as if one can influence the course of events" (Kobasa 1982, 7). People who have a greater sense of control may be more able to see what it is about their circumstance that they can have a hand in directing. Rather than seeing stress as something that will have its way with them, a person with a strong sense of control will look for what it is they can do to help themselves. This may mean that people with a stronger sense of control are more likely to use action-oriented coping (chapter 9) and defuse problems as best they can. Someone with a stronger sense of control who experiences a stressor like financial troubles is more likely to seek expert advice and take action on a plan to minimize their losses as quickly as possible. Someone who lacks a sense of control may believe that there is nothing they can do and, by their own passivity, may let the situation snowball.

The final component of hardiness is *challenge,* "the belief that change, rather than stability, is the normative mode of life" (Kobasa 1982, 7). Challenge may be particularly useful when changes are thrust upon a person. Someone with a sense of control and challenge will be far more likely to see a reason why things are changing and to seek out opportunities they can use to their advantage during change. As the old saying goes, the only constant is change, and being able to see change as bringing opportunity, as opposed to thinking of what one loses with change, is probably a healthy perspective to bring to our ever-changing world. We have known for a long time that people respond better to stress when they have chosen to be under stress rather than when stress is uncontrollable. Having an attitude involving challenge will help people to feel like there is something about the course of events that they can steer. Challenge is also related to the critical ability to tolerate ambiguity, that is, being flexible enough in one's thinking that there is less need for a right way and a wrong way to do things. An example of challenge might be when someone is confronted with a change to their work role, perhaps being asked to work in a different way or simply getting a new job description. Someone with a challenge attitude would see this change, as an opportunity to learn, to shake things up a bit, to try to see the good in change and to be excited about what is happening in their lives. Someone who lacks the challenge attitude may yearn to keep things as they were and may worry that the changes will be difficult to manage.

Presenting these aspects of hardiness would not, all by itself, instill hardiness in people and of course we recognize this. We have presented these ways of coping as a goal to work toward that would be healthy and protective for you. Sometimes people vulnerable to depression, particularly those prone to perfectionism, take these kinds of ideals too literally and begin to measure themselves on how hardy they are. This is mostly counterproductive since the goal is not to be perfect in hardiness but to increase, over time, one's ability to be flexible and to tolerate ambiguity. Keep in mind, too, that hardiness is not presented here as "musts" or "shoulds," in the sense of "I must have a challenge perspective or I'm doomed." Rather, we would say that these are very worthwhile, healthy attitudes to cultivate and work on over the long run. The components of hardiness are ways of seeing yourself and the world, somewhat like the adaptive coping strategies we presented in chapter 9 and the adaptive beliefs or rules in chapter 6. Ways of thinking, feeling, and behaving can be changed and worked on over time, but this is a process with occasional stops and starts.

Values

Part of self-actualization, and positive psychology more generally, is the idea that people who are happy and satisfied believe that they are involved in living a life and doing things that have value. It is in this sense that we use the term values in this chapter, and not in the sense that you ought to have a particular kind of values. For example, the term "values" is often seen in the form of family values or old-fashioned values, and sometimes the term "values" is hijacked for political purposes, as if to say that family values should be some kind of ideal, or take precedence over some other value. We are interested more in the idea of values than in the content of values; content is really in your hands, as it should be. For example, one person living a life consistent with their values may focus on certain ideas and ideals about whom they aspire to be as a mother, wife, or friend. As a mother, you may want to be caring; as a wife, devoted; and as a friend, loyal. Each of these values could be broken down into behaviors and principles, too. But then another person may value their contribution to local, national, or international politics. Their value might be the service to others, and along with that would come specific behaviors. Everyone, somewhere inside themselves, has values of some kind or another, and exactly what those values are is less relevant. What you value is an individual choice and you have only yourself to answer to when it comes to figuring out what those values are.

But let us step back for a moment and try to find a definition of values. One definition comes from Steven Hayes and his colleagues, who say that values are "global desired life consequences" (Hayes, Strosahl, and Wilson 1999, 206). When you define such global values in a number of areas, you can direct your own behavior to be consistent with reaching, or aiming for, those values (Hayes, Strosahl, and Wilson 1999; Frankl 1963). However, just because one has selected a value, does not mean that the path to that goal is straight. In fact, the opposite is often true. You can expect that the path to meeting your values will be winding and sometimes obstructed, and will often involve decisions that you cannot be sure about. Values are almost exactly like headings on a compass (Hayes, Strosahl, and

Wilson 1999): You may determine that you want to end up south by southwest, but you may not be able to go in a straight line. There will be times when you have to go sideways, around mountains, or over bridges and across streams; you may even have to double back if one route does not work out. Despite this, values are necessary because, without them, we go about our lives in circles or randomly. Some psychologists believe that certain kinds of unhappiness are related to an absence of clearly defined values, or to having a life that is not consistent with one's values. If this is true, reflecting on values will be an important part of happiness and satisfaction.

It is all too easy, in everyday life, to avoid thinking too much about values. Our plates are already full with getting up on time, going to work, taking care of family, eating, leisure activities, and so much else that we often spend little time figuring out what it all means or where we are headed. Of course, there is nothing really so terribly wrong with this way of existing in life, particularly if you are not unhappy with how things are. But positive psychologists focus on the idea of enhancement, that is, how much better your life could be if you spent time thinking through your values and arranging your life so that you meet those goals. How much more fulfilled could you be? Are there some things you do that you actually do not truly value? Could you reinvest that energy into something you care about more? Ultimately, there is nothing to lose by looking at your values and how you pursue them. You may find that your daily life is completely consistent with your values, and thus you are simply confirming what you know and experience already. However, if there is a way that your life could be more consistent with your values, there is no telling what kind of benefit you will experience, but it is likely to be significant.

Defining Your Values

Values are hard to describe in a vacuum and it is much easier to describe our values in certain kinds of domains. Hayes and his colleagues (1999) describe nine different domains, though it is important to remember that you may have a value that does not fit nicely into one of the following categories. This is perfectly fine—the categories we describe here, based on Hayes and his colleagues (1999), are really just to start the process. The nine categories are listed below, and we provide some space for you to begin writing down your values in these areas.

Worksheet 14.1
Defining Your Values

1. Intimate relationships—the kind of partner you want to be:

_____

_____

2. Family relationships—the ways you would like to relate to family:

_____

_____

3. Friendships—the kinds of friendships you would like to cultivate:

_____

_____

4. Vocation—jobs or areas that you feel passionate about working on:

_____

_____

5. Education—the sorts of things you would like to learn about:

_____

_____

6. Recreation and leisure—the kinds of ways you want to spend free time:

_____

_____

7. Spirituality and philosophy—the way you want to see the world and the meaning life has (this will be examined in detail in the next section on meaning):

_____

_____

8. Citizenship—how you might like to participate in your local or the global community:

_____

_____

9. Physical well being—the goals you have for maintaining physical health and well-being:

_____

_____

You will notice that in each area you are prompted to be somewhat wishful in your thinking and that is exactly how it should be. Values are things you would like to have, things you would strive for, but, ironically, most values are unreachable and elusive. For example, no matter how much you might value close family relationships, other members of your family could still be difficult, angry, or disengaged for many different reasons. You could be involved in part-time college courses in a field of study you love, but never find enough time to get all the credits you need for a degree. You may want to maintain a certain fitness level but struggle to stay there as decades go by and your body changes. But in the end this is perfectly okay because these values always serve to make you try in a positive direction. Values have no concrete endpoint, no real goal line. If they did, they probably wouldn't be values at all. You will never reach a point where you think to yourself, "Finally, I've achieved my value so I will stop having that value." That would not make sense at all since values are not a thing to do, they are a way of being and believing as you do things.

We realize this concept of values is tricky in many ways, and values are a bit of a squishy concept to get ahold of. This gets back to when we described the difficulties with defining happiness earlier in the chapter. But values are real and they are important. Think of Maslow's list of self-actualized people. All had views, causes, work, and ideas they believed in passionately. Living a life of values will leave less room for negative feelings and emotions, leave less room for doubt about your choices, and lead toward self-actualization.

Meaning

In this final section of this chapter, we describe the need for meaning in life. In a way, meaning probably incorporates concepts like flow, hardiness, and values, but meaning asks the biggest question of all, "What is life about and why am I here?" The idea of meaning entered the world of academic psychology mostly through the work of Viktor Frankl after World War II. The timing here was no coincidence—Frankl had spent years in a concentration camp during the war and under these most horrific circumstances developed his theory of meaning and a new approach to therapy. One could say that Frankl, even as he was developing these ideas, was putting them to the ultimate test. He was trying to maintain his dignity and a sense that life was worth living even under the threat that he, like so many comrades, could end up dying in the gas chambers or fall victim to one of the terrible epidemics that swept through the prisons. More than that, the daily life in the camps, described graphically in his remarkable and emotionally resonant book *Man's Search for Meaning,* was brutal in the smallest and largest possible ways: insufficient food, cramped and uninhabitable shelters, tasks of pure drudgery under constant scrutiny and threat of corporeal punishment, beatings from guards that rained down randomly, and everyday experiences of man's inhumanity to man, both at the hands of the guards and between the prisoners themselves. Remarkably enough, Frankl was able to find some kind of meaning in his experience that kept him looking at the future. Other prisoners lost hope, despaired, and often died after giving up psychologically, but Frankl maintained throughout his experience that a person could *choose* to find meaning, even in the midst of this great suffering. At first Frankl endured the experience by thinking of his wife, who unfortunately did die in a different camp though Frankl did not find this out until after the war. Through the love he had for his wife, he experienced moments of peace and beauty around simple things like tiny fragments of nature he observed or moments of humanity he witnessed. He sometimes believed he saw signs that he was on the right track, that his wife or her spirit were with him somehow. But he also found some meaning in his intellectual ideas and tried hard to keep a record of the insights he was having, even though writing was nearly impossible. Frankl even tried to lend what support he could to other prisoners, though he acknowledged that much of the time the moment-to-moment deprivations and threat to life and limb prevented him from doing anything to help others. But he did what he could.

On one particularly bad day when the guards made the prisoners go completely without food, Frankl elected to speak to his comrades, share some of his ideas, and motivate them to go on. He said in part:

> *I agreed that each of us could guess for himself how small were his chances of survival. . . . I estimated my own chances at about one in twenty. But I also told them that, in spite of this, I had no intention of losing hope and giving up. For no man knew what the future would bring, much less the next hour."* (Frankl, 1963, 82)

He also spoke about meaning:

> *Human life, under any circumstances, never ceases to have a meaning and . . . this infinite meaning of life includes suffering and dying. . . . I said that someone looks down on each of us in difficult hours—a friend, a wife, somebody alive or dead, or a God—and he would not expect us to disappoint him. He would hope to find us suffering proudly—not miserably."* (Frankl, 1963, 83)

When Frankl finished his speech, the men thanked him with tears in their eyes. And the impact he had on his comrades that night and throughout his imprisonment may be the real meaning of Frankl's suffering. If, on the night of that speech or at other times, he inspired one or two or a dozen men to not lose hope that day or the next, he may have saved their lives. This would still be true even if Frankl himself had been killed, and so no matter what, his would have been a life of great dignity. The number of people who have benefited in some way from Frankl's ideas by reading them is larger still, and this too gives meaning to his experiences in the camps.

After the war, Frankl returned to a very productive life as an academic and therapist, and many of his ideas continue to influence existential therapists. The centerpiece of this approach to therapy is that a person constructs their world for themselves, and therefore defines what life means to them. Frankl did not believe the question "what is the meaning of life?" is even the right question, musing instead that "it did not really matter what we expected from life, but rather what life expected from us. We needed to stop asking about the meaning of life, and instead think of ourselves as those who were being questioned by life—daily and hourly" (Frankl 1963, 77). Once this meaning is established, life's ups and downs are more tolerable. On this point Frankl quotes the philosopher Nietzsche, "He who has a *why* to live for can bear with almost any *how*" (Frankl 1963, 76).

The idea of life having a meaning is often associated with spirituality and religion. Certainly, having a strong belief system involving a higher power is one form of meaning, but meaning is not synonymous with religious practice or even belief in God. However, for those interested in looking at meaning, the impact of religion and religious beliefs on psychological health is a good way to start to examine the benefits of meaning. Researchers in this area believe that the relationship between religion and depression is complicated and there is even evidence that religious practices motivated by external factors or social or cultural pressures (for example, when someone does not have faith but goes to church because of outside pressures to do so) may be a risk factor for depression (Murphy et al. 2000). But religious activities and religious beliefs that are internal, that the person really believes and holds onto, seem to actually protect people from depression even when they do not attend church regularly (Braam et al. 2001; McCullough and Larson 1999). Future studies will likely show us whether this protective effect of religion is due to belief in a higher power, or whether it is meaning associated with that higher power that is protective. But it is hard to escape the idea that belief and finding a meaning in life are good.

So in the end, the meaning of life is something we choose for ourselves, and it may be something that is not always easy. As with living up to our values, we never really are able to accomplish this far-reaching goal and then set aside the meaning of life. As Frankl discovered, adversity and suffering can make it very difficult to focus on meaning. Hopefully, no one reading this book will ever be subjected to experiences like the ones Frankl had, but it is almost a guarantee that everyone reading this book will encounter a low point in their life. For some, this could be the return of depression or an unexpected stress or illness. You can only try your best to keep seeing meaning during those low points. Even when things are going just fine with your mood and your life, pursuing meaning may not be simple. For example, if part of the meaning you seek in life revolves around helping others, you still need to choose in what way you want to help. Is it better to hand a homeless person some money for food, or is it better to help hand out blankets to the homeless on cold winter nights, or is better to get politically involved in public assistance programs for the homeless? All three are good deeds, and it takes a great deal of wisdom to choose the right action for you. If part of the meaning of your life is being a good parent, you will already know that you are confronted every day with choices and decisions about what parenting strategies are best for your children. One way of doing things may make a greater positive difference compared to another, so no matter what, people will face some difficult choices around meaning. But this is considered to be a healthy kind of difficult choice since all the options lead to greater fulfillment and all choices are consistent with the meaning your life has. Meaningfulness in living also focuses a great deal on taking action, doing something concrete that is consistent with the meaning that life has for you.

A very easy way to think about and assess the meaning your life has is to ask yourself this question: Is there a reason that I get out of bed that is more important than me and my immediate needs? Keep in mind that this question is in no way meant to suggest that you or your needs are not important. Rather, the question asks whether there is something greater that you believe in that is more important than the fact that you are tired or perhaps don't feel at your best. If the answer to that question is yes, chances are you will get out of bed and set about that bigger goal—whatever it is you are getting out of bed for is probably part of the meaning of your life. That's really all that there is to meaning: finding something greater than yourself, taking action on it, and sticking with it.

Summary

We have taken a different kind of journey in this chapter: there are fewer facts, a lot of loose ends, and perhaps no immediate solutions. By necessity, talking about vital involvement in life requires some amount of philosophy, a little less science, and a much greater focus on what you can do to enhance your life rather than what you can do to protect yourself from relapse. You may not, ultimately, have a choice about whether you have a relapse. Indeed, some part of relapse risk is under your control and you should do whatever you can to prevent relapse, but no one can tell you exactly what percentage of the risk is in your hands. But striving to self-actualize, creating flow, developing hardiness, living your values, and building meaning in your life are all in your control. After all, nothing else and no one else can do these things for you. Enhancing these strengths, aside from reducing relapse risk, may help make those low points more tolerable and may help you sustain yourself even in some dark moments. So there is finally a bottom line: vital involvement is about making sure you don't give up on things and that you continue to take hopeful action for yourself no matter what happens.

Summary Exercise

Record what you believe is the bottom line from this chapter, then record what practices or exercises you would adopt as part of your wellness plan.

Chapter 14, Vital Involvement in Life, examines the importance of positive psychology for increasing quality of life, not just preventing relapse. My bottom line in this chapter is:

_____

_____

The practices, exercises, or actions I will take from this chapter are:

_____

_____

Appendix

Additional Resources

Recommended Readings for Consumers

Depression and Bipolar Disorder

Copeland, M. E. 2001. *The Depression Workbook: A Guide for Living with Depression and Manic Depression.* 2nd ed. Oakland, CA: New Harbinger Publications.

Edwards, V. 2002. *Depression and Bipolar Disorders.* Toronto: Key Porter.

Ellis, T. E., and C. F. Newman. 1996. *Choosing to Live: How to Defeat Suicide through Cognitive Therapy.* Oakland, CA: New Harbinger Publications.

Miklowitz, D. J. 2002. *The Bipolar Disorder Survival Guide: What You and Your Family Need to Know.* New York: Guilford.

Papolos, D., and J. Papolos. 1997. *Overcoming Depression: The Definitive Resource for Patients and Families Who Live with Depression and Manic-Depression.* 3rd ed. New York: Harper Collins.

Solomon, A. 2001. *The Noonday Demon: An Atlas of Depression.* New York: Simon & Schuster.

Cognitive Behavioral Therapy

Burns, D. D. 1999. *The Feeling Good Handbook.* Revised edition. New York: Plume.

Burns, D. D. 1999. *Feeling Good: The New Mood Therapy.* Revised edition. New York: Avon.

Greenberger, D., and C. A. Padesky. 1995. *Mind over Mood: Change How You Feel by Changing the Way You Think.* New York: Guilford Press.

McKay, M., M. Davis, and P. Fanning. 1997. *Thoughts and Feelings: Taking Control of Your Moods and Your Life*. 2nd ed. Oakland, CA: New Harbinger Publications.

Interpersonal Psychotherapy

Weissman, M. M. 2000. *Mastering Depression through Interpersonal Psychotherapy: Patient Workbook*. San Antonio, TX: Psychological Corporation.

Mindfulness Meditation

Kabat-Zinn, J. 1990. *Full Catastrophe Living: Using the Wisdom of Your Body and Mind to Face Stress, Pain, and Illness*. New York: Dell Publishing.

Kabat-Zinn, J. 1994. *Wherever You Go, There You Are: Mindfulness Meditation in Everyday Life*. New York: Hyperion.

Kabat-Zinn, J. 1995. *Mindfulness Meditation: Cultivating the Wisdom of Your Body and Mind* (audiotape). Niles, IL: Nightingale-Conant.

Medication Treatments

Healy, D. 2002. *Psychiatric Drugs Explained*. 3rd ed. New York: Churchill Livingston.

Stahl, S. M. 2000. *Essential Psychopharmacology of Depression and Bipolar Disorder*. New York: Cambridge University Press.

Communication and Relationships

Christensen, A., and N. S. Jacobson. 2000. *Reconcilable Differences*. New York: Guilford.

McKay, M., M. Davis, and P. Fanning. 1995. *Messages: The Communications Skills Book*. 2nd ed. Oakland, CA: New Harbinger Publications.

Perfectionism

Antony, M. M., and R. P. Swinson. 1998. *When Perfect Isn't Good Enough: Strategies for Coping with Perfectionism*. Oakland, CA: New Harbinger Publications.

Basco, M. R. 2000. *Never Good Enough: How to Use Perfectionism to Your Advantage without Letting It Ruin Your Life*. New York: Simon & Schuster.

Stress Management

Davis, M., E. R. Eshelman, and M. McKay. 2000. *The Relaxation and Stress Reduction Workbook*. 5th ed. Oakland, CA: New Harbinger Publications.

Goudey, P. 2000. *The Unofficial Guide to Beating Stress*. New York: IDG Books.

Anxiety Disorders

Antony, M. M., and R. P. Swinson. 2000. *The Shyness and Social Anxiety Workbook: Proven, Step-by-Step Techniques for Overcoming Your Fear.* Oakland, CA: New Harbinger Publications.

Foa, E. B., and R. Wilson. 2001. *Stop Obsessing! How to Overcome Your Obsessions and Compulsions.* Revised edition. New York: Bantam Books.

Hyman, B. M., and C. Pedrick. 1999. *The OCD Workbook: Your Guide to Breaking Free from Obsessive-Compulsive Disorder.* Oakland, CA: New Harbinger Publications.

Matsakis, A. 1996. *I Can't Get Over It: A Handbook for Trauma Survivors.* 2nd ed. Oakland, CA: New Harbinger Publications.

Zuercher-White, E. 1997. *An End to Panic: Breakthrough Techniques for Overcoming Panic Disorder.* 2nd ed. Oakland, CA: New Harbinger Publications.

Recommended Readings for Professionals

Beck, A. T., A. J. Rush, B. F. Shaw, and G. Emery. 1979. *Cognitive Therapy of Depression.* New York: Guilford Press.

Clark, D. A., and A. T. Beck, with B. A. Alford. 1999. *Scientific Foundations of Cognitive Theory and Therapy of Depression.* New York: Wiley.

Gotlib, I. H., and C. L. Hammen. 2002. *Handbook of Depression.* New York: Guilford.

Persons, J. B., J. Davidson, and M. A. Tompkins. 2001. *Essential Components of Cognitive-Behavioral Therapy for Depression.* Washington, DC: American Psychological Association.

Segal, Z. V., J. M. G. Williams, and J. D. Teasdale. 2002. *Mindfulness-Based Cognitive Therapy for Depression: A New Approach to Preventing Relapse.* New York: Guilford.

Weissman, M. M., J. C. Markowitz, and G. L. Klerman. 2000. *Comprehensive Guide to Interpersonal Psychotherapy.* New York: Basic Books.

Where to Get Help

Strategies for Finding a Therapist

In order to find an appropriate therapist, you will need to be resourceful, taking advantage of suggestions from people you know and information from the Internet and other resources. Ideally, the person you see will know a lot about depression and will also have expertise in delivering treatments that have been shown to be effective for depression. Below are some suggestions to keep in mind:

- If you live in a larger city, there is a good chance that there will be a nearby clinic that specializes in the treatment of depression or mood disorders. Alternatively, there may be a nearby clinic that specializes in the types of treatments that have been shown to be useful for depression (such as cognitive behavioral therapy, interpersonal psychotherapy, and pharmacotherapy). These clinics are sometimes located in academic centers, including university-based hospitals or clinical psychology training programs. There may also be excellent specialty clinics in your area that are run privately.

- If you live in a smaller town, you may not have access to specialty clinics. Still, it is important that you make sure that your therapist or doctor is familiar with evidence-based treatments for depression.

- If you are considering taking medication, you typically need to have the medication prescribed by a physician (usually a psychiatrist or family doctor). A good place to start is with a visit to your family doctor. Your doctor may be able to refer you to a specialist, or may recommend that you be treated in his or her office.

- If you are seeking referrals, we recommend contacting some of the organizations listed in the following sections on National Organizations and Additional Internet Resources. Some of these organizations (for example, the ADAA, BPSA, and ACT) offer referrals to experts in different areas around North America. Searching some of the other Internet sites may also be helpful. For example, although the Web site for the International Society for Interpersonal Psychotherapy is aimed at mental health professionals with an interest in interpersonal psychotherapy (IPT), there is an area on the Web site that lists members of the society. If any of those members are in your area, they may be in a position to offer you IPT.

- In addition to the Web sites that we have listed here, there are hundreds of Web sites on the Internet for local clinics around the world that specialize in depression or cognitive behavioral therapy. Take advantage of a good Internet search engine (our favorite is www.google.com/advanced_search). Enter the name of your city, along with other relevant terms (such as CBT, cognitive, or depression), and see what comes up.

- Do a search for the name of an author of one of your favorite books on depression or cognitive behavioral therapy. Many authors have their own Web sites that provide contact information. Sometimes if you e-mail an author to ask for a suggested referral in your area, you may get a helpful response.

- Don't be afraid to shop around. If there are several good therapists in your area, you can switch if the first one doesn't work out. If your area has long waiting lists for treatment, you may want to consider getting your name on more than one waiting list, just in case the first option doesn't work out.

National Organizations (USA)

Anxiety Disorders Association of America (ADAA)
8730 Georgia Avenue, Suite 600
Silver Spring, MD 20910
Tel: 240-485-1001
Fax: 240-485-1035
Web site: www.adaa.org

Depression and Bipolar Support Alliance (BPSA)
(formerly called the National Depressive and Manic-Depressive Association)
730 Franklin Street, Suite 501
Chicago, IL 60610-7224
Tel: 800-826-3632 or 312-642-0049
Fax: 312-642-7243
Web site: www.ndmda.org

National Alliance for the Mentally Ill (NAMI)
Colonial Place Three
2107 Wilson Blvd., Suite 300
Arlington, VA 22201
Tel: 800-950-NAMI (6264) or 703-524-7600
Web site: www.nami.org

National Mental Health Association (NMHA)
1021 Prince St.
Alexandria, VA 22314
Tel: 800-969-NMHA (6642)
TTY Toll Free: 800-433-5959
Web site: www.nmha.org

Additional Internet Resources

Academy of Cognitive Therapy (ACT)
www.academyofct.org

American Association of Suicidology (AAS)
www.suicidology.org

American Foundation for Suicide Prevention (AFSP)
www.afsp.org

American Psychiatric Association (APA)
www.psych.org

American Psychological Association (APA)
www.apa.org

Association for Advancement of Behavior Therapy (AABT)
www.aabt.org

Australian Association for Cognitive and Behaviour Therapy (AACBT)
www.psy.uwa.edu.au/aacbt/

British Association of Behavioural and Cognitive Psychotherapy (BABCT)
www.babcp.com

Canadian Mental Health Association (CMHA)
www.cmha.ca

Center for Mindfulness in Medicine, Health Care, and Society (CFM)
www.umassmed.edu/cfm

Depression and Related Affective Disorders Association (DRADA)
www.drada.org

European Association for Behavioural and Cognitive Therapies (EABCT)
www.eabct.com

International Society for Interpersonal Psychotherapy (ISIPT)
www.interpersonalpsychotherapy.org

National Depression Screening Day
www.mentalhealthscreening.org

National Foundation for Depressive Illness (NAFDI)
www.depression.org

National Institute of Mental Health (NIMH)
www.nimh.nih.gov

References

Abramson, L. Y., M. E. P. Seligman, and J. D. Teasdale. 1978. Learned helplessness in humans: Critique and reformulation. *Journal of Abnormal Psychology* 87, 49–74.

Alden, L. E., and P. J. Bieling. 1996. Interpersonal convergence of personality constructs in dynamic and cognitive models of depression. *Journal of Research in Personality* 30:60-75.

American Psychiatric Association. 2000. *Diagnostic and Statistical Manual of Mental Disorders.* 4th ed., text revision (DSM-IV-TR). Washington, DC: American Psychiatric Association.

Angst, J. 1986. The course of affective disorders. *Psychopathology* 19:47-52.

Antony, M. M., and R. P. Swinson. 2000. *Phobic Disorders and Panic in Adults: A Guide to Assessment and Treatment.* Washington, DC: American Psychological Association.

Antony, M. M., and R. P. Swinson. 1998. *When Perfect Isn't Good Enough: Strategies for Coping with Perfectionism.* Oakland, CA: New Harbinger Publications.

Beck, A. T. 1967. *Depression: Clinical, Experimental, and Theoretical Aspects.* New York: Harper & Row.

Beck, A. T. 1983. Cognitive therapy of depression: New perspectives. In *Treatment of Depression: Old Controversies and New Approaches,* edited by P. J. Clayton and J. E. Barnett. New York: Raven Press.

Beck, A. T., A. J. Rush, B. F. Shaw, and G. Emery. 1979. *Cognitive Therapy of Depression.* New York: Guilford.

Belsher, G., and C. G. Costello. 1988. Relapse after recovery from unipolar depression: A critical review. *Psychological Bulletin* 104:84-96.

Bergin, A. E., and M. J. Lambert. 1978. The evaluation of therapeutic outcomes. In *Handbook of Psychotherapy and Behavior Change: An Empirical Analysis,* 2nd ed., edited by S. L. Garfield and A. E. Bergin. New York: Wiley.

Bezchlibnyk-Butler, K. Z., and J. J. Jeffries. 2002. *Clinical Handbook of Psychotropic Drugs.* 12th ed. Seattle, WA: Hogrefe & Huber Publishers.

Bieling, P. J., and L. E. Alden. 2001. Sociotropy, autonomy, and the interpersonal model of depression: An integration. *Cognitive Therapy and Research* 25:167-184.

Bieling, P. J., and W. Kuyken. 2003. Is cognitive case formulation science or science fiction? *Clinical Psychology: Science and Practice* 10:52–69

Bieling, P. J., A. T. Beck, and G. K. Brown. 2002. *Stability and Change of Sociotropy and Autonomy Subscales in the Treatment of Depression.* Unpublished paper.

Billings, A. G., R. C. Cronkite, and R. H. Moos. 1983. Social-environmental factors in unipolar depression: Comparisons of depressed patients and nondepressed controls. *Journal of Abnormal Psychology* 92:119-133.

Blaney, P. H. 1977. Contemporary theories of depression: Critique and comparison. *Journal of Abnormal Psychology* 86:203-223.

Blatt, S. J. 1974. Levels of object representation in anaclitic and introjective depression. *Psychoanalytic Study of the Child* 29:107-157.

Blatt, S. J. 1995. The destructiveness of perfectionism: Implications for the treatment of depression. *American Psychologist* 12:1003-1020.

Blatt, S. J., and D. C. Zuroff. 1992. Interpersonal relatedness and self-definition: Two prototypes for depression. *Clinical Psychology Review* 12:527-562.

Boland, R., and M. B. Keller. 2001. Chronic and recurrent depression: Pharmacotherapy and psychotherapy combinations. In *Treatment of Recurrent Depression,* edited by J. Greden. Washington, DC: American Psychiatric Press.

Bootzin, R. R., and S. P. Rider. 1997. Behavioral techniques and biofeedback for insomnia. In *Understanding Sleep: The Evaluation and Treatment of Sleep Disorders,* edited by M. R. Pressman and W. C. Orr. Washington, DC: American Psychological Association.

Braam, A. W., P. van den Eeden, M. J. Prince, A. T. F. Beekman, S. L. Kivelae, B. A. Lawlor, A. Birkhofer, R. Fuhrer, A. Lobo, H. Magnusson, A. H. Mann, I. Meller, M. Roelands, I. Skoog, C. Turrina, and J. R. M. Copeland. 2001. Religion as a cross-cultural determinant of depression in elderly Europeans: Results from the EURODEP collaboration. *Psychological Medicine* 31:803-814.

Bressa, G. M. 1994. S-adenosyl-l-methionine (SAMe) as antidepressant: Meta-analysis of clinical studies. *Acta Neurologica Scandinavica* 154(Suppl.):7-14.

Brown, G. W., and T. O. Harris. 1978. *Social Origins of Depression: A Study of Psychiatric Disorder in Women.* New York: Free Press.

Brown, M. A., J. Goldstein-Shirley, J. Robinson, and S. Casey. 2001a. The effects of a multi-modal intervention trial of light, exercise, and vitamins on women's mood. *Women and Health* 34:93-112.

Brown, R. A., and S. E. Ramsey. 2000. Addressing comorbid depressive symptomatology in alcohol treatment. *Professional Psychology: Research and Practice* 4:418-422.

Brown, R. A., M. Evans, I. W. Miller, E. S. Burgess, and T. I. Mueller. 1997. Cognitive behavioral treatment for depression in alcoholism. *Journal of Consulting and Clinical Psychology* 5:715-726.

Brown, T. A., L. A. Campbell, C. L. Lehman, J. R. Grisham, and R. B. Mancill. 2001b. Current and lifetime comorbidity of the DSM-IV anxiety and mood disorders in a large clinical sample. *Journal of Abnormal Psychology* 110:585-599.

Burns, D. D. 1980. The perfectionist's script for self-defeat. *Psychology Today* November, 34-57.

Burns, D. D. 1999. *The Feeling Good Handbook.* Revised edition. New York: Plume.

Carroll, K. M., C. Nich, and B. J. Rounsaville. 1997. Contribution of the therapeutic alliance to outcome in active versus control psychotherapies. *Journal of Consulting and Clinical Psychology* 65:510-514.

Clark, D. A, A. T. Beck, and B. A. Alford. 1999. *Scientific Foundations of Cognitive Theory and Therapy of Depression.* Chichester, UK: Wiley & Sons.

Connors, G. J., K. M. Carroll, C. C. DiClemente, R. Longabaugh, and D. M. Donovan. 1997. The therapeutic alliance and its relationship to alcoholism treatment participation and outcome. *Journal of Consulting and Clinical Psychology* 65:588-598.

Coren, S. 1996. *Sleep Thieves: An Eye-Opening Exploration into the Science and Mysteries of Sleep.* New York: The Free Press.

Coryell, W., J. Endicott, and M. B. Keller. 1991. Predictors of relapse into major depressive disorders in a nonclinical population. *American Journal of Psychiatry* 148:1353-1358.

Coryell, W., J. Endicott, G. Winokur, H. Akiskal, D. Solomon, A. Loen, T. Mueller, and T. Shea. 1995. Characteristics and significance of untreated episodes of major depressive disorder. *American Journal of Psychiatry* 152:1124-1129.

Cotman, C. W., and N. C. Berchtold. 2002. Exercise: A behavioral intervention to enhance brain health and plasticity. *Trends in Neurosciences* 25:295-301.

Coyne, J. C. 1976. Toward an interactional description of depression. *Psychiatry: Journal for the Study of Interpersonal Processes* 39:28-40.

Cronkite, R. C., and R. H. Moos. 1995. Life context, coping strategies, and depression. In *Handbook of Depression.* 2nd ed., edited by E. E. Beckham and W. R. Leber. New York: Guilford.

Csikszentmihalyi, M. 1990. *Flow: The Psychology of Optimal Experience.* New York: Harper & Row.

Csikszentmihalyi, M., and I. S. Csikszentmihalyi. 1988. *Optimal experience: Psychological Studies of the Concept of Flow in Consciousness.* New York: Cambridge.

Daley, S. E., C. Hammen, and U. Rao. 2000. Predictors of first onset and recurrence of major depression in young women during the 5 years following high school graduation. *Journal of Abnormal Psychology* 109:525-533.

Davidson, J. R. T., and K. M. Connor. 2000. *Herbs for the Mind: What Science Tells Us about Nature's Remedies for Depression, Stress, Memory Loss, and Insomnia.* New York: Guilford.

Davila, J., C. Hammen, D. Burge, B. Paley, and S. E. Daley. 1995. Poor interpersonal problem solving as a mechanism of stress generation in depression among adolescent women. *Journal of Abnormal Psychology* 104:592-600.

DeRubeis, R. J., and P. Crits-Christoph. 1998. Empirically supported individual and group psychological treatments for adult mental disorders. *Journal of Consulting and Clinical Psychology* 66:37-52.

DeRubeis, R. J., L. A. Gelfand, T. Z. Tang, and A. D. Simons. 1999. Medications versus cognitive behavior therapy for severely depressed outpatients: Meta-analysis of four randomized comparisons. *American Journal of Psychiatry* 156:1007-1013.

Dewan, M. J., and V. S. Anand. 1999. Evaluating the tolerability of the newer antidepressants. *Journal of Nervous and Mental Disease* 187:96-101.

Diener, E. 2000. Subjective well-being: The science of happiness and a proposal for a national index. *American Psychologist* 55:34-43.

Doogan, D. P., and V. Caillard. 1992. Sertraline in the prevention of depression. *British Journal of Psychiatry* 160:217-222.

Dworkin, S. F., L. Wilson, and D. L. Masson. 1994. Somatizing as a risk factor for chronic pain. In *Psychological Vulnerability to Chronic Pain,* edited by R. C. Grzesiak and D. S. Ciccone. New York: Springer.

D'Zurilla, T. J., and M. R. Goldfried. 1971. Problem-solving and behavior modification. *Journal of Abnormal Psychology* 78:107-126.

Elkin, I., M. T. Shea, J. T. Watkins, S. Imber, S. M. Sotsky, J. E. Collins, D. R. Glass, P. A. Pilkonis, W. R. Leber, J. P. Docherty, S. J. Fiester, and M. B. Perloff. 1989. National Institute of Mental Health treatment of depression collaborative research program: General effectiveness of treatments. *Archives of General Psychiatry* 46:971-983.

Enns, M. W., J. R. Swenson, R. S. McIntyre, R. P. Swinson, S. H. Kennedy. 2001. Clinical guidelines for the treatment of depressive disorders. VII. Comorbidity. *Canadian Journal of Psychiatry* 46(Suppl. 1):77S-90S.

Evans, M. D., S. D. Hollon, R. J. DeRubeis, J. M. Piasecki, W. M. Grove, M. J. Garvey, and V. B. Tuason. 1992. Differential relapse following cognitive therapy and pharmacotherapy for depression. *Archives of General Psychiatry* 49:802-808.

Eysenck, H. J. 1952. The effects of psychotherapy: An evaluation. *Journal of Consulting Psychology* 16:319-324.

Fava, M., A. Giannelli, V. Rapisarda, A. Patralia, and G. P. Guaraldi. 1995. Rapidity of onset of the antidepressant effect of parenteral S-adenosyl-L-methionine. *Psychiatry Research* 56: 295-297.

Fester, C. B. 1973. A functional analysis of depression. *American Psychologist* 28:857-870.

Fleming, J. 1997. *Become Assertive!* Kent, UK: David Grant Publishing.

Flett, G. L., and P. L. Hewitt. 2002. *Perfectionism: Theory, Research, and Treatment.* Washington, DC: American Psychological Association.

Frank, E., R. F. Prien, R. B. Jarrett, M. B. Keller, D. J. Kupfer, P. W. Lavori, A. J. Rush, and M. M. Weissman. 1991. Conceptualization and rationale for consensus definitions of terms in major depressive disorder: Remission, recovery, relapse, and recurrence. *Archives of General Psychiatry* 48:851-855.

Frankl, V. 1963. *Man's Search for Meaning.* New York: Washington Square.

Gatchel, R. J. 1999. Perspectives on pain: A historical overview. In *Psychosocial Factors in Pain: Critical Perspectives,* edited by R. J. Gatchel and D. C. Turk. New York: Guilford.

Gatchel, R. J., and D. C. Turk. 1999. Interdisciplinary treatment of chronic pain patients. In *Psychosocial Factors in Pain: Critical Perspectives,* edited by R. J. Gatchel and D. C. Turk. New York: Guilford.

George, M. S., Z. Nahas, X. B. Li, J. H. Chae, N. Oliver, A. Najib, and B. Anderson. 2001. New depression treatment strategies: What does the future hold for therapeutic uses of minimally invasive brain stimulation? In *Treatment of Recurrent Depression,* edited by J. Greden. Washington, DC: American Psychiatric Press.

Giles, D. E., R. B. Jarrett, M. M. Biggs, D. S. Guzick, and A. J. Rush. 1989. Clinical predictors of recurrence in major depression. *American Journal of Psychiatry* 146:764-767.

Gortner, E. T., J. K. Gollan, K. S. Dobson, and N. S. Jacobson. 1998. Cognitive-behavioral treatment for depression: Relapse prevention. *Journal of Consulting and Clinical Psychology* 66:377-384.

Gotlib, I. H., and C. L. Hammen. 1992. *Psychological Aspects of Depression: Toward a Cognitive Interpersonal Integration.* Chichester, UK: Wiley & Sons.

Greden, J. F. 2000. Antidepressant maintenance medications. In *Pharmacotherapy for Mood, Anxiety, and Cognitive Disorders,* edited by U. Halbreich and S. A. Montgomery. Washington, DC: American Psychiatric Press.

Greenberger, D., and C. A. Padesky. 1995. *Mind over Mood: Change How You Feel by Changing the Way You Think.* New York: Guilford Press.

Greist, J. H. 1987. Exercise intervention with depressed outpatients. In *Exercise and Mental Health,* edited by W. P. Morgan and S. E. Goldston. Washington, DC: Hemisphere.

Hammen, C. 1991. Generation of stress in the course of unipolar depression. *Journal of Abnormal Psychology* 100:555-561.

Hammen, C. 2000. Interpersonal factors in an emerging developmental model of depression: Assessment and treatment implications. In *Stress, Coping, and Depression,* edited by S. L. Johnson, A. M. Hayes, T. M. Field, N. L. Schneiderman, and P. M. McCabe. Mahwah, NJ: Lawrence Erlbaum.

Hanh, T. N. 1976. *The Miracle of Mindfulness: A Manual of Meditation.* Boston, MA: Beacon Press.

Hanh, T. N. 1987. *Being Peace.* Berkeley, CA: Parallax Press.

Hart, A. B., W. E. Craighead, and L. W. Craighead. 2001. Predicting recurrence of major depressive disorder in young adults: A prospective study. *Journal of Abnormal Psychology* 110:633-643.

Hayes, S. C., K. D. Strosahl, and K. G. Wilson. 1999. *Acceptance and Commitment Therapy: An Experiential Approach to Behavior Change.* New York: Guilford Press.

Howland, R. H., and M. E. Thase. 1999. Affective disorders: Biological aspects. In *Oxford Textbook of Psychopathology,* edited by T. Millon, P. H. Blaney, and R. D. Davis. New York: Oxford University Press.

Hypericum Depression Trial Study Group. 2002. Effect of Hypericum perforatum (St. John's wort) in major depressive disorder: A randomized controlled trial. *Journal of the American Medical Association* 287:1807-1814.

Ingram, R. E., J. Miranda, and Z. V. Segal. 1998. *Cognitive Vulnerability to Depression.* New York: Guilford Press.

Jacobson, N. S., K. S. Dobson, P. A. Truax, M. E. Addis, K. Koerner, J. K. Gollan, E. Gortner, and S. E. Prince. 1996. A component analysis of cognitive-behavioral treatment for depression. *Journal of Consulting and Clinical Psychology* 64:295-304.

Jarrett, R. B., D. Kraft, J. Doyle, B. M. Foster, G. G. Eaves, and P. C. Silver. 2001. Preventing recurrent depression using cognitive therapy with and without a continuation phase: A randomized clinical trial. *Archives of General Psychiatry* 58:381-388.

Joiner, T. E. 2000. Depression's vicious scree: Self-propagating and erosive processes in depression chronicity. *Clinical Psychology Science and Practice* 7:203-218.

Joiner, T. E., and J. C. Coyne, eds. 1999. *The Interactional Nature of Depression: Advances in Interpersonal Approaches.* Washington, DC: American Psychological Association.

Judd, L. L. 1997. The clinical course of unipolar major depressive disorders. *Archives of General Psychiatry* 54:989-991.

Kabat-Zinn, J. 1990. *Full Catastrophe Living: Using the Wisdom of Your Body and Mind to Face Stress, Pain, and Illness.* New York: Dell Publishing.

Kabat-Zinn, J. 1994. *Wherever You Go, There You Are: Mindfulness Meditation in Everyday Life.* New York: Hyperion.

Kaelber, C. T., D. E. Moul, and M. E. Farmer. 1995. Epidemiology of depression. In *Handbook of Depression.* 2nd ed., edited by E. E. Beckham and W. R. Leber. New York: Guilford.

Kalb, R., M. Trautmann-Sponsel, and M. Kieser. 2001. Efficacy and tolerability of hypericum extract WS 5572 versus placebo in mildly to moderately depressed patients. *Pharmacopsychiatry* 34:96-103.

Keller, M. B. 1994. Depression: A long term illness. *British Journal of Psychiatry* 165 (Suppl. 26):9-15.

Keller, M. B., D. N. Klein, R. M. A. Hirschfeld, J. H. Kocsis, J. P. McCullough, I. Miller, M. B. First, et al. 1995. Results of the DSM-IV mood disorders field trial. *American Journal of Psychiatry* 152:843-849.

Kendler K. S., L. M. Karkowski, and C. A. Prescott. 1999. Causal relationship between stressful life events and the onset of major depression. *American Journal of Psychiatry* 156:837-841.

Kendler, K. S., L. M. Thornton, and C. O. Gardner. 2000. Stressful life events and previous episodes in the etiology of major depression in women: An evaluation of the kindling hypothesis. *American Journal of Psychiatry* 157:1243-1251.

Kessler, R. C., K. A. McGonagle, S. Zhao, C. B. Nelson, M. Hughes, S. Eshleman, H. -U. Wittchen, and K. Kendler. 1994. Lifetime and 12-month prevalence of *DSM-III-R* psychiatric disorders in the United States: Results from the National Comorbidity Survey. *Archives of General Psychiatry* 51:8-19.

Kilbourn, K., P. Saab, and N. Schneiderman. 2000. Depression and negative affect in post-myocardial infarction patients: Assessment and treatment implications. In *Stress, Coping, and Depression,* edited by S. L. Johnson, A. M. Hayes, T. M. Field, N. L. Schneiderman, and P. M. McCabe. Mahwah, NJ: Lawrence Erlbaum.

Kobasa, S. C. 1979. Stressful life events, personality, and health: An inquiry into hardiness. *Journal of Personality and Social Psychology* 37:1-11.

Kobasa, S. C. 1982. The hardy personality: Toward a social psychology of stress and health. In *Social Psychology of Health and Illness,* edited by G. Sanders and J. Suls. Hillsdale, NJ: Lawrence Erlbaum.

Kuhn, M. A., and D. Winston. 2000. *Herbal Therapy and Supplements: A Scientific and Traditional Approach.* Philadelphia, PA: Lippincott.

Lane, A. M., and D. J. Lovejoy. 2001. The effects of exercise on mood changes: The monitoring effect of depressed mood. *Journal of Sports Medicine and Physical Fitness* 41:539-545.

Lecrubier, Y., G. Clerc, R. Didi, and M. Kieser. 2002. Efficacy of St. John's wort extract WS 5570 in major depression: A double-blind, placebo-controlled trial. *American Journal of Psychiatry* 159:1361-1366.

Lee, T. M., and C. C. H. Chan. 1999. Dose-response relationship of phototherapy for seasonal affective disorder: A meta-analysis. *Acta Psychiatrica Scandinavica* 99:315-323.

Lenze, E. J., M. A. Dew, S. Mazumdar, A. E. Begley, C. Cornes, M. D. Miller, S. D. Imber, E. Frank, D. J. Kupfer, and C. F. Reynolds. 2002. Combined pharmacotherapy and psychotherapy as maintenance treatment for late-life depression: Effects on social adjustment. *American Journal of Psychiatry* 159:466-468.

Levine, J., Y. Barak, M. Gonzalves, H. Szor, A. Elizur, O. Kofman, and R. H. Belmaker. 1995. Double-blind, controlled trial of inositol treatment of depression. *American Journal of Psychiatry* 152:792-794.

Levine, J., A. Mishori, M. Susnosky, M. Martin, and R. H. Belmaker. 1999. Combination of inositol and serotonin reuptake inhibitors in the treatment of depression. *Biological Psychiatry* 45:270-273.

Lewinsohn, P. M. 1974. A behavioral approach to depression. In *The Psychology of Depression: Contemporary Theory and Research,* edited by R. J. Friedman and M. M. Katz. New York: Wiley.

Lin, E. H., W. J. Katon, M. VonKorff, J. E. Russo, G. E. Simon, T. M. Bush, C. M. Rutter, E. A. Walker, and E. Ludman. 1998. Relapse of depression in primary care: Rate and clinical predictors. *Archives of Family Medicine* 7:443-449.

Linde, K., G. Ramirez, C. D. Mulrow, A. Pauls, W. Weidenhammer, and D. Melchart. 1996. St. John's wort for depression. *British Medical Journal* 313:253-258.

Litten, R. Z., and J. P. Allen. 1995. Pharmacotherapy for alcoholics with collateral depression or anxiety: An update of research findings. *Experimental and Clinical Psychopharmacology* 3:87-93.

Mack, A. H., J. E. Franklin, and R. J. Frances. 2001. *Concise Guide to Treatment of Alcoholism and Addictions.* Washington, DC: American Psychiatric Publishing.

Maddi, S. R., S. Kahn, and K. L. Maddi. 1998. The effectiveness of hardiness training. *Consulting Psychology Journal: Practice and Research* 50:78-86.

Marcus, D. K., and M. E. Nardone. 1992. Depression and interpersonal rejection. *Clinical Psychology Review* 12:433-449.

Marx, E. M., J. M. Williams, and G. C. Claridge. 1992. Depression and social problem solving. *Journal of Abnormal Psychology* 101:78-86.

Maslow, A. H. 1968. *Toward a Psychology of Being.* New York: Van Nostrand.

Mattson, M. E., F. K. Del Boca, K. M. Carroll, N. L. Cooney, C. C. DiClemente, D. Donovan, R. M. Kadden, B. McRee, C. Rice, R. G. Rycharik, and A. Zweben. 1998. Compliance with treatment and follow-up protocols in project MATCH: Predictors and relationship to outcome. *Alcoholism: Clinical and Experimental Research* 22:1328-1339.

McCullough, M. E., and D. B. Larson. 1999. Religion and depression: A review of the literature. *Twin Research* 2:126-136.

McGrath, M. J., and D. B. Cohen. 1978. REM sleep facilitation of adaptive waking behavior: A review of the literature. *Psychological Bulletin* 85:24-57.

McKay, M., M. Davis, and P. Fanning. 1995. *Messages: The Communications Skills Book.* 2nd ed. Oakland, CA: New Harbinger Publications.

Melzack, R., and P. Wall. 1965. Pain mechanisms: A new theory. *Science* 50:971-979.

Merriam-Webster, Inc. 1993. *Merriam Webster's Collegiate Dictionary*. 10th ed. Springfield, MA: Merriam-Webster, Inc.

Miller, L. G. 1998. Herbal medicinals: Selected clinical considerations focusing on known or potential drug-herb interactions. *Archives of Internal Medicine* 158:2200-2211.

Monroe, S., and A. D. Simons. 1991. Diathesis-stress theories in the context of life stress research: Implications for the depressive disorders. *Psychological Bulletin* 110:406-425.

Mueser, K. T. 1998. Social skills training and problem solving. In *Comprehensive Clinical Psychology*, Volume 6, edited by A. S. Bellack and M. Hersen. New York: Elsevier.

Murphy, P. E., J. W. Ciarrocchi, R. L. Piedmont, S. Cheston, M. Peyrot, and G. Fitchett. 2000. The relation of religious belief and practices, depression, and hopelessness in persons with clinical depression. *Journal of Consulting and Clinical Psychology* 68:1102-1106.

Nemets, B., Z. Stahl, and R. H. Belmaker. 2002. Addition of omega-3 fatty acid to maintenance medication treatment for recurrent unipolar depressive disorder. *American Journal of Psychiatry* 159:477-479.

Nezu, A. M. 1987. A problem-solving formulation of depression: A literature review and proposal of a pluralistic model. *Clinical Psychology Review* 7:121-144.

Nurnberg, H. G., A. Gelenberg, T. B. Hargreave, W. M. Harrison, R. L. Siegel, and M. D. Smith. 2001. Efficacy of sildenafil citrate for the treatment of erectile dysfunction in men taking serotonin reuptake inhibitors. *American Journal of Psychiatry* 158:1926-1928.

Parikh, S. V., and R. W. Lam. 2001. I. Definitions, Prevalence, and Health Burden. *The Canadian Journal of Psychiatry* 46(supplement), 135–205.

Paterson, R. 2000. *The Assertiveness Workbook: How to Express Your Ideas and Stand Up for Yourself at Work and in Relationships*. Oakland, CA: New Harbinger Publications.

Paykel, E. S., R. Ramana, Z. Cooper, H. Hayhurst, J. Kerr, and A. Barocka. 1995. Residual symptoms after partial remission: An important outcome in depression. *Psychological Medicine* 25:1171-1180.

Paykel, E. S., J. Scott, J. D. Teasdale, A. L. Johnson, A. Garland, R. Moore, A. Jenaway, P. L. Cornwall, H. Hayhurst, R. Abbott, and M. Pope. 1999. Prevention of relapse in residual depression by cognitive therapy: A controlled trial. *Archives of General Psychiatry* 56:829-835.

Philipp, M., R. Kohner, and K. O. Hiller. 1999. Hypericum extract versus imipramine or placebo in patients with moderate depression. *British Medical Journal* 319:1534-1539.

Post, R. M. 1992. Transduction of psychosocial stress into the neurobiology of recurrent affective disorder. *American Journal of Psychiatry* 149:999-1010.

Prien, R. F., L. L. Carpenter, and D. J. Kupfer. 1991. The definition and operational criteria for treatment outcome of major depressive disorder: A review of the current research literature. *Archives of General Psychiatry* 48:796-800.

Project MATCH Research Group. 1998. Matching patients with alcohol disorders to treatments: Clinical implications from project MATCH. *Journal of Mental Health* 7:589-602.

Rehm, L. P., A. L. Wagner, and C. Ivens-Tyndal. 2001. Mood disorders: Unipolar and bipolar. In *Comprehensive Handbook of Psychopathology*, 3rd ed., edited by H. E. Adams and P. B. Sutker. New York: Kluwer Academic/Plenum Publishing.

Reynolds, C. F., E. Frank, J. M. Perel, S. D. Imber, C. Cornes, M. D. Miller, S. Mazumdar, P. R. Houck, M. A. Dew, J. A. Stack, B. G. Pollock, and D. J. Kupfer. 1999. Nortriptyline and interpersonal psychotherapy as maintenance therapies for recurrent major depression: A randomized controlled trial in patients older than 59 years. *Journal of the American Medical Association* 281:39-45.

Reynolds, C. F., and D. J. Kupfer. 1988. Sleep in depression. In *Sleep Disorders: Diagnosis and Treatment,* edited by R. L. Williams, I. Karacan, and C. A. Moore. New York: Wiley.

Rhee, S. H., S. A. Feignon, J. L. Bar, Y. Hadeishi, and I. D. Waldman. 2001. Behavior genetic approaches to the study of psychopathology. In *Comprehensive Handbook of Psychopathology,* 3rd ed., edited by H. E. Adams and P. B. Sutker. New York: Kluwer Academic/Plenum Publishing.

Robinson, M. E., and J. L. Riley. 1999. The role of emotion in pain. In *Psychosocial Factors in Pain: Critical Perspectives,* edited by R. J. Gatchel and D. C. Turk. New York: Guilford.

Russo, E. 2001. *Handbook of Psychotropic Herbs: A Scientific Analysis of Herbal Remedies for Psychiatric Conditions.* New York: Haworth Press.

Segal, Z. V., M. Gemar, and S. Williams. 1999. Differential cognitive response to a mood challenge following successful cognitive therapy or pharmacotherapy for unipolar depression. *Journal of Abnormal Psychology* 108:3-10.

Segal, Z. V., J. M. G. Williams, and J. D. Teasdale. 2002. *Mindfulness-Based Cognitive Therapy for Depression: A New Approach to Preventing Relapse.* New York: Guilford.

Segrin, C. 2001. *Interpersonal Processes in Psychological Problems.* New York: Guilford Press.

Seligman, M. E. P. 1974. Depression and learned helplessness. In *The Psychology of Depression: Contemporary Theory and Research,* edited by R. J. Friedman and M. M. Katz. Washington, DC: Winston-Wiley.

Seligman, M. E. P., and M. Csikszentmihalyi. 2000. Positive psychology: An introduction. *American Psychologist* 55:5-14.

Shea, M. T., I. Elkin, S. Imber, S. Sotsky, J. T. Watkins, J. E. Collins, P. A. Pilkonis, E. Beckham, D. R. Glass, R. T. Dolan, and M. B. Perloff. 1992. Course of depressive symptoms over follow-up: Findings from the National Institute of Mental Health treatment of depression collaborative research program. *Archives of General Psychiatry* 49:782-787.

Shelton, R. C., M. B. Keller, A. Gelenberg, D. L. Dunner, R. Hirschfeld, M. E. Thase, J. Russell, R. B. Lydiard, P. Crits-Cristoph, R. Gallop, L. Todd, D. Hellerstein, P. Goodnick, G. Keitner, S. M. Stahl, and U. Halbreich. 2001. Effectiveness of St John's wort in major depression: A randomized controlled trial. *Journal of the American Medical Association* 285:1978-1986.

Sime, W. E. 1996. Guidelines for clinical applications of exercise therapy for mental health. In *Exploring Sport and Exercise Psychology,* edited by J. L. Van Raalte and B. W. Brewer. Washington, DC: American Psychological Association.

Stevens, D. E., K. R. Merikangas, and J. R. Merikangas. 1995. Epidemiology of depression. In *Handbook of Depression,* 2nd ed., edited by E. E. Beckham and W. R. Leber. New York: Guilford.

Swann, W. B., R. M. Wenzlaff, D. S. Krull, and B. W. Pelham. 1992. Allure of negative feedback: Self-verification strivings among depressed persons. *Journal of Abnormal Psychology* 101:293-305.

Tannen, D. 1991. *That's Not What I Meant: How Conversational Style Makes or Breaks Relationships.* New York: Ballantine Books.

Tannen, D. 2001. *You Just Don't Understand: Women and Men in Conversation.* New York: Quill.

Teasdale, J. D., Z. V. Segal, J. M. G. Williams, V. Ridgeway, J. Soulsby, and M. Lau. 2000. Prevention of relapse/recurrence in major depression by mindfulness-based cognitive therapy. *Journal of Consulting and Clinical Psychology* 68:615-623.

Thase, M. E., and R. H. Howland. 1995. Biological processes in depression: An updated review and integration. In *Handbook of Depression,* 2nd ed., edited by E. E. Beckham and W.R. Leber. New York: Guilford.

Tkachuk, G. A., and G. L. Martin. 1999. Exercise therapy for patients with psychiatric disorders: Research and clinical implications. *Professional Psychology: Research and Practice* 30:275-282.

Wagner, H. R., B. J. Burns, W. E. Broadhead, K. S. Yarnall, A. Sigmon, and B. N. Gaynes. 2000. Minor depression in family practice: Functional morbidity, co-morbidity, service utilization and outcomes. *Psychological Medicine* 30:1377-1390.

Ware, J. C., and C. M. Morin. 1997. Sleep in depression and anxiety. In *Understanding Sleep: The Evaluation and Treatment of Sleep Disorders,* edited by M. R. Pressman and W. C. Orr. Washington, DC: American Psychological Association.

Weishaar, M. E. 1993. *Aaron T. Beck.* Thousand Oaks, CA: Sage Publications.

Weissman, M. M. 2000. *Mastering Depression through Interpersonal Psychotherapy: Patient Workbook.* San Antonio, TX: Psychological Corporation.

Weissman, M. M., M. Bruce, P. Leaf, L. Florio, and C. Holzer. 1991. Affective disorders. In *Psychiatric Disorders in America,* edited by L. Robins and E. Regier. New York: Free Press.

Weissman, M. M., P. J. Leaf, M. L. Bruce, and L. Florio. 1988. The epidemiology of dysthymia in five communities: Rates, risks, comorbidity, and treatment. *American Journal of Psychiatry* 145:815-819.

Weissman, M. M., J. C. Markowitz, and G. L. Klerman. 2000. *Comprehensive Guide to Interpersonal Psychotherapy.* New York: Basic Books.

Wilhelm, K., G. Parker, J. Dewhurst-Savellis, and A. Asghari. 1999. Psychological predictors of single and recurrent major depressive episodes. *Journal of Affective Disorders* 54:139-147.

Wong, A. H. C., M. Smith, and H. S. Boon. 1998. Herbal remedies in psychiatric practice. *Archives of General Psychiatry* 55:1033-1044.

About the Authors

Peter J. Bieling, Ph.D.

Peter J. Bieling, Ph.D. is Assistant Professor in the Department of Psychiatry and Behavioural Neurosciences at McMaster University and Director of Mood and Anxiety Services of St. Joseph's Healthcare, Hamilton, Ontario. Dr. Bieling completed his Ph.D. in clinical psychology at the University of British Columbia and did his postdoctoral training at the Center for Cognitive Therapy, University of Pennsylvania and the Beck Institute for Cognitive Therapy. He has authored many articles in the area of depression, particularly the psychological factors that are associated with depression and vulnerability to depression. Dr. Bieling is also a Founding Fellow in the Academy of Cognitive Therapy and has written extensively about therapy for depression. In addition to his research activities and academic work, he is an active therapist and teacher of cognitive behavioral therapy and a consultant in private practice.

Martin M. Antony, Ph.D.

Martin M. Antony, Ph.D. is Associate Professor in the Department of Psychiatry and Behavioural Neurosciences at McMaster University. He is also Chief Psychologist and Director of the Anxiety Treatment and Research Centre at St. Joseph's Healthcare in Hamilton, Ontario. He received his Ph.D. in clinical psychology from the University at Albany, State University of New York, and completed his predoctoral internship training at the University of Mississippi Medical Center. Dr. Antony has published nine books, including *The Shyness and Social Anxiety Workbook* (2000) and *When Perfect Isn't Good Enough*

(1998). He has also published more than eighty scientific papers and book chapters in the areas of cognitive behavioral therapy and anxiety disorders. Dr. Antony has received early career awards from the Society of Clinical Psychology (American Psychological Association), the Canadian Psychological Association, and the Anxiety Disorders Association of America, and is a Fellow of the American and Canadian Psychological Associations. He was recently President of the Anxiety Disorders Special Interest Group of the Association for Advancement of Behavior Therapy (AABT) and was Program Chair for the 2001 AABT meeting. Dr. Antony is actively involved in clinical research in the area of anxiety disorders, teaching, and education, and maintains a clinical practice.

Some Other
New Harbinger Titles

Your Surviving Spirit, Item 3570 $18.95

Coping with Anxiety, Item 3201 $10.95

The Agoraphobia Workbook, Item 3236 $19.95

Loving the Self-Absorbed, Item 3546 $14.95

Transforming Anger, Item 352X $10.95

Don't Let Your Emotions Run Your Life, Item 3090 $17.95

Why Can't I Ever Be Good Enough, Item 3147 $13.95

Your Depression Map, Item 3007 $19.95

Successful Problem Solving, Item 3023 $17.95

Working with the Self-Absorbed, Item 2922 $14.95

The Procrastination Workbook, Item 2957 $17.95

Coping with Uncertainty, Item 2965 $11.95

The BDD Workbook, Item 2930 $18.95

You, Your Relationship, and Your ADD, Item 299X $17.95

The Stop Walking on Eggshells Workbook, Item 2760 $18.95

Conquer Your Critical Inner Voice, Item 2876 $15.95

The PTSD Workbook, Item 2825 $17.95

Hypnotize Yourself Out of Pain Now!, Item 2809 $14.95

The Depression Workbook, 2nd edition, Item 268X $19.95

Beating the Senior Blues, Item 2728 $17.95

Shared Confinement, Item 2663 $15.95

Handbook of Clinical Psychopharmacology for Therpists, 3rd edition, Item 2698 $55.95

Getting Your Life Back Together When You Have Schizophrenia, Item 2736 $14.95

Do-It-Yourself Eye Movement Technique for Emotional Healing, Item 2566 $13.95

Stop the Anger Now, Item 2574 $17.95

The Self-Esteem Workbook, Item 2523 $18.95

The Habit Change Workbook, Item 2639 $19.95

The Memory Workbook, Item 2582 $18.95

Call **toll free, 1-800-748-6273,** or log on to our online bookstore at **www.newharbinger.com** to order. Have your Visa or Mastercard number ready. Or send a check for the titles you want to New Harbinger Publications, Inc., 5674 Shattuck Ave., Oakland, CA 94609. Include $4.50 for the first book and 75¢ for each additional book, to cover shipping and handling. (California residents please include appropriate sales tax.) Allow two to five weeks for delivery.

Prices subject to change without notice.